Teaching Science is Phenomenal

Using Phenomena to Engage Students in Three-Dimensional Science Performances Consistent with the NRC Framework and NGSS

Teaching Science is Phenomenal

Using Phenomena to Engage Students in Three-Dimensional Science
Performances Consistent with the NRC Framework and NGSS

Organizing Student Science Performances Using
5E and **Gather, Reason, Communicate Instructional Sequences**

Brett D. Moulding & Rodger W. Bybee

Teaching Science is Phenomenal: Using Phenomena to Engage Students in Three-Dimensional Science Performances Consistent with the NRC Framework and NGSS

Photos courtesy of Dr. Michael Dahlby, Ken Huff, Brett Moulding, Erin Moulding

Printed in the United States of America

First Printing, 2017

First Printing: ISBN 978-0-9990674-0-6

Second Printing: ISBN 978-0-9990674-2-0

ELM Tree Publishing
953 N Ocotillo Drive
Washington, UT 84780

www.TeachingScienceIsPhenomenal.com

Preferred Citation:

Moulding, B. & Bybee, R. (2017). *Teaching Science is Phenomenal.* ELM Tree Publishing: Washington, UT. ISBN:978-0-9990674-0-6

Acknowledgments

We would like to thank our friends and colleagues for the many hours of their support and encouragement in the development of this book. We greatly appreciate their talents and time in reviewing this book and discussing key aspects of teaching and learning with us as the book was being developed. They are inspirational people, dedicated educators, and critical friends.

Lesa Rohrer, Oklahoma Public Schools,
Ken Huff, Science Teacher, Mill Middle School, Williamsville, New York,
Sam Shaw, South Dakota State Department of Education,
Catherine Mackey, Arkansas State Department of Education
Juan-Carlos Aguilar, Georgia State Department of Education

We would also like to thank Dr. Louise Moulding and Dr. Lindsay Beddes for editorial support.

Most importantly, we are grateful for the many teachers we have had the honor of working with over the past many years, who inspired us to write this book and share the many instructional strategies we learned from them.

About the Authors

Brett Moulding has spent his career as a science educator. In addition to 20 years of classroom experience, he has state-level administrative experience and served as a member of the National Research Council's (NRC) Board on Science Education, National Assessment of Educational Progress Framework committee, NRC Framework for K-12 Science Education Committee, and *Next Generation Science Standards* writing team.

Rodger Bybee has spent his career in science education in both school and research settings. He served as executive director of the NRC Center for Science, Mathematics, and Engineering Education. He was chair of the content working group of the NRC report that established the *National Science Education Standards* and served on the *Next Generation Science Standards* writing team. Rodger served as the executive director of Biological Sciences Curriculum Study (BSCS), retiring in 2007, during which he served as principal investigator for many significant projects.

During the past 10 years, Brett and Rodger have been engaging teachers in professional learning experience across the United States, consistent with the vision for teaching and learning described in the *Framework* including classroom observation of teachers. These experiences were made more poignant by the simultaneous work of the authors on the *Framework* and *NGSS* writing committees. The experiences of their careers in science education have led to unique insights into the structure of effective science instruction and the nature of effective teaching and learning.

Preface

Classroom teachers of science have a wonderful opportunity to change instruction as states move to new three-dimensional state science standards. In this book, we recognize the challenges and opportunities educators face, and address in a practical way the needed changes in instruction to implement the new standards. We also describe how instructional changes embrace and accommodate the innovations expected with the new science education standards.

Instruction is best accomplished when it has structure. In this book, the BSCS 5E Instructional Model and the Gather, Reason, and Communicate performance sequence are integrated as a way to structure science instruction around student science performances. This approach is an effective way to engage students in science learning by making sense of phenomena. Phenomena are observable occurrences or events that can be investigated to support a scientific explanation. Phenomenon-initiated instruction is driven by questions that encourage students to make sense of the world in which they live. Providing a structure for students to engage with phenomena builds critical thinking and reasoning skills. The book features everyday science phenomena and scaffolds so that teachers might use them to engage students in science performances at the intersection of the three dimensions of science described in the NRC report, *A Framework for K-12 Science Education: Practices, Crosscutting Concepts, and Core Ideas (Framework)*.

This book is a sequel to the book *A Vision and Plan for Science Teaching and Learning* and expands the ideas by providing classroom-tested examples of phenomenon-based performances, linked to science standards, that make student thinking visible. A Vision and Plan for Science Teaching and Learning is available at: http://pestl.org/sciencebook.html and is a useful tool for teachers who wish to change their instructional approaches to implement the NGSS and/or state standards aligned to the *Framework*.

Rationale and research to support this approach to science teaching and learning comes from the *Framework* and the findings from the past nine years of professional learning experiences of the Partnership for Effective Science Teaching and Learning (PESTL) professional development program. The PESTL program included over 2,000 hours of classroom observation of science instruction, as well as evaluation of teacher efficacy specific to science teaching and learning.

The vision for science education presented in this book builds an argument for why and how science instruction is accomplished using science phenomena to present three-dimensional science performances that actively engage students in science and engineering practices using a clear set of disciplinary core ideas and crosscutting concepts.

Brett D. Moulding

Rodger W. Bybee

TABLE OF CONTENTS

Everything must be made as simple as possible. But not simpler.

~ Albert Einstein

CHAPTER 1

INTRODUCTION

Contemporary standards for science education, whether developed at the national, state, or district level, require teachers to rethink classroom instruction because the methods and strategies of teaching and learning represent the most fundamental and essential level of reform. Therefore, instruction in the science classroom is our focus. But first, we must step back and understand both how students learn, described in *How People Learn* and the vision for science education, described in *A Framework for K-12 Science Education* (*Framework*). The former provides the research basis for instruction, and the latter presents a vision for contemporary standards and their ultimate influence on classroom instruction.

Research on how students learn highlights three ideas that have implications for our discussion of instruction (adapted from *How People Learn*).

- Students come to the classroom with conceptual models and explanations about how the world works. These initial concepts must be used in order for students to develop more accurate science concepts.

- Students should (a) develop deep foundations of science knowledge, (b) develop an understanding of facts and ideas within the context of a conceptual framework, and (c) organize knowledge in ways that facilitate retrieval and application to make sense of new phenomena they encounter beyond the classroom.

- A metacognitive approach to teaching and learning can help students take control of their own education by defining learning goals and monitoring their progress in achieving them.

The *Framework* recommends that standards be organized using three dimensions of science (i.e., science and engineering practices, crosscutting concepts, and disciplinary core ideas). Science standards spawn from the *Framework* describing performance expectations at the intersection of the three dimensions, but neither the *Framework* nor new standards provide educators with clear descriptions of *how* to teach at that intersection. It would be inappropriate for standards or a document designed for developing standards to tell teachers how to teach science; however, the *Framework* does provide insights into the research describing how students learn and implications for teaching. This book presents the integration of the BSCS 5E instructional model and the Gather, Reason, and Communicate (GRC) student performance sequence. We argue the integration of these two instructional approaches provides an effective structure for teaching science consistent with the vision of the *Framework*.

What Are the Innovations Described in The *Framework*?

There are six innovations expressed here in the context of how science learning would change for students.

1. Students engage in three-dimensional learning—science and engineering practices, disciplinary core ideas, and crosscutting concepts.

2. Classroom learning focuses on students constructing scientific explanations for causes of natural phenomena and engineering solutions to problems.

3. Students learn about the nature of science and engineering design.

4. Students experience a coherent K-12 science curriculum.

5. Science programs include explicit connections to English language arts and mathematics for all students.

6. Assessments for student learning are aligned with performance expectations as stated in contemporary standards.

The *Framework* recommends that science education in grades K-12 establish and integrate three dimensions of science as its foundation. A summary of the three dimensions are provided in the appendices. The colors shown here are consistent with those found in most resources for the three dimensions. You will see these used throughout this text.

- **Scientific and engineering practices**: The practices include the methods and processes of scientific inquiry and of engineering design. See Appendix A and C.

- **Crosscutting concepts**: These concepts unify scientific disciplines and domains of engineering. See Appendix B and D.

- **Disciplinary core ideas**: These are basic concepts of physical, life, Earth and space science, and engineering that progress through grades K-12. See Appendix E.

The *Framework* proposes the synthesis of the three dimensions into statements of contemporary standards and the subsequent implementation of those standards in curriculum, assessment, and instruction. The synthesis requires integrating the three dimensions to increase coherence among curriculum, assessment, and instructional sequences. In accomplishing this aim, the *Framework* further recommends that students construct explanations for causes of natural phenomena in science, and design solutions to human problems in engineering. Finally, standards should be stated as performance expectations that have implications for curriculum, assessments, and instruction. Specifically, students should (1) be actively engaged; (2) begin and complete investigations; and, (3) act in the manner of scientists and engineers as they answer scientific questions and solve engineering problems.

There were other innovations presented in the *Framework*. For example, the report stressed the use of learning progressions for K-12 programs, emphasized the importance of diversity and equity, and underscored the nature of science and technology. Here, we direct attention to the *Framework*'s implications for classroom instruction.

The complexity of contemporary standards presents significant challenges for educators with the task of classroom instruction. The question, "How do I incorporate three dimensions into my teaching?" is not unreasonable. We have reduced the complexity while maintaining the integrity of the central innovation of the *Framework*. By combining the BSCS 5E instructional model and the GRC student performance sequence, designed to integrate the *Framework's* Science and Engineering Practices, we have developed a practical and effective way for teachers to meet the expectations and innovations set forth in the *Framework*. Figures 1-1 and 1-2 briefly summarize the BSCS 5E instructional model and GRC performance sequences.

This book centers on the process of teaching, the essential component of any educational reform. In light of contemporary reform, we address the implications of the *Framework* for standards as they pertain to classroom instruction. The *Framework* has several innovations, but the one we address in this book is the recommendation of engaging students in making sense of phenomena using the three dimensions: scientific and engineering practices, crosscutting concepts, and disciplinary core ideas.

In order to accomplish this complex goal, classroom instruction should be based on our contemporary understanding of how students learn science and the integration of a general instructional model that uses the application of a learning sequence for science. Specifically, the BSCS 5E instructional model and the GRC performance sequence. The integration of these two models enhances students' learning of science by integrating the three dimensions around phenomena.

Throughout the book, reference is made to science phenomena and student performances. When we use the term "phenomena," we are referring to natural science phenomena as well as human engineered phenomena. Our use of "student performances" refers to the active engagement of students in making sense of phenomena. These performances include mental as well as physical engagement and the implied hands-on investigation of natural phenomena. The following chapters develop and refine the ideas, models, and concepts briefly introduced in this chapter.

Figure 1-1. The BSCS 5E Instructional Model

Engagement	Students engage in making sense of a phenomenon by using concepts and practices in short activities that promote curiosity and elicit current knowledge.
Exploration	Students engage in exploration experiences that provide them with a common base of activities within which their current concepts (i.e. preconceptions) and practices are identified and conceptual change is facilitated.
Explanation	Students focus attention on a particular aspect of the engagement and exploration experiences which provide opportunities for them to demonstrate their conceptual understanding and science practices. An explanation from the teacher or other resources may guide learners toward a deeper understanding, a critical part of this phase.
Elaboration	Students apply their understanding of the concept and their abilities by conducting additional activities. The new activities challenge and extend students' conceptual understanding and practices. Through these experiences, the students develop deeper and broader understanding, more information, and adequate practices.
Evaluation	Students assess their understanding and abilities, and teachers evaluate student progress toward achieving the learning outcomes.

Figure 1-2. The Gather, Reason, and Communicate Performance Sequence

Gather	Students are provided with a relevant phenomenon or problem that acts as the launching point for them to (1) obtain information by asking questions and defining problems for causes of the phenomenon within and among systems; (2) investigate the interactions of components of systems to determine the changes in terms of flow of energy and cycling of matter; and (3) determine the proportion of components in systems and interactions/feedback among systems. Gathering may include reading, listening, investigating, and using models.
Reason	Students use information they gathered to make sense of phenomena. Reasoning includes analyzing data and information, constructing explanations for the cause(s) of the phenomenon, engineering solutions to problems, and developing arguments for how the evidence supports or refutes explanations or solutions. Reasoning occurs in our brains, but may utilize models, speaking, and writing to organize the relationship between causes of phenomena and the evidence supporting the explanations.
Communicate Reasoning	Students communicate their reasoning by developing arguments for how evidence supports explanations. Communicating includes speaking, writing, and/or models to present explanations and arguments to themselves and others.

Teaching Science is Phenomenal

Bibliography

Bybee, R. (2015). *The BSCS 5E Instructional Model: Creating Teachable Moments*. Washington, DC: NSTA Press.

Moulding, B., Bybee, R., & Paulson, N. (2015). *Vision and Plan for Science Teaching and Learning*. Salt Lake City, UT: Essential Teaching and Learning.

National Research Council. (1999). *NRC Report How People Learn*. Washington, DC: The National Academies Press.

National Research Council. (2012). *A Framework for K-12 Science Education: Practices, Crosscutting Concepts, and Core Ideas*. Washington, DC: The National Academies Press.

National Research Council. (2015). *NRC Report Guide to Implementing the Next Generation Science Standards*. Washington, DC: The National Academies Press.

NGSS Lead States. (2013). *Next Generation Science Standards: For States, By States*. Washington, DC: The National Academies Press.

Science is a way of thinking much more than it is a body of knowledge.

~Carl Sagan

CHAPTER 2

A STRUCTURE AND FUNCTION FOR SCIENCE TEACHING

How Can We Best Organize Science Instruction?

Students come to school ready to learn science in the same way they have been investigating the natural world for as long as they can remember. In the National Research Council Report *Taking Science to School*, Richard Duschl states

All young children have the intellectual capability to learn science. Even when they enter school, young children have rich knowledge of the natural world, demonstrate causal reasoning, and are able to discriminate between reliable and unreliable sources of knowledge. In other words, children come to school with the cognitive capacity to engage in serious ways with the enterprise of science. (p. vii)

Children bring many experiences to school; it is important that instruction builds on their experiences and curiosity.

Not all children learn the same way; we should value differences and build on individual students' ways of learning.

Reading is only one way of learning; valuing other ways children learn is essential for building on the experiences they bring to the classroom.

The teacher's role is to organize science experiences and knowledge in ways that support all students in making sense of phenomena, consistent with how scientists construct knowledge. It is not enough for teachers to understand science; they must also structure teaching in ways that enhance student learning. We propose a structure for science teaching based on the BSCS 5E instructional model and the Gather, Reason, and Communicate (GRC) student performance sequence.

The BSCS 5E Instructional Model

More than 25 years ago, the 5E Instructional Model was developed by a team at BSCS, led by Rodger Bybee. It is composed of five phases arranged in an instructional sequence.

The BSCE 5E Instructional Sequence

Students *Engage* with Phenomena

In this phase, students' attention and interest are focused on a situation, event, object, demonstration, or problem that involves the content and abilities that are the aims of instruction. From a teaching point of view, asking a question, posing a problem, or presenting phenomena are all examples of strategies to engage learners. If students look puzzled, expressing "How did that happen?" or "I have wondered about that," and "I want to know more about that," they likely are engaged and ready to learn. Students have some ideas, but the expression of concepts and use of their abilities may not be scientifically or technologically accurate and productive.

The engagement activity needs to provide opportunities to assess students' prior knowledge. Teachers might, for example, provide a brief description of a natural phenomenon and ask students how they would explain the situation. The main point is that the students are motivated to think about content related to the learning outcomes of the instructional sequence. The second point about this phase is that it presents opportunities for teachers to informally determine students' current understanding of ideas and concepts, and ideas they are using to make senses of phenomena. The core ideas and crosscutting concepts used to make sense of the phenomenon in this phase will be used throughout the subsequent phases.

Students *Explore* Phenomena

In this phase, students have time and opportunities to resolve the disequilibrium of the engagement experience. The exploration activities provide concrete, hands-on experiences where students express their current conceptions and demonstrate their abilities as they try to clarify puzzling elements of the Engage phase.

Exploration experiences should be designed for later introduction and description of the concepts, practices, and skills of the instructional sequence. Students should have experiences with sufficient time and opportunities to formulate explanations, investigate phenomena, observe patterns, and develop their explanations of phenomena. Briefly, students should gather, reason, and communicate evidence for their current understanding of the phenomenon under investigation.

Teaching Science is Phenomenal

The teacher's role in the Explore phase is to initiate the activity, describe appropriate background information, provide adequate materials and equipment, and to counter any misconceptions. After this, the teacher steps back and becomes a cognitive coach with the tasks of listening, observing, and guiding students as they clarify their individual understanding and begin reconstructing scientific concepts and developing scientific and engineering practices.

Students and Teacher Explain Phenomena

Scientific explanation for phenomena is prominent in this phase. The concepts, practices, and abilities with which students were originally engaged and subsequently explored, are now made clear and comprehensible. The teacher directs students' attention to key aspects of the prior phases by first asking students for their explanations.

Using students' explanations and experiences, the teacher introduces scientific or technological concepts briefly and explicitly. Here, using an *NGSS* example, the disciplinary core ideas including vocabulary, science or engineering practice, and crosscutting concepts are presented, clearly and simply. Students' prior experiences revealed during the Engage and Explore phases should be used as contexts for the explanation.

We would make the point here that verbal explanations are common in this phase. However, use of video, the web, prepared readings, or software also may provide content to facilitate development of accurate explanations. During this phase, it is important for the teacher to synthesize the students' explanations from group discussions and individual writing in order to validate and/or redirect the explanations into a cogent and scientifically accurate explanation or technologically acceptable solution shared by all students.

Students Elaborate Scientific and Engineering Concepts and Abilities

In the elaboration phase, the teacher challenges students with a new situation and encourages interactions among students and with other sources such as written material, databases, simulations, and web-based searches from which they gather, reason, and communicate their response and apply their learning to the new situation.

Learning experiences extend, expand, and enrich the concepts and abilities students developed in the prior phases. The intention is to facilitate the transfer of concepts and abilities to related, but new phenomena. A key consideration for this phase is to use phenomena that are challenging yet achievable by students.

Students and Teacher Evaluate Students' Learning

Students receive feedback on the adequacy of their performance of the practices and abilities to accurately use crosscutting concepts and disciplinary core ideas. Of course, informal, formative evaluations will occur from the initial phase of the instructional sequence, but as a practical matter, teachers must assess and report on educational outcomes. Hence, the Evaluate phase serves to address the issue of assessment. In the Evaluate phase, the teacher should involve students in experiences that are understandable and consistent with those of prior phases and congruent with the explanations. The teacher should determine the evidence for student learning and means of obtaining that evidence as part of the Evaluate phase.

The BSCS 5E Instructional Model is based on a contemporary understanding of how students learn and is generally applicable for all classroom instruction. Next, we present a model that is specifically applicable to science teaching and can be integrated with the 5E model to support the pedagogy needed to realize the instructional implications laid out in the *Framework*.

The Gather, Reason, and Communicate Performance Sequence

Gather, Reason, and Communicate (GRC) is a performance sequence that has utility for organizing instruction within the 5E model and provides a structure for students to use in making sense of science phenomena. The GRC sequence is anchored in the science and engineering practices described in the *Framework* with the purpose of engaging students in formulating explanations of phenomena based on evidence, in which they use crosscutting concepts and core ideas.

The GRC Performance Sequence

The relationship between the GRC sequence and the science and engineering practices as described in the *Framework* can be seen in Figure 2-1. You will notice that some of the practices appear in multiple locations across GRC and are used by students in different ways within the performance sequence. For example, students might "use models" to (a) gather information or data, (b) reason the relationship between components of systems, or (c) communicate reasoning. Notice that the same science and engineering practice (use models) can be implemented in each step of the sequence. Here are two more examples.

- The practice of "develop arguments" could be used when students reason about information, but also when students communicate an argument to support or refute explanations.

- The practice of "obtain, evaluate, and communicate information" can be used by students to gather information, to reason by evaluating information, and to communicate information both orally and in writing.

The GRC performance sequence engages students in using specific science and engineering practices, or components of practices, during performances and leads to making students' thinking visible. When the GRC sequence is used proficiently, teachers are able to distinguish among student performances of gathering (e.g., investigations, observations, obtaining information); reasoning (e.g., constructing explanations, designing solutions, analyzing data, developing arguments); and communicating (e.g., written or oral presentations). The essential expectation in science is for students to reason. Simply making observations and then communicating these observations may be useful but is not sufficient. Our goal is for students to use science and engineering practices, core ideas, and crosscutting concepts to reason causes of phenomena. Gathering provides raw materials for reasoning. Communicating is how students make their reasoning visible to both the teacher and themselves. Engaging students in reasoning is an important goal of science education; this performance sequence is a structure to help attain that goal.

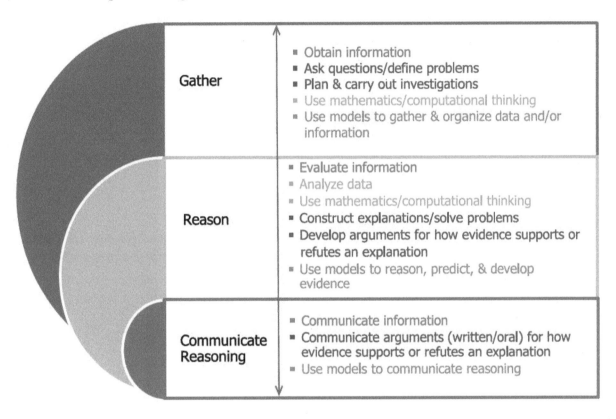

Figure 2-1. Science and Engineering Practices Organized by the GRC Sequence.
The practices are not specific to a part of the sequence but can be used at any time. In this figure, the practices are color coded to identify linked practices. Red= obtain, evaluate, and communicate information; Blue= construct explanations and developing arguments; Orange= analyze and interpret data, use mathematical/computational thinking; and Aqua= develop and use models.
Model developed by B. Moulding, 2012

The purpose of the GRC sequence is to focus instruction on experiences that lead to students' reasoning and then communicating their reasoning. The emphasis within performances may vary with the phenomenon, but ultimately should lead to students reasoning and making their thinking visible through speaking, writing, and/or using models to communicate their reasoning. Here is an example:

Students visit a natural area near their school to investigate small ecosystems as part of a school science activity. On the visit, students look under rocks, leaves, and logs, investigating the ecosystems. Students take notes in their log book on the types and number of insects, bugs, plants, and worms they observe. Students return to the classroom and draw pictures of the ecosystems, gather information from the Internet or are provided readings about the names of the organism observed, and write a summary of their observations.

When using a GRC sequence, students are prompted to engage in performances such as those listed below. Please note that the science and engineering practices are shown in blue, and the crosscutting concepts are shown in green.

Elementary level prompt example

- Use models to organize observations and find patterns across multiple small ecosystems under the rocks and logs, to use as evidence to support an explanation for causes of differences in the two ecosystems.

Middle or High School level prompt example

- Develop a model to show the flow of energy and cycling of matter in an observed ecosystem and the interactions of organisms within that ecosystem.

GRC then goes a step further by prompting students to use reasoning to develop and communicate their explanation through speaking, writing, and/or using models. Prompts to engage students in communicating their reasoning focus on explanations or arguments.

Elementary level prompt example

- Use models to communicate an explanation for how matter cycles and energy flows into, out of, and within ecosystems.

Middle or High School level prompt example

- Develop and communicate an argument for how the evidence you collected in the investigation supports or refutes the explanation that energy for the organisms comes from stored chemical energy in plant matter brought into the ecosystems by one of the organisms in the ecosystem.

Tasks that only engage students in gathering information and communicating information are not sufficient to meet the goal of engaging students in reasoning. The GRC sequence meets the goal by intentionally structuring the sequence to provide prompts for student performances that engage them in using the information they have gathered to then reason and construct explanations for how the ecosystem operates. Figure 2-2 describes the elements of a GRC performance sequence for the small ecosystem experience.

Figure 2-2. Example of GRC and Student Investigation of a Small Ecosystem

Gather	Reason	Communicate
Students observe the types and numbers of various organisms living under rocks.	Students analyze data and observations to determine if patterns exist among organisms in the different environments.	Students write an argument for how the evidence they have collected supports their explanation for why more organisms are found under rocks on moist soil than under rocks on dry sand.
Students pose questions about numbers of organisms living under rocks sitting on dry sand compared to numbers under rocks on moist clay.	Students develop a model for the input and output of matter and energy into and out of the small system.	
Students determine the proportion of the various organisms under different rocks.	Students construct an explanation for why organisms live together under the rock.	Students use models and writing to help communicate their findings and explanations.
Students gather information from the Internet on the needs of the specific organisms found under the rocks.	Students construct explanations for why there is a greater variety of organisms under the rock that has moisture than under the dry rocks.	
Students pose questions to seek information for how organisms obtain matter and energy from the ecosystem in which they live.	Students use data from the class as well as information gathered online as evidence to support their explanations.	

The Explain and Evaluate phases rely on the gathering of information from previous phases. Typically, the lessons are structured as (1) Engage, (2) Explore and Explain, (3) Elaborate and Evaluate. However, it is important to note that the core ideas and crosscutting concepts used in student performances for Explain and Evaluate build from all prior phases of instruction as well as prior knowledge students bring to the learning experience. At appropriate points, the instruction should specifically address students' understanding of the nature and limitation of models, the nature of specific practices being used (e.g., good questions seek empirical evidence, models provide insights into the structure and function of systems, explanations are supported by evidence) and how the crosscutting concepts are used in making sense of phenomena (e.g., the proportion of the components in the system affect the rate of change, the stability of the system is a result of the flow of energy into or out of the system, matter in the system in conserved and can be accounted for when it leaves the system).

So far, we have provided one illustration (shown in Figure 2-1) of student-centered performances utilizing the GRC sequence. In Figure 2-2, we showed the GRC applied to an example. Next, in Figure 2-3 we show how the two models can be integrated to support three-dimensional science teaching and learning through the lens of both the students and the teacher. In Chapters 7 and 8, we will present other examples of instructional sequences that integrate the 5E and GRC models.

Figure 2-3. Phases of the 5E and GRC Integrated Instructional Model

GRC SEQUENCES	WHAT STUDENTS DO	WHAT TEACHERS DO
5E Engage Phase		
Gather **Reason** **Communicate Reasoning**	• Begin thinking about causes of natural and/or engineered phenomena. • Define the system under investigation in terms of matter; forces or energy; stability and change; scale, proportion, or quantity. • Ask questions, collect information, plan and carry out investigations to obtain data and information about causes of phenomena. • Use information, observations, and data to construct initial explanations of causes of phenomena. • Communicate current knowledge and explanations for causes of phenomena and evidence that supports explanations.	• Present phenomena in ways that initiate student questions or engage students in experiences with phenomena that capture students' interest. • Ask questions to help students define the system in terms of the crosscutting concepts. • Provide opportunities for students to investigate and assemble information. • Ask questions that focus on core ideas specific to the explanation of phenomena. • Listen to explanations. Listen for students' preconceptions.
5E Explore Phase		
Gather **Reason** **Communicate Reasoning**	• Obtain information from various sources for causes of phenomena and/or analogous phenomena. • Investigate the variables affecting phenomena. • Continue developing explanations for causes of the phenomena. • Continue examining patterns, clarifying the system, and gathering information. • Use information from experiences to formulate an initial explanation and arguments for how the evidence supports this explanation. • Communicate, using writing, speaking, and/or models, how evidence supports the explanation of causes of phenomena.	• Supply materials and structure for students to investigate phenomena. • Focus students' attention on valid sources of information. • Guide students' investigation by asking questions and giving advice. • Focus students on summarizing information. • Ask students for current explanations, and how they are using information/ data from investigations, models, and reliable sources as evidence to support explanations. • Provide expectations for student presentations.

Teaching Science is Phenomenal

	5E Explain Phase	
Reason **Communicate Reasoning**	• Express knowledge and demonstrate abilities relative to phenomena. • Combine data and information in a logical manner to formulate an explanation of phenomena. • Collaborate with other students to share ideas and reasoning for causes of phenomena from Engage/Explore phases. • Present an explanation of causes of phenomena. • Reflect on learning and application of knowledge to analogous phenomena. • Reflect on learning evident in the feedback from formative assessment.	• Clarify students' use of concepts, practices, and ideas. Adjust students' use of specific vocabulary. • Make provisions for students to present explanations, and guide the students' formulation of an explanation. • Formatively assess the accuracy of students' explanation, synthesize students' explanations into a scientifically accurate common class understanding for causes of phenomena. • Reflect on teaching and learning.
	5E Elaborate Phase	
Gather **Reason** **Communicate Reasoning**	• Use crosscutting concepts to define the system. • Obtain information about new phenomena by defining the systems, finding patterns, and determining causes of the phenomena. • Apply knowledge from previous phases to make sense of analogous phenomena. • Construct an explanation for causes of phenomena using disciplinary core ideas and crosscutting concepts to make sense of the phenomena and arguing how the evidence supports the explanation. • Communicate through writing, models, and speaking the arguments for how the evidence supports the explanation for causes of the new phenomena.	• Present new analogous phenomena. • Provide time and opportunity for students to investigate new phenomena. • Guide students' synthesis of arguments for how the evidence from observations, data, core ideas, and/or concepts supports an explanation consistent with accepted science. • Listen, analyze student models, and/or read students' work to formatively assess their ability to transfer knowledge and apply concepts and practices. • Formatively assess students' understanding and, based on that, make instructional decisions.
	5E Evaluate Phase	
Reason **Communicate Reasoning**	• Express understanding of analogous phenomena. • Identify essential data and information that are necessary to use as evidence. • Combine concepts and evidence in a logical manner. • Present writing and models to communicate an explanation of phenomena and arguments of how evidence supports the explanation.	• Design and present an assessment that will provide evidence of students' knowledge and abilities. • Allow students to investigate phenomena. • Provide opportunities to construct explanation. • Describe expectations and mode of presentation. • Evaluate the reasoning and scientific understanding presented by students.

Questions, Recommendations, and Implications

In presentations and workshops, teachers have asked about the synthesis of the 5E and GRC models. This section addresses some of the issues raised by curriculum developers, assessment specialists, and classroom teachers during professional development. We preface this discussion by pointing out the rationale for the respective models. The 5E model is based on the psychology of learning and the observation that students need time and opportunities to formulate or reconstruct concepts and develop abilities. These two factors justify the perspective and the sequence of each phase of the 5Es.

The GRC sequence is anchored in the science and engineering practices described in the *Framework* with the purpose of engaging students in formulating explanations of phenomena in which they combine evidence and concepts in a logical manner. The latter requires a sequence of structured experiences, the function of which is to provide time and opportunities for students to use scientific and engineering practices to construct conceptual understanding of core ideas and crosscutting concepts to explain phenomena.

What is the Appropriate Use of this Integrated Instructional Model? Should the instructional model be the basis for a lesson? A unit of study? An entire program? The optimal use of the integrated model is a unit lasting two to three weeks where each phase is used as the basis for one or more lessons (with the exception of the Engage phase, which may be less than a lesson). We assume some cycling of lessons within a phase; for example, there might be two lessons in the Explore phase and three lessons in the Elaborate phase. Using the model as the basis for a single lesson decreases the effectiveness of the individual phases due to reducing the time and opportunities for students to challenge and restructure concepts and abilities for learning. Conversely, going through the model once as the basis for an entire program increases the time and experience of the individual phases to the point that the perspective for the phase loses its effectiveness.

Ideally, the Explain phase is used to facilitate a group discussion, to synthesize, and more accurately represent the use of core ideas, conceptual models, and/or crosscutting concepts. During this phase, it is critical for the teacher to help students conceptualize the knowledge needed to make sense of analogous phenomena and to develop accurate science language to communicate their reasoning. This aspect of "explaining" can be misunderstood leading teachers to use the phase to tell students explanations rather than guiding them to reason out their own explanations. It is the intent that the Explain phase leads to deeper understanding for students to apply learning and make sense of analogous phenomena presented during the Elaborate phase and Evaluate phase. The Evaluate phase is similar to the Explain phase but focuses on application of ideas to a new phenomenon and creates an opportunity to assess individual student learning.

Can a Phase Be Omitted? No, we recommend that you do not omit a phase. Earlier research found a decreased effectiveness when phases were omitted or their position shifted. From a contemporary understanding of how students learn, there is integrity to each phase and the sum of the phases, as originally designed. This question is based on prior ideas about teaching and learning that would omit earlier phases and go immediately to a teacher's explanation of phenomena.

Can Phases Be Repeated? Yes, it is sometimes necessary to repeat a phase. This change should be based on the curriculum developer or teacher's judgment relative to students' need for time and experiences to learn a concept or develop an ability. Repeating the Explore phase using different performances with analogous phenomena provides a way for students to build deeper knowledge about key aspects of the core ideas or crosscutting concepts needed to construct explanations.

Shouldn't Evaluation Be Continuous? Yes, effective teachers continuously evaluate their students' understanding. In the 5E instructional model, the Evaluate phase is intended as a summative assessment conducted at the end of a unit. Certainly, meaningful informal assessment should continuously inform teacher and learners throughout the instructional sequence; however, there also is need for an evaluation at the end of the unit. During formative assessments, teachers should anticipate students' responses and plan prompts based on these. Student learning, as revealed in these formative assessments, should be reflected upon by the teacher to inform instruction, and by the students to inform learning.

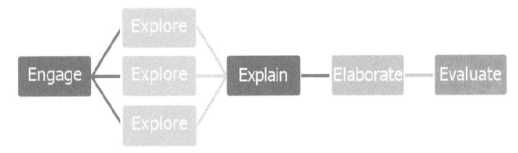

Figure 2-4. Multiple Explore Phases Can Be Used to Build Student Understanding.

What If I Need to Explain an Idea Before (or After) the Explanation Phase? This may be necessary as some ideas are prerequisite to students' understanding the primary concepts of a unit. Teachers will have to make a judgment about the priority and prerequisite nature of the core ideas. One should maintain an emphasis on the primary or major core ideas, concepts, and required abilities of the unit that will help students develop conceptual models for making sense of many phenomena. It is critical, however, to understand that the intent of the instructional model is to have students learn within a context. We recommend that the Engage phase be initiated with an opportunity for students to wonder, ask questions, and explore the phenomenon in a safe setting. The information, ideas, and questions gathered and generated by students through the Engage phase are designed to build a reserve of appropriate and generally accurate core ideas, conceptual models, and crosscutting concepts. This reserve fuels the discussion during the Explain phase, where the teacher's role is to synthesize students' ideas into a scientifically accurate explanation of the phenomenon. The students should gather information in each phase from accurate sources including selected readings, online sites, models, texts, and the teacher to further develop their conceptual understanding as evidenced through student performances.

Summary: How Do GRC and 5E Operate Together?

A vision for science teaching and learning inspires a plan of action that provides specific direction for how and when effective science teaching and learning should progress. A clear structure of instruction is essential for effective science teaching and learning. It is not enough to make the right instructional decisions, we need to understand how learning progresses and why a specific approach to teaching leads to meaningful learning. Meaningful learning occurs when students can apply and transfer their learning to make sense of new phenomena they encounter beyond the classroom. Educators need to be competent and conscious of why and how specific instructional approaches are successful so we can repeat these approaches with fidelity in future instruction. In this way, these approaches become habits of the mind leading to consistent instructional changes. Many instructional approaches work in practice, the question we should be asking is, does this approach work in theory?

Standards describe the aims or goals of science learning and do not provide specific directions for teaching and learning. Standards are only indicators that support our direction. An effective instructional plan for science teaching and learning should include a clear instructional sequence for engaging students in the development of accurate scientific explanations. This structure depends greatly on the learning goals. If the goal is to prepare students to make sense of phenomena, then the sequence should engage students in science performances and provide a structure for reasoning. An important aspect of

any instructional plan is the development of the teacher's conceptual understanding of how to sequence instruction in ways that lead to students' reasoning, and the development and application of effective strategies for shifting the teaching by the teachers into learning by the students.

The 5E instructional model is grounded in theory and creates a focus with each phase that carries forward students' use of core ideas and crosscutting concepts to make sense of a series of phenomena that have the same causes. This sequence provides cohesiveness for students' reasoning and opportunities to apply what they have learned in previous lessons to making sense of new phenomena. GRC is an effective way to engage students in scientific reasoning, supported by evidence, and to make their thinking visible through the intentional use of science and engineering practices. This integration of the two models supports the vision for teaching and learning at the intersection of the three-dimensions by shifting the focus from the teacher to the student.

Strategies for extending student thinking may include the teacher modeling science reasoning with problems or phenomena, for which even the teacher may not have a ready answer. This strategy allows the teacher to model the challenges, struggles, and opportunities for making sense of the phenomena. Instruction shifts to a new level of student engagement when teachers view unanswered questions about phenomena as exciting opportunities.

Reflecting on The Structure and Function of Science Teaching and Learning

1. How does having a clear structure for teaching science support learning?

2. Why are the student performances for GRC organized around the science and engineering practices?

3. How does the 5E model create opportunities for students to engage in the expectations of the NRC *Framework* to "Use the core ideas and crosscutting concepts to make sense of phenomena" in settings beyond the classroom, and to conceptualize science learning into useful tools?

4. Why is it important for teachers to engage in science learning along with the students?

Bibliography

Bybee, R. (2015). *The BSCS 5E Instructional Model: Creating Teachable Moments*. Washington, DC: NSTA Press.

Moulding, B., Bybee, R., & Paulson, N. (2015). *Vision and Plan for Science Teaching and Learning*. Salt Lake City, UT: Essential Teaching and Learning.

Lawson, A. E., Abraham, M. R., & Renner, J. W. (1989). A Theory of Instruction: Using the Learning Cycle to Teach Science Concepts and Thinking Skills (Monograph, Number One). Manhattan, KS: National Association for Research in Science Teaching.

National Research Council. (1999). *NRC Report How People Learn*. Washington, DC: The National Academies Press.

National Research Council. (2007). *Taking Science to School: Learning and Teaching Science in Grades K-8*. Washington, DC: The National Academies Press.

National Research Council. (2012). *A Framework for K-12 Science Education: Practices, Crosscutting Concepts, and Core Ideas*. Washington, DC: The National Academies Press.

National Research Council. (2015). *NRC Report Guide to Implementing the Next Generation Science Standards*. Washington, DC: The National Academies Press.

NGSS Lead States. (2013). *Next Generation Science Standards: For States, By States*. Washington, DC: The National Academies Press.

Taylor J., Van Scotter, P., & Coulson, D. (2007). Bridging Research on Learning and Student Achievement: The Role of Instructional Materials. *Science Educator, 16*(2), 44–50.

The best scientist is open to experience and begins with romance — the idea that anything is possible.

~Ray Bradbury

CHAPTER 3

USING SCIENCE PHENOMENA TO INITIATE STUDENT PERFORMANCES

How Can Science Phenomena Initiate Teaching and Learning?

The word phenomenon, like many science words, has Greek roots; however, the public commonly uses this term in a somewhat different way. In the general lexicon, the term phenomenon is reserved for extraordinary occurrences that are directly perceivable, or an unusual event. In science, the term phenomenon refers to any observable event or fact that can be investigated to gather evidence in order to support a scientific explanation. In addition, phenomena do not have to be phenomenal. Everyday phenomena that exist in a student's world provide a useful way to initiate learning. Engaging students with phenomena, including observing, being curious, and gathering evidence to support explanations for causes of phenomena, is a central tenet to science.

It is important for students to engage in scientific investigation to make sense of phenomena. Investigations are meaningful for students when the phenomena (1) are engaging and interesting; (2) are observable and connected to their lives; (3) can be explored in the classroom with hands-on investigations that generate meaningful data and evidence; (4) are observable in a video or simulation; and/or (5) are connected to their culture and place. Additionally, good phenomena for use in the classroom should require students to engage in performances described by the science standards.

Students should regularly engage in constructing explanations for why (causes) or how (mechanisms) phenomena occur to build conceptual understanding of core ideas and crosscutting

concepts. Effective science instruction engages students in making sense of phenomena in ways that provide them with the skills, knowledge, and dispositions to construct explanations for causes of phenomena they will encounter beyond the classroom. Effective science instruction also supports students in conceptualizing core ideas for use in reasoning. The crosscutting concepts provide a useful lens to focus students on essential aspects of phenomena (e.g., what caused the phenomenon, how is matter cycling in the system, is energy flowing into or out of the system, how are the patterns observed in the system related to causes of the phenomenon).

What is a Phenomenon?

Science seeks to explain causes of phenomena. We observe phenomena and do not immediately see the underlying causes. When we wonder why something happens, "why" is the cause, and what "happens" is the phenomenon or effect. Why does the sun appear to rise in the east each morning? The phenomenon (effect) is the sun appearing over the horizon; the cause of the sun appearing to move from east to west is the rotation of Earth on its axis from west to east, causing the sun to appear to rise in the east and move toward the west.

The first time you walk on a beach you quickly discover the wet sand is firmer and easier to walk on than the dry sand. This is a phenomenon and has a cause; the goal is for students to use reasoning to construct an explanation. Student explanations may range from "my feet sink in dry stand, but not in wet sand," to "wet sand is denser," to high school student explanations that the "intermolecular forces among water molecules and sand hold the sand together."

Science teaching and learning that leads students to observe science phenomena in their daily lives, wonder about the phenomena, and seek explanations for causes of the phenomena, requires a different structure than students listening to teachers telling them about science or reading about science to answer a list of questions. Instruction that engages students in science performances is focused on science and engineering practices that lead students to develop (1) a conceptual understanding of the core ideas, (2) a cadre of examples and coherent explanation they can apply to similar phenomena, and (3) the ability to use crosscutting concepts to make sense of phenomena. We advocate for using the crosscutting concepts as the tool for this sense-making (see Chapter 6). The *Framework* clearly states the expectation that students engage in science performances that facilitate their formation of explanations at the intersection of the three dimensions.

The broad set of expectations for students articulated in the framework is intended to guide the development of new standards that in turn guide revisions to science-related curriculum, instruction, assessment, and professional development for educators. A coherent and consistent approach throughout grades K-12 is key to realizing the vision for science and engineering education embodied in the framework: that students, over multiple years of school, actively engage in science and engineering practices and apply crosscutting concepts to deepen their understanding of each field's disciplinary core ideas. (*Framework*, p. 2)

Our task as teachers is helping students develop a logical and useful structure for making sense of phenomena beyond the classroom.

Using Bigger Core Ideas to Make Sense of Phenomena

Describing core ideas as "Conceptual Models" is one way of addressing the use of the core ideas across many phenomena. The *Framework* develops a set of core ideas with a large grain size. The intent of this approach is to engage students in using the science and engineering practices to develop a deep understanding of a specific set of generalizable crosscutting concepts and core ideas to use in making sense of a broad range of phenomena.

If students have developed conceptual models, they can draw on these and experiences to make sense of new phenomena. Using crosscutting concepts is one way to focus students' explanations across many phenomena. This is a useful way to facilitate reasoning strategies and subsequently make sense of novel phenomena. See Appendix A and B if not familiar with the science and engineering practices and/or crosscutting concepts.

Making sense of the phenomenon of seeing your breath on a cold day is made easier if a student understands how water condenses on the outside of a glass of ice water, clouds form, or fog forms over a warm lake or river. Figure 3-1 shows an example of a common science phenomenon and the ways

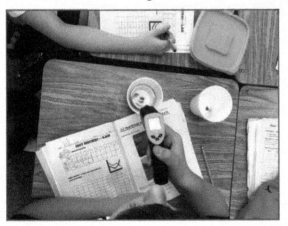

students might engage in making sense of its causes. Knowing the changes in matter and the flow of energy is key to all of these similar phenomena; but so too is an understanding of the core idea that matter changes phase when sufficient energy is added or removed. We will be referring to phenomena with the same or similar causes as **analogous phenomena**. A series of phenomena with the same or similar causes helps students to conceptualize their understanding of causes of new phenomena they may encounter outside of the classroom.

Figure 3-1. Example of Performances for Using Core Ideas

MAKING SENSE OF A PHENOMENON AND ANALOGOUS PHENOMENA

Phenomenon: Sometimes on a very cold day you can see your breath.

To make sense of this phenomenon we could engage students with the following series of performance prompts. Note that the science and engineering practices are shown in blue, with crosscutting concepts in green.

Plan and carry out an investigation to gather evidence that supports an explanation for causes of your breath being visible when you exhale on a very cold day.

Middle school or high school students' thinking might follow a path such as:

Ask Questions – Students might ask, "What causes a change in the appearance of my breath on a cold day? Where did the fog-like cloud come from? Why don't I see it on warm days? What is the white stuff I see? Where else have I seen similar phenomena? Would any warm air cause clouds?"

Construct Explanations – Students use information from the investigation and prior knowledge to construct an explanation. For example - "When I exhale my breath has nitrogen, carbon dioxide, water, and oxygen gases in it. At least one of these gases is changing from invisible to visible. On cold days, my breath looks like a cloud or fog. I know that clouds and fog are made of water droplets that are visible because they reflect light causing invisible water gas to become visible water liquid droplets. Energy flows from particles with higher energy to particles with lower energy. When water vapor in my breath loses energy to the surrounding systems, it changes to liquid droplets that can be observed as clouds. Matter is moving from my body system to the surrounding air system. Once in the air system, the matter loses energy to the air causing it to change from a gas to liquid droplets I can see."

Plan Investigations to Support an Explanation – Students develop a series of investigations to gather supporting evidence. First, they determine how they can gather evidence to support their explanation. Brainstorming, they might think, "Maybe I could investigate breathing into a baggie in the house and releasing it outside to see if it changes. Or I could use air collected on a warm day and air collected on a cold day and observe how it changes at various temperatures. I could breathe into two bags and then release the air from one into a refrigerator and the other in the freezer. I could also breathe onto a cold water bottle or cold window glass. I need to obtain information about the temperature at which the gases in my breath changes into liquid."

Develop a Model – Students develop a model to show the relationships between matter and energy and describe the systems involved, representing relationships between states of matter and inputs or outputs of energy into and out of a system. As you walk around the room, you see students' diagrams with circles and squares showing the movement of particles of water from their body to the surrounding air. The model shows the transfer of energy from the particles of water gas in the breath to the surrounding cold air particles causing the water to change from a gas to a liquid.

Construct Explanations and Develop Models – Students construct explanations supported by evidence (e.g., heat energy transfers from high to low, matter is conserved, matter changes state, matter is made of particles, clouds are small droplets in the cold air, organisms give off water as a gas). A sample student explanation is "The water we exhale is a gas. When it moves into the cold air the water quickly loses enough energy to change into tiny droplets of liquid water that reflect light, so we see our breath as a white cloud."

Communicate Explanations – Students communicate causes of changes in the systems and use models and arguments to reflect on these explanations. Students use evidence from the investigation to communicate an explanation that the water changes from a gas to a liquid. They use their models to show the changes from gas to a liquid that occur in the systems and describe why liquid water is visible as a white cloud and water as a gas cannot be seen.

Teaching Science is Phenomenal

When students engage in making sense of phenomena they use multiple practices, crosscutting concepts, and core ideas. The performances create opportunity for students to gather information and data, reason the data's relationship to the phenomenon, and communicate explanations supported by evidence they gathered and/or developed through the investigation.

Multiple core ideas are needed to make sense of a seemingly simple phenomenon. Consider the core ideas students may use to make sense of this phenomenon.

- Matter is made of particles and particles from one system can move to another system.
- Energy flows from the system with more heat energy to the system with less heat energy.
- Energy is involved when matter changes.
- Matter cycles and energy flows among living and nonliving parts of systems and ecosystems.

It is important to describe performance in broad enough terms such as "causes of change in matter and energy" to help students generalize their reasoning to analogous phenomena. For example,

- On a cold winter morning, you can see your breath.
- Water condenses on the outside of a glass of ice water.
- Clouds form as air passes over mountains tops.
- Clouds generally have flat bottoms.
- Fog forms over a lake on a cool Fall morning.
- Airplanes leave contrails when flying at high altitudes.

How Are Analogous Phenomena Used in an Instructional Sequence?

Analogous phenomena are multiple phenomena with the same causes. Science phenomena travel in packs. When students are making sense of a novel phenomenon they can rely on the conceptual models and crosscutting concepts previously used to make sense of analogous phenomena. The use of analogous phenomena is greatly aided by students' thinking organized around (1) broad core ideas (conceptual models); and (2) crosscutting concepts. Using questions based on crosscutting concepts helps organize and focus students' thinking to make sense of causes of phenomena. For example,

- How is energy flowing into, out of, and/or within a system affecting the changes in the system?
- Why does the proportion of salt in a solution affect the movement of water across the cell wall?
- Why does the proportion of carbon dioxide in the atmosphere fluctuate seasonally as the atmosphere interacts with other Earth systems?
- How does the scale of the system affect how the system operates?

To support reasoning about analogous phenomena, use questions structured like the following:

- How are the transfers of energy between systems similar as water condenses on a glass and water condenses on a blade of grass?
- How is the movement of matter and flow of energy in the formation of a cloud analogous to the appearance of a person's breath on a cold day?

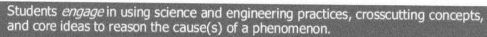

Students *engage* in using science and engineering practices, crosscutting concepts, and core ideas to reason the cause(s) of a phenomenon.

Students gather, reason, and communicate their reasoning for the cause(s) of the phenomenon.

Students *explore* causes of **analogous phenomena** using practices, crosscutting concepts, and core ideas to construct explanations.

Students gather information and data to use as evidence to support reasoning.

Students communicate their reasoning with *explanations* and arguments about how the evidence supports the explanation.

Students and teacher use accurate science language to communicate causes of phenomena, and agree upon explanations consistent with accepted science principles.

Students *elaborate* their understandings by applying their learning to construct explanations of causes of **analogous phenomena**.

Students and teacher *evaluate* understanding of the causes of the phenomenon and reflect on students' learning.

Figure 3-2. An Initial Phenomenon in the Engage Phase of the 5E and GRC Sequences.
Student understanding progresses by using analogous phenomena in the subsequent phases.

In the 5E instructional model a single phenomenon may be used across all phases. However, we have found it more effective to use two or three analogous phenomena for helping students to apply their learning to new contexts. In Figure 3-2 we show how analogous phenomenon can be used to support learning in each phase. Notice how one phenomenon is used to initiate the Engage phase, an analogous phenomenon is used for the Explore and Explain phases, and yet another analogous phenomenon is used for the Elaborate and Evaluate phases.

This approach provides students with a broader understanding of how to use the core ideas and crosscutting concepts, and leads to students transferring this learning to make sense of phenomena beyond the classroom. Figure 3-3 presents examples of a series of analogous phenomena that can be used to structure science teaching and learning. One way to think about a phenomenon is to consider it as the effect; hence, our students should be seeking causes of phenomena to establish "cause and effect" relationships. These phenomena are most effective when they are based on observations students make in their own context. Many, but not all of the crosscutting concepts and core ideas are taken directly from the *Framework*.

Figure 3-3. Examples of Analogous Phenomena

RELATED NGSS STANDARDS	ANALOGOUS PHENOMENA	CROSSCUTTING CONCEPTS AND CORE IDEAS TO SUPPORT EXPLANATIONS OF THE CAUSES OF PHENOMENA
ONE MS-PS1-4 5-PS1-1 5-PS1-2	• On a cold winter morning, you can see your breath. • Water condenses on the outside of a glass of ice water. • Clouds form as air passes over mountains tops. • Clouds generally have flat bottoms. • Fog forms over a lake on a cool Fall morning. • Airplanes leave contrails when flying at high altitudes.	*Crosscutting Concepts* – Cause and Effect; Systems and System Models *Core Ideas* - Energy transferring out of systems causes the water to change from gas to liquid. Matter is made of particles that can move from one system to another. Energy is involved when matter changes, the energy in the water is leaving so the water changes from a gas to a liquid.
TWO 5-PS1-4 5-PS1-1 5-PS1-2 MS-PS1-2 MS-PS1-5 HS-PS1-6 HS-PS1-7	• Steel wool changes color and gains mass when it rusts. • When magnesium ribbon is strongly heated, it glows and gains mass. • If baking soda and vinegar are mixed in an open container the resulting mixture weighs less than the starting materials. • When Alka-Seltzer is placed in an open container of water the mass of the system (water and Alka-Seltzer) is less after the reaction.	*Crosscutting Concepts* – Systems and System Models; Energy and Matter *Core Ideas* – The total number of each type of atom is conserved, and thus the mass does not change. Substances react chemically in characteristic ways. In a chemical process, the atoms that make up the original substances are rearranged and grouped into different molecules. These new substances have different properties than those of the reactants. The mass of matter involved in a chemical change can be accounted for in terms of movement among systems. The source of additional mass is oxygen from the air (tracing the movement from one system to another).
THREE MS-ESS1-1 1-ESS1-1 5-ESS1-2	• The moon appears to move across the sky from east to west; however, the moon orbits the Earth from west to east. • Mars and Jupiter sometimes appear to move backwards in the sky in a "retrograde" motion. • Constellations and stars observed in the night sky change position seasonally.	*Crosscutting Concepts* – Systems and System Models; Patterns *Core Ideas* – Patterns of the apparent motion of the sun, moon, planets, and stars in the sky can be observed, described, predicted, and explained. The Earth spinning on its axis and orbiting the sun results in the apparent motion of the moon, sun, planets, and stars.
FOUR 3-PS2-1 3-PS2-2 4-PS3-3 MS-PS2-2 HS-PS2-1 5-PS1-1	• The leaves on trees move when the wind blows. • Sailboats are pushed across the lake by wind. • When a golf ball rolls across the floor and collides with another golf ball the second ball moves. • Water flowing downhill moves the sand and rocks as it flows. • Rivers and streams meander across the valley in S-shaped patterns.	*Crosscutting Concepts* – Cause and Effect *Core Ideas* – When an object collides with another object, energy is transferred. Matter is made of particles that have mass and, when moving, can transfer a force. Change in the Earth surface are due to interactions of forces.

RELATED NGSS STANDARDS	ANALOGOUS PHENOMENA	CROSSCUTTING CONCEPTS AND CORE IDEAS TO SUPPORT EXPLANATIONS OF THE CAUSES OF PHENOMENA
FIVE 4-PS4-1 MS-PS4-1 MS-PS4-2 HS-PS4-1	• Flags wave in the wind. • Fly fishing line surfing downstream moves in sideways waves in the current. • Clouds sometime form into a wave pattern. • Water in a lake forms waves when the wind blows. • Sand on the bottom of a stream has a wave pattern.	*Crosscutting Concepts* – Patterns *Core Ideas* – Waves transfer energy. A simple wave has a repeating pattern with a specific wavelength, frequency, and amplitude. A sound wave needs a medium (e.g., air, water) through which it is transmitted.
SIX 3-PS2-1 3-PS2-3 MS-PS2-5 MS-PS2-2 MS-PS2-3 MS-PS2-5 HS-PS1-3	• A falling drop of water has a spherical shape. • A needle can float on water. • Water mounds up above the rim of a glass. • Water moves up the xylem in a tree. • Water moves up a paper towel.	*Crosscutting Concepts* – Structure and Function *Core Ideas* – Electromagnetic forces between water molecules cause molecules to be attracted to one another (hydrogen bonding), resulting in surface tension, capillary action, adhesion, and cohesion.
SEVEN MS-PS2-4 MS-ESS1-2	• Planets are spherical in shape. • Stars, including our sun, are spherical in shape. • Comets and asteroids have irregular shapes.	*Crosscutting Concepts* – Structure and Function *Core Ideas* – Gravity is a force that acts at a distance, pulling objects toward center of mass. Objects at the scale of planets or larger have sufficient mass and time for gravity to pull them into spheres.
EIGHT 3-PS2-1 4-PS4-1 MS-PS2-2 MS-PS4-2 MS-PS4-1 HS-PS2-2 HS-PS3-5 HS-PS4-1	• Waves will appear and move to the center of a glass of water sitting on a table when you tap on the legs of the table or stomp on the floor. • Earthquakes occurring near Alaska created tsunami (tidal wave) in Hawaii 5 hours later. • Liquid in a cup splashes out if you carry it while walking.	*Crosscutting Concepts* – Cause and Effect *Core Ideas* – Waves can transfer energy. The movement of energy and transfer of a force through a medium can take the form of a wave.
NINE MS-PS4-2 HS-PS4-1	• When a pencil is placed in a glass of water it appears to be bent. • Mirages appear over the desert or arctic. • Sometimes a green flash of light can be observed shortly after the sun sets below the ocean horizon. • Rainbows appear when there is sunshine and rain.	*Crosscutting Concepts* – Patterns; Structure and Function *Core Ideas* - When light shines on an object, it is reflected, absorbed, or transmitted through the object, depending on the object's structure and the frequency (color) of the light. The path that light travels can be traced as straight lines, except at interfaces (surfaces) between transparent materials with different refractive indices (e.g., air and water, air and glass) where the light path bends. Lenses and prisms are applications of this effect.

Teaching Science is Phenomenal

RELATED NGSS STANDARDS	ANALOGOUS PHENOMENA	CROSSCUTTING CONCEPTS AND CORE IDEAS TO SUPPORT EXPLANATIONS OF THE CAUSES OF PHENOMENA
TEN 2-PS1-4 5-PS1-1 MS-PS1-4 MS-PS3-3 MS-PS3-4 MS-PS3-5 HS-PS3-4	• The propane tank on a barbeque becomes cold and water condenses on the tank while in use. • After a workout, the sweat on your shirt feels cool. • Eyeglasses fog up on a cold day when you walk into the house from the outside. • Eyeglasses fog up on a hot and humid day when you walk outside from an air-conditioned room.	*Crosscutting Concepts* – Cause and Effect *Core Ideas* – Energy is involved when matter changes from one state to another. As water changes from a liquid to a gas, heat energy is transferred from one system to another system.
ELEVEN HS-PS3-4	• Air released from the valve stem of a tire feels very cold, even if the tire is not cold. • The air inside a large syringe seems to cool when the plunger is drawn out quickly. • When a parcel of air in the atmosphere rises in altitude it gets colder. • Clouds form over mountains.	*Crosscutting Concepts* – Cause and Effect *Core Ideas* – When a gas expands, energy is absorbed from the surrounding systems. The cooling results from the work which the gas does against its internal van der Waals cohesive forces. This is referred to as the Joule-Thompson effect. A rising parcel of air expands, decreasing atmospheric pressure and temperature. This is referred to as adiabatic cooling.
TWELVE MS-PS2-2	• Maple syrup moves in a curved path from the center to the edge of a spinning plate. • Seen from space, clouds on Earth appear to be moving in a swirling motion. • When going around a corner in a car drinks slosh in the opposite direction of the turn.	*Crosscutting Concepts* – Cause and Effect *Core Ideas* – The motion of an object is determined by the sum of the forces acting on it; if the total force on the object is not zero, its motion will change. Centrifugal force is an inertial force directed away from the axis of rotation. The frame of reference is rotating so the objects move in relationship to the rotation in a curved path as viewed from the observer's frame of reference.
THIRTEEN MS-LS4-4 HS-LS4-4 HS-LS4-5	• Few native Hawaiian plants have thorns. • Lizards that live on the dunes of the Sahara Desert of Africa and lizards living in the Painted Desert of America look different and are different colors. However, both have webbed feet and can move quickly over loose sand. • Near deep ocean hydrothermal vents, the food chain does not involve photosynthesis.	*Crosscutting Concepts* – Structure and Function *Core Ideas* – Organisms best adapted to an environment are able to survive, grow, and reproduce. Organisms across multiple ecosystems engage with the environment in similar ways. Natural selection leads to adaptation by organisms that are anatomically, behaviorally, and physiologically well suited to survive and reproduce in a specific environment.

RELATED NGSS STANDARDS	ANALOGOUS PHENOMENA	CROSSCUTTING CONCEPTS AND CORE IDEAS TO SUPPORT EXPLANATIONS OF THE CAUSES OF PHENOMENA
FOURTEEN MS-LS1-1 MS-LS3-2 HS-LS1-4	• A log from a Russian Olive tree left on wet soil grows roots and eventually grows into a tree. • Earth's largest known living organism is a Quaking Aspen grove in Utah known as "Pando." • Raspberry plants, like the ones in my neighbor's yard, have started growing in my yard.	*Crosscutting Concepts* – Cause and Effect *Core Ideas* – Asexual reproduction is when an organism reproduces by cell division and results in organisms with the same genetic make-up.
FIFTEEN MS-LS1-1 MS-LS1-2 HS-LS1-3	• A carrot placed in salt water becomes limp; a carrot placed in fresh water becomes crisp. • Bacteria does not grow in fruit jams and jellies. • Only three organisms live and reproduce in the very salty water of the Great Salt Lake. • If a slug or snail crawls across salt, it shrivels up and dies.	*Crosscutting Concepts* – Structure and Function *Core Ideas* – Systems of specialized cells within an organism help perform essential functions of life. Feedback mechanisms maintain an organism's internal conditions within certain limits. The parts of the cell perform functions necessary for the cell to live.
SIXTEEN HS-PS2-2 HS-PS2-3	• Falling on grass does not hurt as much as falling on concrete. • Running on the track at the high school feels better on your feet and knees than running on the street. • Water balloons dropped on the sidewalk break less often than water balloons dropped on the lawn.	*Crosscutting Concepts* – Structure and Function *Core Ideas* - When objects collide, contact forces transfer energy which change the motion of the objects. When two objects interact, each one exerts a force on the other, and these forces can transfer energy between them. The effect of unbalanced forces on an object result in a change of motion.
SEVENTEEN 5-PS1-3	• When water freezes into ice it floats. • When ice is placed in rubbing alcohol it sinks, but floats on the water formed by the melting ice. • It is warmer upstairs than downstairs. • Helium-filled balloons float, but air-filled balloons do not float.	*Crosscutting Concepts* – Change and Stability; Cause and Effect *Core Ideas* – The density of objects determines how they sort themselves in a gravitational field.
EIGHTEEN 5-PS1-1 5-PS1-2 MS-PS1-2 MS-PS1-5 HS-PS1-2 HS-PS1-6 HS-PS1-7	• If you leave things like nails or dad's saw and hammer outside on the lawn the metal parts rust. • New pennies are shinier than old pennies. • When an apple is cut, it turns brown over time.	*Crosscutting Concepts* – Change and Stability; Cause and Effect *Core Ideas* – Chemical change causes difference in the properties of substances. Oxygen from the atmosphere reacts with other substances.

RELATED NGSS STANDARDS	ANALOGOUS PHENOMENA	CROSSCUTTING CONCEPTS AND CORE IDEAS TO SUPPORT EXPLANATIONS OF THE CAUSES OF PHENOMENA
NINETEEN MS-LS4-1 MS-LS4-3 HS-LS4-1	• A horse has more genetic information in common with a fish than with a pine tree. • The genetic code for a dog is more closely related to a wolf than to a cat. • The genetic code of a dolphin is more similar to a cow than to a shark.	*Crosscutting Concepts* – Patterns; Structure and Function *Core Ideas* – Adaptation by natural selection acting over generations changes species in response to changes in environment. Genetic information provides evidence of evolution. DNA sequences vary among species. Genetic lines of descent can be inferred by comparing DNA sequences of different organisms.
TWENTY MS-PS4-2	• Sometimes the sunset appears orange in color. • Sometimes the moon appears orange in color. • Sometimes the water in Horsetail Waterfall in Yosemite National Park glows with an orange light. • The ice in a glacier is a different color than ice on a lake surface or ice from your freezer.	*Crosscutting Concepts* – Scale, Proportion, and Quantity; Cause and Effect; Structure and Function *Core Ideas* - Light travels in waves of different wavelengths that interact differently with matter. Some wavelengths of light are reflected, refracted, or scattered by particles in the atmosphere and other wavelengths are not. When light shines on an object, it is reflected, absorbed, or transmitted through the object, depending on the object's material and the frequency (color) of the light.
TWENTY-ONE MS-ESS2-4 MS-ESS2-5	• The rainfall totals in Reno, Nevada are less than Salt Lake City, Utah, although both cities are near large mountain ranges. • Buffalo, New York, on the east side of Lake Erie, receives much more snow than Detroit, Michigan, on the west side of Lake Erie. • Storms from the north produce greater snow on the south end of a large lake.	*Crosscutting Concepts* – Cause and Effect; Systems and System Models *Core Ideas*– Water continually cycles among land, ocean, and atmosphere via transpiration, evaporation, condensation, crystallization, and precipitation, as well as downhill flows on land. The complex patterns of the changes and the movement of water in the atmosphere, determined by winds, landforms, and ocean temperatures and currents, are major determinants of local weather patterns.
TWENTY-TWO MS-LS1-6 MS-LS2-1 MS-LS2-3 HS-LS2-5	• Canada geese migrate north at different times each Spring. • Northern right whales migrate each spring up the eastern coast of the United States. • Mule deer migrate up and down elevation with the seasons	*Crosscutting Concepts* – Systems and System Models; Cause and Effect; Stability and Change *Core Ideas* – Living organisms obtain the things they need to live from the environment. Plants use energy from the sun to change carbon dioxide and water into sugar.

ENGINEERING CHALLENGES

RELATED NGSS STANDARDS	ANALOGOUS PHENOMENA	CROSSCUTTING CONCEPTS AND CORE IDEAS TO SUPPORT EXPLANATIONS OF THE CAUSES OF PHENOMENA
A MS-PS2-1 MS-PS2-2 HS-PS2-2 HS-PS2-3	• Design a running track surface that makes running less painful. • Design a playground material that is safer to fall onto than dirt. • Design a car bumper that keeps people safer in a car crash.	*Crosscutting Concepts* – Cause and Effect; Structure and Function; Systems and System Models; Energy and Matter *Core Ideas* - Energy is conserved. For every force, there is an equal but opposite force.
B K-PS2-1 K-PS2-2 3-PS2-1 3-PS2-4 5-PS2-1 MS-PS2-2	• Design a sippy cup for children that does not spill when turned upside down. • Design a canoe/kayak that is lighter but more difficult to capsize. • Design a cup holder for a car that prevents drinks from spilling and takes up less space. • Design a step stool that is easy to move but stable to stand on.	*Crosscutting Concepts* – Structure and Function; Stability and Change *Core Ideas* – The motion of an object is determined by the sum of the forces acting on it; if the total force on the object is not zero, its motion will change. The greater the mass of the object, the greater the force needed to achieve the same change in motion. For any given object, a larger force causes a larger change in motion. Gravity is a force directed down.
C MS-PS3-3 MS-P S3-4	• Design a more energy efficient water heater. • Design a more efficient way to heat the air in a house. • Design clothing that keeps you warmer in winter and cooler in summer.	*Crosscutting Concepts* – Cause and Effect; Systems and System Models; Energy and Matter; Stability and Change *Core Ideas* – Temperature is a measure of the average kinetic energy of particles of matter. Heat is energy and can be transferred.
D MS-LS2-5 LS-4. D ETS1.B HS-LS2-2 HS-LS2-7	• Design ways to increase biodiversity of native plants and animals in an ecosystem. • Design ways to connect ecosystems that have been isolated by highways and, at the same time, make the highways safer without sacrificing efficiency. • Design ways to return biodiversity to regions that are dominated by human agriculture, and at the same time improve the success of the farms.	*Crosscutting Concepts* – Cause and Effect; Systems and System Models *Core Ideas* – Biodiversity describes the variety of species found in Earth's terrestrial and oceanic ecosystems. The completeness or integrity of an ecosystem's biodiversity is used as a measure of its health. Changes in biodiversity can influence humans' resources, (e.g., food, energy, and medicines), as well as ecosystem services on which humans rely (e.g., water purification and recycling). There are systematic processes for evaluating solutions with respect to how well they meet the criteria and constraints.
E 3-LS4-4 MS-LS2-1 MS-LS2-3 MS-ESS2-4 MS-ESS3-3	• Design ways to improve the quality of water produced in a watershed. • Design ways to increase oxygen levels in stagnant water, such as in wetlands. • Design a system to reduce sediment buildup in streams, reservoirs, and lakes.	*Crosscutting Concepts* – Systems and System Models; Cause and Effect; Scale, Proportion, and Quantity *Core Ideas* – Water flows through watersheds and picks up soluble substances and suspension of substances that affect the quality of the water.

Teaching Science is Phenomenal

	• Design a system that reduces the effects of runoff over parking lots and other hard surfaces during heavy rain.	
F MS-PS3-3 HS-PS3-1 HS-PS3-1	• Design a safer handle for a frying pan. • Design ways to improve a mug so it keeps hot beverages hot and cold beverages cold. • Design windows so they keep the house cooler in the summer and warmer in the winter.	*Crosscutting Concepts* – Systems and System Models; Structure and Function; Scale, Proportion, and Quantity; Energy and Matter; Stability and Change *Core Ideas* – Heat transfers from where there is more heat to where there is less heat. The thermal conductivity of materials depends on the properties of the substances and the distance between the particles.
G 2-ESS1-1 2- ESS2-1 4-ESS2-1 4-ESS3-2	• Design ways to slow the weathering of the concrete at the bottom of a rain gutter spout. • Design ways to slow the erosion of soil on the hillside of the school playground. • Design ways to reduce the amount of soil that washes out of flowerbeds and onto the sidewalk. • Design a system that reduces movement of pesticides from farms into streams during extreme rainfall.	*Crosscutting Concepts* – Structure and Function; Cause and Effect; Change and Stability. *Core Ideas* – Water flows through watersheds and picks up soluble substances and suspension of substances that affect the quality of the water. Wind and water can change the shape of the land. Rainfall helps to shape the land and affects the types of living things found in a region. Water, ice, wind, living organisms, and gravity break rocks, soils, and sediments into smaller particles and move them around.

Why Should We Use Phenomena to Initiate Student Science Performances?

An important innovation coming from the *Framework* is the shift from learning about science to engaging students in doing science. Engaging students in making sense of phenomena by investigating and communicating causes mimics what scientists do. Science phenomena are interesting and, when used in classroom instruction, engage students in making sense of their world, now and in the future. Science instruction is not about teaching students "the core ideas," it is about providing students with the skills and knowledge to use core ideas over time to make sense of phenomena they encounter beyond the classroom. Science instruction shifts phenomena sense-making from a non-scientific approach to a scientifically accurate, evidence-based approach. This is why it is so important to not only engage students in making sense of phenomena, but to provide them with the skills and knowledge to verify their explanations through arguing how the scientifically accurate evidence supports their explanations.

How Are Phenomena Related to Performance Expectations?

Instruction is much broader than standards. *NGSS* and state science standards based on the *Framework* were never intended to be the only set of performance expectations for engaging students in science learning. Students should regularly engage in three-dimensional performances of science that are beyond the performance expectations described in the standards. In standards documents, there is generally only a single practice, crosscutting concept, and core idea in each performance expectation. This is because the standards describe what is to be assessed rather than all that is to be learned.

Instruction is not as limited as assessment; coupling multiple practices and crosscutting concepts within a single performance expectation helps to focus student performances.

Below is an example of performance expectations with coupled practices in blue and coupled crosscutting concepts in green:

- Develop models to communicate an explanation for the changes in an ecosystem in terms of matter cycling and energy flowing, when the total mass of grass growing in the ecosystem decreases by 25% due to drought.

- Develop questions to obtain information for causes of seasonal changes in the intensity of sunlight.

- Use models to analyze data for changes in barometric pressure and wind speed to find pattern of change in the weather conditions.

The quickest way to detect error in analogy is to carry it out as far as it will go—and further. Every analogy will break down somewhere.

~Henry Hazlitt

Science lesson performance expectations are most useful when they describe the performance of the students and not just what the teacher is expected to do. The use of "lesson performances" describe three-dimensional student performances within a lesson that are important but different than performances described in the standards. In Figure 3-4, we use a complex phenomenon to show how a series of lesson performances initiate a series of student performances. As you read through the lesson, notice the intentional focus on student-centered science performances. Information for teachers to support the students' performances are presented as teaching suggestions. As before, science and engineering practices are blue, crosscutting concepts are green, and core ideas are red.

Figure 3-4. Sample Lesson Used to Engage Students in Making Sense of a Phenomenon

THE MOON AND MORNING STAR

Phenomenon – The position of Venus and the moon relative to one another and their positions above the horizon change each night.

Lesson Performance Expectation:
Construct an explanation for causes of the changes to objects in the solar system that results in both the motion and apparent motion of moon, Venus, and Earth.

(Teaching Suggestions: If possible have students observe Venus and the moon in the night sky on a day such as December 5 at 6pm (the day was selected using the simulator Stellarium for a position when the moon and Venus are close at a reasonable time of day. If it is not possible, use pictures from the Stellarium to show changes in the position of the moon and Venus each day for three days).

1. Students obtain information from reliable sources to develop a model that describes changes in the motion of Earth, moon, and Venus.

2. Students construct an explanation for why changes in the position of the moon and Venus are caused by the moon orbiting the Earth, Earth spinning on its axis, and Venus moving as it orbits the sun.

Class Discussion:

Q: Why do the positions of Venus and moon change each day?

Q: How do the movements of the moon, Venus, and the Earth result in the observed phenomenon?

Q: Why does the motion of the Earth affect the appearance of the moon and Venus?

Q: How would the motion of the moon and Venus appear if we observed them from Mars?

(Teaching Suggestions: The Earth turns (revolves) from west to east. This causes the objects in the night sky to appear to rise in the east and set in the west. The moon orbits Earth from west to east, so each day at the same time the moon appears about 13 degrees further to the east. Venus is moving much slower than the moon (less than 1 degree each day) so the position does not appear to move over three or four days of observation).

3. Students construct an explanation for causes of the changes in the relative position of objects in the solar system, based on the motion and apparent motion of moon, Venus, and Earth.

Each of the three student performances above use the following criteria:

- Student uses core ideas to explain the phenomenon.
- Crosscutting concepts focus students on specific aspects of the phenomenon.
- Students use practices to gather evidence and make sense of the phenomenon.

Example: Plan and carry out an investigation to gather evidence to explain causes of changes over time in the relative positions of the moon in the night sky.

Science reasoning begins with engaging students in making sense of a phenomenon. When the student performances are consistently organized across the GRC performance sequence, students become proficient at engaging in a structure centered on constructing explanations and developing arguments for how the evidence they gathered supports an explanation. When the GRC sequence is placed within the 5E instructional model, and students apply it to analogous phenomena, their learning deepens. These two organizational tools are useful for structuring instruction in ways that create opportunities for students to apply their learning to make sense of phenomena. The Elaboration phase in the 5E sequence allows students to apply learning to new, analogous phenomena. The true measure of learning is applying knowledge in new situations. The 5E instructional model leads to application in the Elaboration phase.

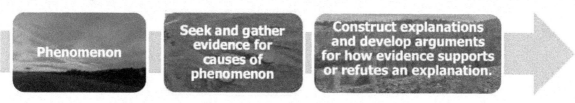

Figure 3-5. Reasoning Initiated by a Phenomenon

The GRC performance sequence centers on students reasoning with the information they have gathered. The purpose of the communicate reasoning component is to establish a time for students to restate and reflect on their reasoning and make it visible to others. This is the best way for teachers and others to have evidence of the degree to which students can logically explain evidence and reflect understanding of essential concepts and ideas.

Figure 3-6. Example of GRC Performances and 5E Instructional Sequence

EXAMPLE OF TYPICAL GRC STUDENT PERFORMANCES

Gather
1. Observe a phenomenon and ask questions to plan an investigation and/or gather information for causes of the phenomenon
2. Observe and/or obtain information specific to the phenomenon
3. Investigate causes of the phenomenon
    a. Establish causality of the phenomenon
    b. Determine interactions among systems related to the phenomenon
    c. Seek patterns related to causes of the phenomenon
4. Obtain information from reliable sources

Reason
5. Construct explanations supported by evidence for causes of the phenomenon
6. Develop arguments for how the evidence supports the explanation

Communicate
7. Communicate explanations for causes of phenomenon by speaking, writing, and/or using models

EXAMPLE OF TYPICAL 5E INSTRUCTIONAL SEQUENCE

Engage   Develop questions to gather information and/or plan investigations of causes of a phenomenon. Focus on the core ideas supporting explanations of the phenomenon.

Explore   Gather additional information about the phenomenon and the core ideas underlying causes of the phenomenon.

Explain   Construct explanations individually and collectively to establish a shared understanding of the phenomenon and the core ideas and crosscutting concepts supporting explanations of causes.

Elaborate   Apply what they have learned to make sense of analogous phenomena.

Evaluate   Students' ability to use core ideas, practices and crosscutting concepts to make sense of a phenomenon is evaluated by the teacher and student.

Central to science are practices of *constructing explanations supported by evidence* and *developing arguments for how the evidence supports the explanation*. Performance of the other practices leads to these two central practices. When GRC performances are sequenced in meaningful ways, students can use evidence they have gathered to support their explanations. The phases of the 5E instructional model are designed to bring coherence and intentionality to teaching and learning. Using GRC within the 5E model shifts instruction from activities to student performances centered around reasoning. Using the 5E instructional model ensures that students purposefully apply their learning to construct explanations for causes of phenomena.

We encourage instruction that begins with engaging students in asking questions about a phenomenon, and then progresses through a series of gathering performances, which leads to students constructing explanations and arguments, and finally to communicating their reasoning. Any number of practices, crosscutting concepts, and core ideas are used in the process, but culminate in students communicating an argument for how their explanation is supported by the evidence they have gathered. Figure 3-7 shows the basic flow of these performances. A more detailed chart can be found at #Going3Dw/GRC. Regardless of the complexity of the series of steps, students asking questions and constructing explanations for causes of the phenomena are central to student reasoning.

Figure 3-7. GRC Student Performance Sequence

OBSERVE PHENOMENA		
Students ask questions	to	better understand phenomena and plan investigations.
GATHER INFORMATION		
Students use investigations and observation, obtain information from reliable sources, and use models to organize information and data about phenomena	to	gather the "stuff" for reasoning.
REASON EXPLANATIONS		
Students analyze data, evaluate information, and use models and mathematical reasoning to determine relationships among components of systems to use as evidence	to	construct explanations for causes of phenomena and develop arguments for how the evidence supports or refutes explanations.
COMMUNICATE REASONING		
Students use models, speaking, and writing	to	communicate explanations and arguments supported by evidence for causes of phenomena.

How does an educator go about finding and using phenomena to initiate lessons?

Using phenomena to initiate lessons can be a fairly systematic process. Identifying the phenomenon to use in lessons requires creativity and practice. Fortunately, professional teachers are creative people, and often the phenomena come from observations made by students. We recommend that you keep a notebook of phenomena. As it turns out, phenomena are easier to forget than they are to find! Once a phenomenon you believe has promise is found, we recommend the following process to vet the usability of the phenomenon for lessons.

1. Find a phenomenon and consider ways to engage students' curiosity and interest in asking questions to make sense of causes of the phenomenon.
2. Research explanations for causes of the phenomenon and the science and engineering practices students can use to gather evidence to support explanations of causes of the phenomenon.
3. Determine how to use crosscutting concepts to provide insights and focus students' reasoning about the system in which the phenomenon occurs and causes of the phenomenon.
4. Determine the specific standards most closely aligned to the phenomenon.
5. Identify two analogous phenomena (e.g. fog over a lake, dew on the lawn, clouds forming on a mountain top).

These five steps begin with the phenomenon, move to the standards, and then identify analogous phenomena. At times, educators seek phenomena that are aligned to a specific standard. Starting with the standards is more difficult and can lead to forced fits, mismatches, and the use of inappropriate words or concepts. We recommend starting with the phenomenon and then aligning the lesson to the standards. If the phenomenon does not align with a standard at your grade-level, oh well, now you have a phenomenon to share with your colleagues!

How Does the GRC Performance Sequence Merge with the 5E Instructional Model?

The 5E model provides an instructional sequence that allows students to engage in making senses of phenomena, explore how the core ideas are used to support explanations of the phenomena, and then apply the core ideas to make sense of an analogous phenomena. What follows is an example using GRC performances in a 5E Instructional sequence.

Figure 3-8. GRC Performance Sequence Incorporated into the 5E Instructional Model

STRUCTURE FOR INSTRUCTION	SERIES OF STUDENT PERFORMANCES
Engage • Engaging students in making sense of phenomena.	**Gathering Information** • Ask questions to obtain information and/or plan investigation to find causes of the phenomenon. • Plan and carry out investigations to gather evidence to support explanations of causes of the phenomenon. **Reasoning** • Construct preliminary explanations for causes of the phenomenon. **Communicating** • Communicate reasoning through writing, speaking, and/or models of the initial explanation and/or argument for causes of the phenomenon.

STRUCTURE FOR INSTRUCTION	SERIES OF STUDENT PERFORMANCES
Explore and Explain	**Gathering Information**

Explore and Explain

- Students explore additional information about the cause(s) of phenomenon, core ideas, and crosscutting concepts to support explanations of the cause(s) of the phenomenon from the Engage phase and/or an analogous phenomenon.
- Students make sense of central aspects of the Engage and Explore experiences and demonstrate their current conceptual understanding of core ideas, crosscutting concepts, and use of science practices.
- The teacher helps students synthesize explanations and/or use of resources to guide learners toward understandings consistent with accepted science concepts and principles.
- The teacher helps students build more precise use of accepted science language to support reasoning.

Gathering Information
- Explore other aspects of the phenomenon from Engage phase and/or explore one or more analogous phenomenon.
- Obtain information and data to support explanations of causes of the phenomenon.
- Plan and carry out investigations to add to the evidence for causes of the phenomenon.

Reasoning
- Construct explanations and develop arguments for how the evidence supports the explanation for causes of the phenomenon.

Communicating
- Use models to show the interactions of the components of a system and how the interactions cause changes in the system due to flow of energy and/or cycling of matter.
- Use accepted science language and as a class come to a common understanding of causes of the phenomenon that is scientifically accurate.

Elaborate and Evaluate

- Students apply knowledge and skills learned in earlier phases to make sense of an analogous phenomenon and/or an unexplained aspect of the original phenomenon.
- Students' understanding and use of essential science crosscutting concepts and core ideas are evaluated by both the teacher and student.
- The students' knowledge and skills to engage in science and/or engineering practices and apply core ideas and crosscutting concepts to make sense of the phenomenon are assessed and reflected on by both the teacher and learner to develop deeper insights about learning.

Gathering Information
- Students engage in making sense of a new but analogous phenomenon by obtaining information and data to support explanations about causes of the phenomenon.
- Plan and carry out investigations to add to the evidence for causes of the phenomenon.

Reasoning Causes of Phenomenon
- Construct explanations for how evidence supports the explanation.

Communicating Reasoning
- Use models to show the interactions of the components of a system and how the interactions cause changes in the system due to flow of energy and/or cycling of matter.
- Reflect on individual learning and the conceptual understanding of the core ideas and crosscutting concepts to make sense of the phenomenon under study and analogous phenomena.

Each step of the GRC engages students in three-dimensional science performances. In order to move the performances from single events in the classroom to coherent sequences we need to build a structure wherein the students:

1. Engage in a 3-D performance to make sense of a phenomenon, exploring other aspects of the phenomenon using core ideas and crosscutting concepts to make sense of the phenomenon and/or analogous phenomena.

2. Revise and refine explanations of the phenomenon and use of the practices, core ideas, and crosscutting concepts, with guidance and more accurate language from the teacher, into a shared, class-wide understanding that is more consistent with accepted science explanations.

3. Apply the knowledge and skills in an elaboration of the learning to a new analogous phenomenon.

4. Evaluate learning to provide both student and teacher with insights into the student's learning and opportunities to reflect on the learning experience.

These steps are essential for science learning to be internalized by students in ways that allow them to use the core ideas and crosscutting concepts to make sense of novel phenomena. One goal of science education is to help students develop the tools and skills to make sense of phenomena beyond the classroom.

Reflecting on Using Phenomena to Initiate Student Performances in Science

1. How should statements of expectations for student science performances be written in order to bring the three dimensions together in meaningful ways?

2. Try writing a three-dimensional science performance that is initiated with a phenomenon.
   a. Select a phenomenon.
   b. Use practices that help the student make sense of the phenomenon.
   c. Use crosscutting concepts that focus the students on the important aspects of the phenomenon that help them make sense of it.
   d. Identify the core ideas that students need to know to make sense of the phenomenon.

3. Consider ways that you would engage students in asking questions about the phenomenon you selected for the prior question.

4. Use Figure 3-7 to think about how students might engage in making sense of a phenomenon.
   a. Identify a phenomenon (e.g., not all apples taste the same; Canada geese fly north in the spring; large rocks fall off the road cuts and onto the road in the winter, but seldom in the summer).
   b. Write a series of practices across Gather and Reason that would help students gather the information they need to make sense of the phenomenon.
   c. Identify a Communicate statement that could be used to assess students' reasoning (e.g., develop an argument to support the explanation that geese fly north in the spring to find better grass to eat; use a model to communicate causes of rocks falling off the road cuts during the winter, but not during the summer).

Bibliography

Bybee, R. (2015). *The BSCS 5E Instructional Model: Creating Teachable Moments*. Washington, DC: NSTA Press.

Moulding, B., Bybee, R., & Paulson, N. (2015). *Vision and Plan for Science Teaching and Learning*. Salt Lake City, UT: Essential Teaching and Learning.

National Research Council. (1999). *NRC Report How People Learn*. Washington, DC: The National Academies Press.

National Research Council. (2012). *A Framework for K-12 Science Education: Practices, Crosscutting Concepts, and Core Ideas*. Washington, DC: The National Academies Press.

National Research Council. (2015). *NRC Report Guide to Implementing the Next Generation Science Standards*. Washington, DC: The National Academies Press.

NGSS Lead States. (2013). *Next Generation Science Standards: For States, By States*. Washington, DC: The National Academies Press.

CHAPTER 4

MEANINGFUL STUDENT PERFORMANCES IN SCIENCE AND ENGINEERING

How Can Student Performances Lead to Evidence-Based Explanations?

Simply stated, science performances are what students do to develop explanations for causes of phenomena. Engaging students in science and engineering *investigation* using phenomena develops proficiency with the practices, crosscutting concepts, core ideas, and habits of mind needed to effectively engage in science beyond the classroom. Extending students' ability to make sense of novel phenomena requires students to have utility with a useful set of core ideas and crosscutting concepts that support constructing explanations for causes of many phenomena. Performances also involve students gathering the information they need to use as evidence and communicating their reasoning. Investigation is not limited to one practice but engages students in a full suite of science and engineering practices that support logical and coherent reasoning to understand science and engineering.

GRC is an instructional sequence built around the use of the practices; however, the crosscutting concepts and disciplinary core ideas must be used in order for performances to be three-dimensional. Figure 4-1 represents the three dimensions of science coming together in a GRC sequence. In later chapters, the three dimensions are described in detail and their role in student science performances illustrated. Understanding that all three dimensions are essential to a science performance is necessary for developing meaningful ways to engage students in science performances.

The practices describe what the student is doing in the performance. The practices come from the disciplines of science and describe the skills scientists use when pursuing knowledge and describe how students engage in science performances. Science and engineering practices, such as asking questions, obtaining information from reliable sources, or planning and carrying out investigations, are ways for students to gather information and data for use as evidence to support their reasoning. Reasoning practices engage students in analyzing data, constructing explanations, and developing arguments to show how the evidence supports their explanations. The reasoning practices engage students in critical thinking. Students should communicate reasoning both to make their thinking visible to others, but more importantly, to reflect on how their evidence supports the reasoning. The communicate performances of the GRC sequence and the Explanation and Evaluation phases of the 5E instructional model, prompt students with three-dimensional science performances. These performances are formative assessment opportunities that may be used by teachers to reflect on instruction and used by students to reflect on learning.

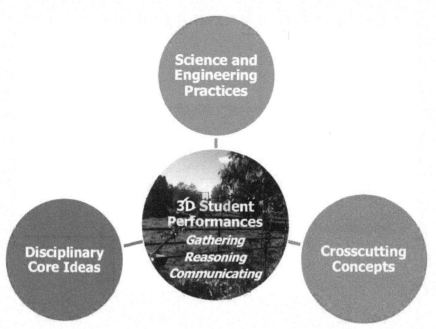

Figure 4-1. Student Science Performances at the Intersection of the Three Dimensions.

Student performances at the intersection of three dimensions are used as a structure for them to organize their thinking. The crosscutting concepts dimension is perhaps the most useful of the three for organizing and focusing the prompts and questions teachers use to engage student in performances, but both the core ideas and practices serve important roles as well. Each of the dimensions work together to contribute to student performances.

Instruction that engages students in reasoning requires a structure that leads students to engage in sense-making, explore additional ways to understand the phenomenon, and then apply (Elaboration) this knowledge and skill to make sense of analogous phenomena. The 5E model provides a structure that is well suited and effective at organizing this iterative approach to teaching and learning. Subsequent chapters make clear the ways 5E and GRC come together in a coherent instructional sequence that organizes and enhances student learning.

Gather Performances

Gather performances provide students with the necessary raw materials, observations, and information to make sense of phenomena. These performances are important on multiple levels, not the least of which is to help the student develop value for pursuing evidence-based explanations for phenomena. Gathering performances provide meaningful ways to engage in science and engineering practices for the purpose of compiling and synthesizing information.

Asking questions and defining problems is an essential practice for engaging students in making sense of phenomena. Students' questions are at the center of curiosity. Curiosity motivates students to persist in seeking the solutions to problems and the explanations for phenomena. When students learn how to frame their questions using crosscutting concepts, the questions become

Teaching Science is Phenomenal

powerful tools for gathering information and/or data relevant to explanations of phenomena. The practices are what students do; the role of the teacher is to create curiosity using phenomena to engage students in asking questions and/or defining problems. Shifting the questioning about phenomena from the teacher to the student requires a significant change in classroom culture.

Planning and carrying out investigations is frequently done as activities and not as student performances. Investigations are more significant performances than doing experiments or activities to play with phenomena. Investigations provide students with a systematic way to obtain information and delve deeply into phenomena, and are mechanisms by which students formally gather information and data to use as evidence for making sense of causes of phenomena. Investigations may be obtaining information in systematic ways, finding answers to science questions, and/or planning and carrying out experiments in which students control variables, change variables, and observe the changes to a system. As described in the *Framework*, investigations are an important way to engage students in multiple practices and provide the context for analyzing data, developing models, and obtaining information. Student-centered investigations provide motivation for students to gather evidence to support their explanations. When students plan and carry out investigations they own the evidence they use to support arguments for causes of phenomena.

Obtaining information is an under-appreciated science practice. Using this practice, students gather much of the raw materials for developing evidence needed to support their explanations. Students gather information by accessing online resources, reading articles, listening to the teacher and other students, and reading instructional material provided in eBooks, open educational resources (OERs), or in texts. Obtaining information should be driven by students' questions about phenomena, but it may be necessary for the teacher to initiate the direction of student thinking. Prompts, using crosscutting concepts, frame students' thinking and support them in obtaining information. For example:

- *What caused the changes in the system?*
- *How did the input of heat energy affect the changes in the matter in the system?*
- *How does the proportion of organisms with these alleles affect the appearance of this trait in the population?*

In the 21st century, efficiently gathering valid information from reliable sources is a critically important skill we must teach our students.

Developing and using models is an effective way for students to gather and organize data, observations, and information obtained from multiple sources into accessible and coherent tools for seeking patterns, determining relationships, and accounting for the components of systems. Models such as T-charts, data tables, graphs, charts, pictures, and diagrams are all useful tools for organizing data.

Additionally, they serve as tools to initiate the reasoning of the relationships between components of systems or determining mathematical relationships.

Using mathematics and computational thinking is an important practice while gathering data and information. Engaging students in using this practice during the gathering performances includes utilizing technology to obtain data/information, establishing mathematical relationships within the data/information, and organizing numerical data into comprehensible relationships. While gathering information and data, students should be considering how to organize the mathematical relationships to reveal meaningful patterns. Students can use computational tools to support gathering reliable and accurate information. This may be as simple as using formulas within spreadsheets to refine data as it is collected or using a cellphone to gather the sounds of song birds or the motion of falling objects.

The function of education is to teach us to think intensively and to think critically. Intelligence plus character – that is the goal of true education.

~Martin Luther King, Jr.

Reason Performances

Engaging students in reasoning is a central goal of science education. The other performances of gathering and communicating should serve to support reasoning. We help students become self-actualized learners by supporting them as they develop a structure for science reasoning based on evidence. Successful science education leads students to question and seek reasons for causes of the phenomena they observe in their daily lives, to question other's reasoning, and value and use science as a way of knowing based on empirical evidence. Science reasoning leads to students' constructing explanations supported by evidence for causes of phenomena and developing arguments for how the evidence they have gathered supports or refutes an explanation. Providing students with the tools to reason is the goal of science education — classrooms should be think tanks, not echo chambers.

The reasoning performances provide a structure by which students construct explanations supported by evidence. Some practices are used in both gathering and reasoning performances, however their function changes depending on when they are used. Structuring the sequence of practices moves students from gathering evidence to using evidence. Using evidence to support explanations is an important habit of mind central to students understanding *science as a way of knowing based on empirical evidence*. The practices and their use in reasoning performance are describe below.

Evaluating information for accuracy and reliability helps students understand how to justify using the information as evidence to support explanations of causes of phenomena. Students should evaluate the merits of the information, consider using multiple sources, and evaluate the validity of information specific to the needed explanations and solutions. The sources and methods for how the source generated the information should be considered in establishing a basis for credibility of causal explanations. The convergence of information and ideas from multiple sources are important considerations when evaluating the validity and reliability of information.

Analyzing and interpreting data is necessary to determine the significance and relevance of data in terms of causality. When students analyze data, they are establishing the meaning of observations and measurements. Investigations might provide data and observations that lack meaning until analyzed, evaluated, and/or interpreted in the context of the phenomenon. Analyzing data and information, using a number of tools and techniques (e.g., graphs, statistical analysis, charts, tables, models), provides greater insights into the significance of the data as evidence to support explanations. Some tools are used to identify patterns in data or determine if a finding is statistically significant or functionally meaningful.

The ability to analyze data (e.g., determining the accuracy of data, developing visualizations of data) has been greatly enhanced by modern computational tools. Analyzing data that are generated when testing engineering designs is useful in determining the best solution to a problem or providing a fair test to compare the efficiencies of multiple designs. Data can be summarized to better see patterns using mathematical processes such as mean, median, mode, and/or chi-square. The validity of the evidence is improved when students use appropriate measures to collect data. The reliability of data is measured through its ability to be repeated with similar patterns and results.

Using mathematical reasoning is a fundamental tool for establishing relationships among variables. Reasoning the relationship between the proportion of the (a) components in systems (e.g., concentration of a solution, ratio of grazing animals to grass in a prairie, ratio of the number of cogs on a gear wheel system), and (b) changes in systems are examples of performances that engage students in using mathematics to reason the expectations and/or predict outcomes. Mathematical reasoning, such as developing computer simulations, solving equations, expressing relationships algebraically, and applying quantitative relationships, can help students provide evidence to support an explanation. Mathematical reasoning is a powerful tool for predicting how changes to one component of a system affects other components of the system.

Using models in reasoning performances helps students determine relationships between variables, causes of change in systems, ways the proportion of components affect the system, and/or changes in systems caused by inputs or outputs of matter and energy. Models support reasoning the effects of interactions among components of systems. Useful models for reasoning include physical models, equations, relational data charts, graphs, and more. Often students use symbols, diagrams, or even doodles to account for components of systems or interactions among multiple systems. The performances move from gathering information to reasoning the interactions among components of systems. Examples of models used to support reasoning causal relationships include:

- Model of the sun, Earth, and moon used to reason the relationship of the relative position of the moon and phases of the moon;
- Equation to analyze the relationship of force, mass, and acceleration ($F = ma$);
- Model of an ecosystem to account for the changes in the matter available at each trophic level;
- Equation to predict relationship of pressure and volume in a closed system ($P_1V_1 = P_2V_2$); and
- Balance chemical equation to reason the conservation of mass, identity of atoms, and conservation of energy.

Constructing explanations is the central practice of science and centers on causes of phenomena. Thus, engaging students in performances to construct explanations is central to learning science. Constructing explanations for causes of phenomena requires students to understand the role of evidence in reasoning. Reasoning is the process by which students support or refute proposed explanations with evidence.

Student writing, models, and oral presentations provide the best opportunities to understand students' reasoning. Value these glimpses into their thinking.

It is human nature to construct explanations for things that happen in our life (e.g., it rains because it is cloudy, my golf swing is getter better because I play more golf, when I think pleasant thoughts I enjoy the day more). Because students construct explanations for phenomena they encounter (whether supported by evidence or not), we encourage any series of science performances to include a performance wherein students construct an explanation for the cause(s) of the phenomenon.

Developing Arguments for how the available evidence supports or refutes explanations is the practice students usually find most challenging, and yet the nature of this practice is an attribute that distinguishes science from other ways of knowing. Students should regularly engage in this practice.

Communicate Reasoning Performances

Student performances of communicating are critical for three purposes. First, reasoning is enhanced when students hold themselves to the expectation that *explanations are supported by evidence*. This creates significant opportunity for self-reflection about the logic behind the reasoning, including students reflecting on the veracity of the evidence supporting their explanation and revising the explanation and/or argument, if needed. Communicating an argument is presenting how each line of evidence supports or refutes the explanation.

Using models, writing, and speaking should not be thought of as separate ways for students to communicate their reasoning. In the communicate performances of the GRC sequence, students first write in order to structure their thinking, then read what they have written and/or develop a model based on their writing. This strategy allows students to see and hear their explanation, providing an opportunity for them to rethink the relationship between the evidence in an argument and the way the evidence logically supports an explanation.

Second, when students write, develop models, or speak, their thinking becomes visible to the teacher and others. This creates a wonderful opportunity for the teacher and fellow students to question the student's thinking, which can clarify reasoning and/or clarify how the evidence supports the argument for a specific explanation. This is a chance for the student to provide further explanation of the mechanism by which a phenomenon operates.

Finally, communicate performances provide a structure through which students can use the practices to make their thinking visible. When students make thinking visible through writing and speaking, the teacher can formatively assess both student learning and the instruction that led to the students' reasoning. Communicating through classroom discourse benefits all students by providing models of evidence-based reasoning. The practices and their instructional utility during this part of the GRC performance sequence are outlined below.

Communicating explanations, as described above, is central for making student reasoning about phenomena visible. The students' explanations should be communicated at some point in the instructional sequence, and evidence supporting the explanations should be presented using speaking, writing, and/or models.

Using models to communicate explanations of causes and/or mechanisms by which phenomena occur allows students to think deeply about the relationships among the components and interactions of systems, the relationships among variables observed and/or measured in investigations, and how the structure affects the function of systems. Many times, models are the best way for students to communicate their reasoning about the mathematical relationships used as evidence. Developing and using models are important practices for students to communicate the evidence supporting their explanations.

Communicating arguments for how evidence supports or refutes an explanation of causes of phenomena is an important practice for students to demonstrate understanding of the nature and process of science. An argument is how students reason the relationship between the evidence and an explanation. Students should provide a separate argument for how each line of evidence—whether it comes from data, core ideas, observations, and/or gathered information—supports or refutes an explanation.

Communicating Information and Classroom Discourse

Supporting students in accurately and meaningfully communicating information, data, core ideas, and models requires discussions centered on the relevance of evidence used to support an explanation of the phenomenon. It is insufficient for students to parrot back information. Rather, students should share the reasoning that connects evidence to their explanation and the relevance of the specific core ideas and crosscutting concept supporting their explanation. Phenomena generally have multiple causes, which necessitates using more than one core idea or crosscutting concept in the explanation. Conceptualizing core ideas and crosscutting concepts increases the utility of these dimensions for making sense of phenomena.

Information is not knowledge.

~Albert Einstein

Classroom discourse is a critical instructional tool for teaching and learning science. This discourse can effectively occur in large group settings, small groups, and/or pairs of students. A safe classroom culture is necessary for productive discourse that makes student reasoning visible. Creating a safe and productive classroom environment requires teachers to listen more than talk, create time for students to think before responding to others, and value all students' ideas.

Wait time/think time is a crucial component of classroom discourse, but so too is valuing students' ideas, which empowers them to extend their thinking and communicate in meaningful ways. One of the most productive "thinking time" strategies is to have students write and/or draw models prior to the classroom discourse. Students are better prepared and feel safer to contribute to classroom discussion when given time to think and write prior to the discussion. This contributes significantly to a safe classroom environment.

Figure 4-2. Relationship between Evidence and Arguments

STUDENTS DEVELOP AN EXPLANATION FOR A PHENOMENON

Phenomenon: Rubbing a stick on a piece of wood causes the end of the stick to get hot.

Student explanation: The mechanical energy put into the system is transformed into heat energy.

Lines of evidence to support explanation:	Arguments for each line of evidence:
1. The more the stick is rubbed, the more heat is produced.	1. Energy is conserved, so all of the energy going into the system can be accounted for as energy transformed or transferred within and/or out of the system.
2. When oil is put on the wood, less heat is produced with the same amount of rubbing.	2. Oil reduces the friction between the stick and board so less mechanical energy is transformed into heat energy. Friction changes mechanical energy into heat energy.
3. Rubbing the stick on the wood slower causes less heat to be produced.	3. When the stick is moved slower less mechanical energy is put into the system for a given time. When less mechanical energy is put into the system less energy is available to be converted into heat energy.
4. Pressing down harder on the stick causes more heat energy to be given off.	4. It requires more mechanical energy to press down harder on the stick so more mechanical energy is put into the system, so more energy is available to be transformed into heat energy.

"Small group" student discussions are an important part of classroom discourse. They provide the space for students to share their reasoning among peers. Small group discussions are enriched when students have gathered information from reliable sources *prior* to the discussion and applied the information to support explanations of causes of phenomena. An effective way to organize the small group discussion is by using a prompt that described the group performance. Here are three examples of structured prompts for small group discussion.

- *Gather information from the reading and use it to develop a model that illustrates why the scale at which fish in a large lake die may or may not affect the growth of plants in the lake.*

- *Explore placing a pencil in water and then obtain information about causes of changes in the appearance of the pencil. Use the information to construct an explanation for causes of changes in the appearance of light as it travels through air and through water.*

- *Observe the crystals in the five samples of granite. Develop questions to use as you obtain information from reliable sources for why the crystals in the rocks are different sizes.*

The small group discussions are excellent springboards into full class discussions. The time spent in pairs or small groups provides an excellent opportunity for students to reason through their ideas prior to presenting them during full class discussion.

Student writing is an artifact of engaging students in performances of gathering, reasoning, and communicating and it supports classroom discourse. As teachers, we have limited time to carefully read students' papers and make insightful and relevant feedback that motivates additional thinking. This means that we should carefully plan the year to include multiple formal assessments using writing. Additionally, less formal writing can be assessed more frequently and quickly by walking around the room as students write, reading over their shoulder, or asking them to read aloud during classroom discourse. Too often we ask students to write or draw models representing their reasoning, but then during classroom discussion only have them paraphrase their writing. If students spend five to eight minutes writing their reasoning, we should have at least three students read their writing aloud to the class. This serves three purposes. First, the student's reasoning is modeled to the entire class; second, student writing now "counts" and the quality of future writing improves; and third, it provides an opportunity to synthesize science reasoning for the entire class.

Formal student writing creates wonderful platforms for teachers to think about student reasoning and ask questions about the students' thinking. The red pencil marks about punctuation and word choice should be replaced with green pencil comments about reasoning, evidence, and alternative explanations. These comments encourage deeper thinking and questioning critical for cultivating student reasoning. Comments should focus on the presented reasoning and encourage students to consider additional lines of evidence to support their explanations and/or arguments.

Teachers should utilize three-dimensional writing prompts that establish clear expectations. The prompt should intentionally direct students to use crosscutting concepts to explain specific aspects of the phenomenon and elicit the core ideas needed to make sense of the phenomenon.

Examples of prompts to initiate science performances with practices in blue and crosscutting concepts in green:

- *Construct a written explanation* for why the *proportion* of carbon dioxide in an open soda can *changes* more quickly when left at room temperature than when kept in the refrigerator.

- *Develop* and *use a model* to support a written *explanation* for why *changes* in the *rate* of movement of tectonic plates *changes* the frequency of volcanoes at the subduction zone.

- *Develop a written argument* for how the evidence collected in the *investigation* supports the *explanation* - "Rubbing a wooden dowel more quickly on a piece of wood *causes* more heat energy to be given off because more mechanical energy was put into the *system* which *causes* more heat energy be given off of the *system*."

Elaborating Student Thinking: When a Word is Not Enough

Students often use a single word to reply to a well-considered question from the teacher. Far too frequently, in the midst of instruction, we allow a single word or short phrase to represent complex ideas that the student may not yet fully understand. When students use a word and/or phrase like "density," "hydrogen bonding," "photosynthesis," or "natural selection" to represent complex ideas, we cannot be confident about what they really understand. We suggest the use of follow-up questions or even rethinking our initial questions to make them more effective.

In the movie *Princess Bride* (Scheinman & Reiner, 1987), the villainous Vizzini—in hopes of killing the hero Westley— cuts the rope Westley is using to climb up the high cliff; yet Westley continues to climb. Vizzini and Indigo have the following exchange.

> *Vizzini: He didn't fall?! Inconceivable!*
>
> *Inigo: You keep using that word. I do not think it means what you think it means.*

Just like Vizzini, our students use words they do not fully understand. Even when students use a word or phrase properly, they may not fully understand the meaning of the word or phrase. Sometimes students are just repeating a word in a similar context and may not know the concept that word represents. Our role in evaluating students' classroom discourse and students' writing is to request sufficient elaboration to have evidence of students' understanding of a concept, idea, or cause of a phenomenon. This requires us to listen carefully and ask students to explain themselves with more details.

In a 1991 episode of the television series "Star Trek: Next Generation" Captain Picard was stranded on a planet with an alien life form (not an unfamiliar plot). The alien and Captain Picard needed to communicate to survive; however, the alien only spoke in parables. The alien communicated his solution for defeating the villains and escaping the planet using the statement, "Darmok and Jalad at Tanagra." For the alien, the title of this parable communicated all that was needed to solve the problem and save their lives. Picard could only repeat the words without understanding the concepts and solution the alien intended (*Darmok episode – 102, Season 5 Episode 2, September 30, 1991*). Sometimes we use science language that is alien to our students or accept their parroted responses (e.g., Why does the water move up the capillary tube – hydrogen bonding; Why does a piece of wadded up paper fall faster than a flat sheet of paper needle – air pressure; Why are planets spherical – gravity). When students are allowed to respond with one or two-word phrases, we really do not know what they know.

Students are better able to transfer conceptual understanding to multiple analogous phenomena when they are able to truly make sense of the underlying principles of complex ideas, such as "hydrogen bonding." This requires teachers to insist that students conceptualize and express complex ideas with meaningful principles about matter, energy, and/or forces that underlie causes of phenomena. Additionally, when teachers expect students to describe causes of a phenomenon and the interactions of matter, energy and/or forces, students will begin to see how core ideas apply across many phenomena. Let's see how this plays out in Vignette 1, which provides an example of this type of student interaction.

Students are given a paper towel and asked to explore how water moves through the towel to develop questions to investigate the phenomenon. What follows is an example of classroom discourse from a high school chemistry class.

Phenomenon: Liquid water moves up through a paper towel despite gravity pulling down on the water.

Carlotta: "Why does the water move up hill?"

Teacher: "That's a good question, why do you think it moves up through the paper?"

David: "Hydrogen bonding!"

Teacher: "What do you mean when you say, 'hydrogen bonding'?"

David: "You know it is hydrogen and it is bonding."

Teacher: "Help me understand what you are saying."

David: "Well, water has hydrogen.... And it bonds."

Teacher: "Does anyone else have more information on how this hydrogen bonding is causing wicking of water up the paper towel?"

Makayla: "I found it on Wikipedia!"

Teacher: "Is that a pun?"

Makayla: "It is really there, and I quote – '*Capillary action (sometimes capillarity, capillary motion, or wicking) is the ability of a liquid to flow in narrow spaces without assistance of, or even in opposition to, external forces like gravity. The effect can be seen in the drawing up of liquids between the hairs of a paint-brush, in a thin tube, in porous materials such as paper and plaster, in some non-porous materials such as sand and liquefied carbon fiber, or in a cell. It occurs because of intermolecular forces between the liquid and the surrounding solid surfaces.*'"

Teacher: "So, what does that mean? Is the movement of water up the paper towel caused by matter, energy, or forces?"

Kesha: "Forces!"

Teacher: "So, how are these forces causing the water to move UP the towel?"

Carlotta: "Well, there is a force between the fibers in the towel and the water, this causes the water to move through the towel. The force is between the molecules of the water and the molecules of the towel. This causes water molecules to move up the towel, overcoming gravity."

Teacher: "What type of forces are we talking about here that are stronger than gravity?"

Max: "It would have to be electromagnetic forces."

Teacher: "What are electromagnetic forces?"

Max: "You know, the forces between the positive end of one molecule and the negative end of another molecule, in this case between the paper and the water."

Teacher:	"So, restating this idea, the intermolecular forces between the water and the paper cause the water to move up between the fibers of the towel. The attraction of the water to the paper is due to electromagnetic forces, in this case we could call this adhesion, attraction of one material to another rather than cohesion, attraction of water to itself which causes drops to form spheres."

~Teacher allows 30 seconds of think time~

Teacher:	"So, can anyone else think of another phenomenon that has the same causes?"
Gabby:	"This is just like when the colored water moved up the stem of the cut carnation flower in biology. We put a flower in blue colored water and the next day the flower had turned blue!"
Teacher:	"Do you remember what that was called?"
Gabby:	"No."
Teacher:	"Does anyone know what that is called?"
Makayla:	"Oh, that was also on Wikipedia, but it didn't make sense to me so I didn't read it out loud earlier. Now it makes sense! It says, '*When the contact length (around the edge) between the top of the liquid column and the tube is proportional to the radius of the tube, while the weight of the liquid column is proportional to the square of the tube's radius. So, a narrow tube will draw a liquid column higher than a wider tube will, given that the inner water molecules cohere sufficiently to the outer ones.*' The tubes in the plant are very small!"
Teacher:	"This is very interesting. So, the smaller the size of tube, the greater the proportion of tube that has electromagnetic attraction pulling on the water."
Kesha:	"This make sense now. Hydrogen bonding causes capillary action. The forces are between molecules that make up the tube and the water. The greater the force, the more the water wicks up the plant."
Teacher:	"Yes, and this is what I call a 'Wiki-Leak!' .... I will explain that joke to you tomorrow. OK, I want everyone to look for a phenomenon with the same causes as the wicking paper towel and we will share tomorrow, see you tomorrow."

When teachers require students to use more than a one-word response, students' ideas begin to grow into conceptual models. These conceptual models can then be applied to make sense of analogous phenomena. As students apply conceptual models to new phenomena their ideas are continuously remodeled and refined to include additional examples. Building a cadre of conceptual models better equips students to seek additional information and engage in reasoning about the interactions of matter, energy, and forces. During class discussion, the teacher's role is significant because it requires the teacher to listen carefully and synthesize students' understanding into a common and accurate scientific explanation across the entire class. This is not front-loading information, rather it is well-planned and structured discussion to provide additional information and language within the context of the phenomenon. The "need" for information is created by the intentional planning of instruction and guided discussion to direct students toward meaningful science ideas. The teacher's ability to know when and how to extend thinking at the important teachable moments is equally critical.

This aspect of the interaction is the result of planning and listening: planning the lesson and questions to extend thinking and listening to students' responses to adjust instruction and help students construct meaningful connections to prior knowledge and experiences. We cannot overstate the importance of teachers listening to students' responses, questions, and explanations then responding appropriately to extend learning.

Why is an Instructional Sequence Critical for Meaningful Student Science Performances?

Science instruction that only uses one phenomenon, or one performance with a single core idea does not provide sufficient opportunities for students to apply learning to new contexts and conceptualize the science core ideas. During the Elaboration phase, students apply what they learn. This well-articulated instructional sequence provides opportunities for students to apply what they have learned. Students making sense of one phenomenon and then transferring that same set of core ideas to make sense of analogous phenomena is an model for science learning. The 5E instructional model provides a true application of what students learn and develops conceptual knowledge of core ideas and crosscutting concepts within an engaging context. When GRC is used within each of the 5E phases, student thinking is structured and reasoning is more central to the teaching and learning. The structure of instruction is important for the teaching and learning process.

Summary

Science in the broadest sense is engaging in investigation. Investigation in science and engineering goes beyond the practice of "plan and carry out;" it includes a suite of practices, crosscutting concepts, and core ideas. Instruction should have a logical and effective sequence in which students apply their new knowledge and skills, as well as knowledge from prior experiences. When students have engaged in investigation, they have a set of skills and knowledge to make sense of novel phenomena they encounter in the world. We believe this preparation is best accomplished through a sequence that returns the student to applying their knowledge and skills to make sense of analogous phenomena. It is important that the instruction uses effective instructional strategies (e.g., classroom discourse, hands-on investigations, engaging phenomenon). Students need to apply what they know, not just parrot back information to the teacher. Classrooms should be "think tanks" and not echo chambers!

Reflecting on Student Science Performances

1. How are student science performances important for application of the science and engineering practices they have learned?

2. Reflect on the vignette of the paper towels wicking up water and write a similar vignette from your own experience that starts with a phenomenon.

3. Why is it important for teachers to use crosscutting concepts in their prompts of student performances?

4. Why are standards aligned to the *Framework* called performance expectations?

5. Why do the authors place so much emphasis on the teacher listening to students?

6. How are Gather, Reason, and Communicate performances different from one another, and what are the key aspects of each of these three types of performance?

Bibliography

Bybee, R. (2015). *The BSCS 5E Instructional Model: Creating Teachable Moments*. Washington, DC: NSTA Press.

Moulding, B., Bybee, R., & Paulson, N. (2015). *Vision and Plan for Science Teaching and Learning*. Salt Lake City, UT: Essential Teaching and Learning.

National Research Council. (1999). *NRC Report How People Learn*. Washington, DC: The National Academies Press.

National Research Council. (2012). *A Framework for K-12 Science Education: Practices, Crosscutting Concepts, and Core Ideas*. Washington, DC: The National Academies Press.

National Research Council. (2015). *NRC Report Guide to Implementing the Next Generation Science Standards*. Washington, DC: The National Academies Press.

National Research Council. (2007). *Taking Science to School: Learning and Teaching Science in Grades K-8*. Washington, DC: The National Academies Press.

NGSS Lead States. (2013). *Next Generation Science Standards: For States, By States*. Washington, DC: The National Academies Press.

Except for children (who don't know enough not to ask the important questions), few of us spend time wondering why nature is the way it is.

~Carl Sagan

CHAPTER 5

SCIENCE AND ENGINEERING PRACTICES

Why Should Students Engage in Doing Science?

Science and Engineering Practices

When used as a teaching strategy, the science and engineering practices become central to student engagement in science. Simply stated, the practices are what students do when they make sense of phenomena. Descriptions of the eight science and engineering practices are provided in Appendix A. In the previous four chapters the instructional sequence of Gather, Reason, and Communicate (GRC) was described around the practices. The 5E instructional model was described as a way to organize iterations of the GRC into an instructional sequence that supports students as they apply core ideas and crosscutting concepts and engage in science and engineering practices. In this integrated sequence, it is important to remember that the practices are what students *do.* The teacher's role is to create an environment and structure for students to use the practices to make sense of phenomena. This is not an easy task, since it must result in students becoming proficient at asking question, planning and carrying out investigations to gather evidence, constructing explanations, arguing for how the evidence supports the explanation, and communicating that explanation and argument.

Constructing explanations based on evidence and developing arguments for how that evidence supports the explanation are the central tasks of scientific inquiry. Gathering practices serve to obtain data, observations, and information to use as evidence supporting explanations. The communicating practices serve to make student reasoning visible. The natural center for student thinking is the reasoning practices couplet of ***constructing explanations*** and ***developing arguments*** for the evidence that supports the ***explanation*** (see Figure 5-1).

Pairing the Practices

Situating science and engineering practices in a sequence is an important aspect of promoting student reasoning. The practices each have a role across GRC. There is also an interrelationship among some of the practices that makes "pairing of practices" an effective way to enhance student reasoning. Some practices have a natural pairing with other practices and/or crosscutting concepts. For example, models and systems function well together: *Develop a model for the interaction of the components of a defined system.* The following paragraphs discuss some of the natural pairings of practices.

SCIENCE AND ENGINEERING PRACTICES

Gather	Reason	Communicate
Developing the data, making observations, and obtaining information that can be used to reason.	Constructing explanations. Developing arguments to support how the evidence supports the explanation.	Presenting arguments through speaking and/or writing for how the evidence supports the explanation.
Using models to organize information (e.g., data charts, tables) and/or gathering data using a simulation and/or physical models.	Using models to analyze data and/or organize relationships between the components of systems. Evaluating information.	Using models to communicate reasoning and arguing for how the evidence supports the explanation.

Note. Some of the practices appear in multiple places. Integrating the GRC within the 5E instructional model engages students in using the practices in a sequence that supports using the practices beyond the classroom.

Planning and carrying out investigations that generate data and information is linked to students *analyzing the data* they collect. There are a number of reasons for pairing investigations with analyzing data, not the least of which is that data students collect has a context and meaning for the students. Analyzing data collected by students contributes significant meaning to supporting the use of the data as evidence in explanations. When students are asked to analyze data sets from other sources, the data lacks context, which makes the analysis unnecessarily difficult and the learning less relevant. This is not to say that students should only analyze the data they generate, but when students analyze others' data, a context and purpose must be supplied to make the task meaningful. Science is not a spectator sport. Groups with two or three students are ideal when carrying out investigations. When groups are greater than three, some students are relegated to the role of spectator and do not engage physically or intellectually in the investigation.

The practices of *obtaining, evaluating, and communicating information* are essentially three connected but separate practices. In the GRC sequence, obtaining information resides within Gather, evaluating information and determining the relevance of the information as evidence to support an explanation resides in Reason, and presenting the reasoning that connects the evidence to explanations of causes of phenomena resides in Communicate. The performance of communicating information makes students' reasoning visible through speaking, writing, and/or models. Obtaining, evaluating, and communicating information is an important practice that resides within each of the phases of the 5E instructional model, but is instructionally significant for the Explore phase, when students focus on gathering information to use as evidence to support explanations of the phenomenon introduced in the Engage phase.

Asking questions should always be linked to other practices: asking questions to *obtain information*, asking questions to *plan an investigation* of phenomena, asking questions to *determine the best solution to solve a problem*, asking questions about the attributes of a *model*, or asking questions to *determine mathematical relationships*. Asking questions is an excellent practice to lead into any phase of the 5E instructional model and an essential component of gathering in the GRC performance sequence. The most important thing to remember is that students are the ones asking the questions. The teacher's role is much more difficult; we must create the conditions that invite good questions, that pique curiosity, and support students in asking better and better questions as they delve more deeply into making sense of phenomena.

Constructing explanations is best paired with *developing arguments* for each line of evidence. When these two practices are linked, they focus students' reasoning on developing an argument for how the gathered evidence supports or refutes an explanation. Students construct or identify an explanation and then develop arguments for how each of the various lines of evidence support the explanation. The pairing of these two practices is central to science reasoning and emphasizes the role of evidence in science. Engaging in argumentation changes and refines the initial explanation. "Engaging in argumentation from evidence about an explanation supports students' understanding of the reasons and empirical evidence for that explanation, demonstrating that science is a body of knowledge rooted in evidence" (*Framework*, p. 34).

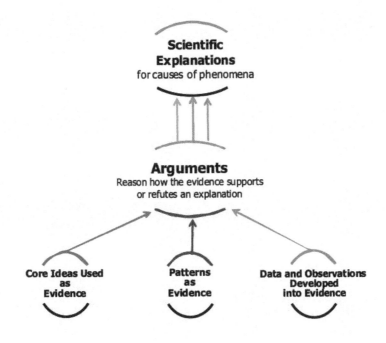

Figure 5-2. Relationship of Explanations and Argumentation

Argumentation is not limited to the students' own explanations, but includes explanations presented by others. When students develop arguments for how evidence supports or refutes a specific explanation, they are engaged in an important habit of the mind. Science explanations are based on evidence. The use of evidence is what distinguishes science from other ways of knowing.

Situating the Practices within Lessons

A natural pairing and sequence of the practices tends to exist across the 5E instructional model and within GRC performances. For instance, students engage in gathering information and constructing explanations in the Engage and Explore phases; focus on explanations and argumentation in the Explain phase; and then apply these practices once again in the Elaborate and Evaluate phases. These sequences provide students with the tools to move from one practice to the next in logical steps toward communicating their understanding of causes of phenomena.

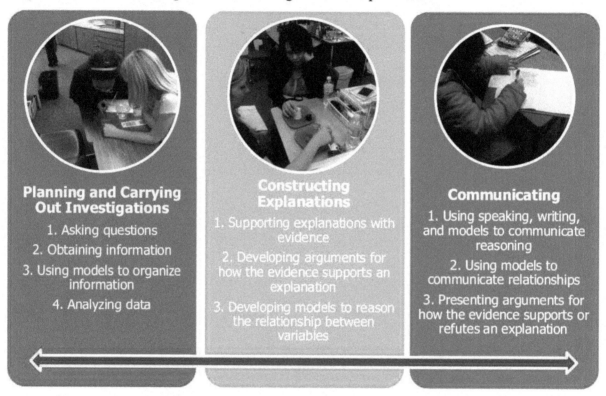

Figure 5-3. Practices Naturally Situated within Sequences of Learning. It is important to note that these sequences of learning performances may not be linear.

Asking Questions to Obtain Information and/or Plan Investigations

Lessons initiated with phenomena are more effective when students use the practice of asking questions to either obtain information and/or plan and carry out investigations. Engaging students in asking questions for these purposes creates a natural way for teachers to assess students' interest in a specific phenomenon. More importantly, asking questions is a tool for students to determine the information needed to make sense of the phenomenon. The strategies teachers use to engage students in asking good questions require planning meaningful prompts that help students seek the information

Teaching Science is Phenomenal

needed to determine causes of phenomena. The 5E instructional model adds benefit by creating a structure for students to build additional skills and obtain information through the Explore phase, and then apply skills and knowledge in subsequent student performances in the Elaborate phase. Throughout the GRC sequence, and within each phase of the 5E instructional model, students are building a foundation of skills and knowledge to apply in the next phases (i.e., Explain and Elaborate). The iterative nature of the 5E instructional model leverages earlier learning for application in later phases to make sense of analogous phenomena.

The practices students use across the phases of the 5E instructional model tend to shift from foreground to background perspective, or primary to secondary emphasis. During the Engage phase, students are introduced to science phenomena and should focus on the practices of asking questions and obtaining information. While these two practices may be used in any of the phases, they should receive special attention in the Engage phase.

During the Explore phase there is a shift from asking general questions about the phenomenon to asking questions that can be investigated. More focused questions lead students to the practices of planning and carrying out investigations, analyzing and interpreting data, using mathematics and computational thinking, and constructing explanations. As appropriate, the latter may include developing models.

In the Explain phase students clearly construct explanations and use models, writing, and speaking to communicate their explanations of the phenomenon. Generally, in the Explain phase students develop and communicate arguments for how the evidence they have collected in the Engage and Explore phases supports their explanations.

Finally, the Elaboration phase should include practices emphasized in the instructional sequence and in the performance expectations for the standards addressed in the lesson. The GRC sequence is not necessarily linear and students may need to return to gathering additional information to support their reasoning, develop and revise models, and continuously communicating their reasoning in many forms.

When students begin to communicate an argument, they may realize that additional evidence is needed to support the explanation or model. The additional information may lead to a revision of the argument.

Developing and Using Models

Students should develop and use models to organize data and information, reason relationships, and/or communicate their reasoning about experiences they have had with the phenomenon. If not, we may end up with little more than memorization of the attributes of a model and not meaningful understanding of the science concepts and ideas underlying the explanation of causes of a phenomenon. More importantly, we find that student curiosity and interest is more significantly leveraged by using the phenomenon first and then moving to the model.

Engage Students in Phenomena First – Then Use Models to Support Reasoning

Refer back to Figure 2-1 and note how the practices are used multiple times across the performance sequence of GRC, with only the practice of developing and using models appearing as students gather, reason, and communicate reasoning. Models should be used to make sense of phenomena. We advocate that students experience the phenomena first rather than using models as the initial learning experience. Later in the sequence, students can use the model to better understand their observations and experiences with actual phenomena. We sometimes make the error of teaching the model rather than the phenomenon. For example, when asked "which direction does the moon orbit the Earth," students and teachers frequently respond, "counter clockwise." But when asked, "So if we go out and observe the moon directly overhead at 9pm on Monday, where will the moon be on Tuesday at 9pm, further east or further west?" both students and teachers struggle to answer. When asked, "What evidence would you need to determine the direction the moon orbits the Earth – east to west or west to east?"– students and teachers say they need a globe of the earth to decide which direction counter clockwise is before they can decide. These responses are grounded in a model-based understanding and not a phenomenon-based understanding, which underscores the importance of teachers and students engaging with phenomena first and then using models to make sense of their observations. If we want students to have a phenomenon-based understanding of the motion of objects in the sky such as the moon's orbit of Earth, instruction needs to be initiated with observation of the moon from the same spot at the same time on two consecutive clear nights. When our understanding is model-based, we rely on exploring the model without connecting it to the phenomenon.

Some phenomena can only be explained using core ideas that are best conceptualized using models, due to the complexity or scale of the interactions (e.g., atomic scale particles, plate tectonics, transformation of light into heat energy). When students are constructing explanations for causes of phenomena involving forces, models are useful to help the students both reason about the phenomena and communicate their reasoning. Models, whether a diagram or a data chart, are useful tools to help students keep track of multiple components and interactions of systems. Sometime we are limited in the phenomena we can bring into our classrooms, but videos, simulations, and/or pictures can help students contextualize phenomena.

Here are a few simple ways to introduce and engage students with phenomena before using models:

- Observe the motion of the moon on three consecutive days before using a model to make sense of the actual and relative motion of the moon.

- Observe an ecosystem of plants and animals in a pond prior to developing a model of a pond ecosystem.

- Investigate various sedimentary rocks and watch a video of the weathering process prior to using a model to explain the processes of weathering, erosion, deposition, sedimentation, and cementation.

- Observe or view pictures of roadside weathering and erosion prior to using stream tables.

The *Framework* states, "Models serve the purpose of being a tool for thinking with, making predictions, and making sense of experiences" *(Framework, pp. 56-7)*, and goes on to address how scientists use models to describe their understanding of systems being investigated, support ways to organize reasoning, pose meaningful questions, support reasoning about relationships among variables, and support development of explanations. The use of models has utility in communicating the thinking of both scientists and students when words are not sufficient to communicate the full intent of complex multidimensional ideas. Developing and using models is a practice that students use across GRC. Models should not be limited to communicating ideas and concepts. Models should also be used to (1) gather and organize information, data, and ideas; (2) reason the relationship between variables and among components of systems; (3) make predictions; and (4) communicate reasoning to others.

Using Models to Gather

Gathering information, observations, and/or data generally initiates the practice of using models in the sequence of GRC. Models are useful tools for gathering and organizing information. Examples of the use of charts, tables, writing, and diagrams to organize information, observations, and data are shown in Figure 5-4. Additionally, models can be used to generate data and/or information about phenomena.

Using Models to Reason

Reasoning requires students to evaluate information, analyze data in ways that reveal logical connections of the data to the phenomena, use mathematical and computational thinking to reason relationships among variables, and relate current ideas and concepts to causes of phenomena. Models are an effective way to determine important relationships between variables and the interactions among the components of systems. The relationship among variables may be modeled using equations (e.g., $F=ma$, $E=\frac{1}{2}MV^2$, $6CO_2 + 6H_2O = C_6H_{12}O_6 + 6O_2$). Reasoning with models is strongly linked to making sense of the interactions of variables (e.g., weather models used to forecast; Earth, moon, sun model used to determine phases of the moon; models used to show the flow of energy in ecosystems). Using models to support reasoning should provide students with ways to generalize, make predictions, and connect cause and effect, or structure and function, to make sense of phenomenon. Models can be used to manipulate data and/or information to make it more useful as evidence when **constructing explanations** and **developing arguments** for how the evidence supports or refutes an explanation.

Using Models to Communicate Reasoning

Communicating the reasoning that supports explanations is an essential practice for science teaching and learning. Communicating makes thinking visible to both the teacher and the student. Students can use models to effectively communicate the mechanisms by which phenomena occur, account for changes in systems, and/or provide the evidence to support an explanation. Students can communicate the key aspects of their explanations through written and oral descriptions of models and/or use the actual model to show key interactions and relationships. Students are able to use models to communicate reasoning they are unable to put into words. The nature of science communication should focus on arguing how evidence supports or refutes an explanation. Models are an important way for students to communicate their arguments in well-organized and cogent ways.

Figure 5-4. Using Models in GRC Performance Sequences

PHENOMENON	PURPOSE	MODELS	HOW STUDENTS USE A MODEL
The moon appears to change shape each night throughout the month.	Gather	Bright light representing the sun, white ball on stick for moon, own head representing the Earth.	As the moon orbits the Earth, different portions of the moon appear to be lit. Student use a chart to record the lit portion at different orbital positions.
	Reason	Student draws a model of the change in phase of the moon at various positions.	Use the same model the student used to gather information on relative positions of the moon and sun to now predict positions when full and/or new moons occur.
	Communicate Reasoning	Diagram of the relative position of the sun, moon, and Earth with lines showing light going to the moon and the light reflecting to Earth from the visible portion of the moon.	Share their understanding of the relative positions of Earth, moon, and sun for various moon phases, knowing half of the moon is always lit, but from our perspective we only see part of the lit portion.
One child can balance the weight of two children on a teeter totter by moving the position where they sit.	Gather	Ruler as a lever, large eraser as a fulcrum, weight of pennies on one side of lever to represent the "effort" and a quarter on the other side to represent the "load." Use T-chart or data chart to record data.	Obtain data for how changing the position of the fulcrum affects the number of pennies (force of effort) needed to lift a "load" when the "effort" is moved further from the fulcrum.
	Reason	Force = mass X distance Force of effort X distance = Force of load X distance.	Use the equation to predict the balance point of two masses on a "teeter totter" when mass is known.

PHENOMENON	PURPOSE	MODELS	HOW STUDENTS USE A MODEL
	Communicate Reasoning	Use a diagram showing a lever, fulcrum, and effort needed to lift an object of given mass. Use equation to show the relationship.	Use model to communicate the relationship between the force and distance for levers and "teeter totters."
Carrot sticks placed in fresh water become crisper, but when placed in salt water limper.	Gather	Chart to record observation of the crispness of carrots in 5 solutions with different salt concentrations.	Collect observations in an organized way to see observable difference in the flexibility of the carrots.
	Reason	Model of cell wall and the ions of salt inside and outside of the cell.	Patterns in the data are analyzed to use as evidence that the concentration of the salt affects the cells. Cell models are used to analyze changes in a system at the cellular scale.
	Communicate Reasoning	Model of cells, ions, and molecules are used to show water movement to balance concentration.	Models of the cell membrane, salt ions, and water molecules are used to show concentration difference that causes movement of water into or out of cells.
When seeds are planted, a living organism grows.	Gather	Charts to record daily changes in the growth of the seeds.	Collect observations and measurements of the daily changes in the stages of the life cycle.
	Reason	Diagram of life cycle showing patterns in the plants and the system of soil, water, light, air, and sunlight needed for growth.	Use model to show patterns of observations across multiple types of plants and stages in life cycle.
	Communicate Reasoning	Pictures organized in a sequence to show changes over time of the life cycle of plants.	Show understanding of the life cycle and how patterns exist across multiple types of plants.
Develop your own models	Gather		
	Reason		
	Communicate Reasoning		

Reflecting on Science and Engineering Practices

1. In this chapter, the authors provide a number of examples of paired practices. Consider other practices that are meaningful when paired and write a short rationale for how you might use them in describing a student performance.

2. In the blank spaces at the end of Figure 5-4, develop a specific model may be used by students to gather information/data, reason relationships, and communicate explanations.

3. Why are the practices useful for engaging students in science learning?

4. The authors argue that we should engage students in making sense of the actual phenomenon before using the model as a proxy. Describe an advantage of starting with the phenomenon and then using models in instruction that the authors did not share in the chapter?

5. The authors state that some students can only share their reasoning using models. Reflect about your students who rely on models rather than responding in writing. How can you use this behavior with models to help them become better writers?

Bibliography

Bybee, R. (2015). *The BSCS 5E Instructional Model: Creating Teachable Moments*. Washington, DC: NSTA Press.

Moulding, B., Bybee, R., & Paulson, N. (2015). *Vision and Plan for Science Teaching and Learning*. Salt Lake City, UT: Essential Teaching and Learning.

National Research Council. (1999). *NRC Report How People Learn*. Washington, DC: The National Academies Press.

National Research Council. (2012). *A Framework for K-12 Science Education: Practices, Crosscutting Concepts, and Core Ideas*. Washington, DC: The National Academies Press.

National Research Council. (2015). *NRC Report Guide to Implementing the Next Generation Science Standards*. Washington, DC: The National Academies Press.

National Research Council. (2007). *Taking Science to School: Learning and Teaching Science in Grades K-8*. Washington, DC: The National Academies Press.

NGSS Lead States. (2013). *Next Generation Science Standards: For States, By States*. Washington, DC: The National Academies Press.

Be less curious about people and more curious about ideas.

~Marie Curie

CHAPTER 6

CROSSCUTTING CONCEPTS AND DISCIPLINARY CORE IDEAS

*How do students use crosscutting concepts and disciplinary core ideas
to make sense of phenomena?*

When making sense of phenomena, students use the crosscutting concepts and disciplinary core ideas in similar, yet different, ways. Students use these two dimensions to support explanations for causes of phenomena. The difference lies in how these two dimensions are conceptualized by students and used to organize their thinking. The crosscutting concepts generally provide a framework for reasoning and the core ideas provide the accumulated evidence/principles supporting explanations and arguments. The crosscutting concepts of patterns, conservation of energy, and conservation of matter are often effectively used by students as evidence. For example:

Figure 6-1. Examples of Crosscutting Concepts Related to Phenomena and Explanations

CROSSCUTTING CONCEPT	PHENOMENON	EXPLANATION
Conservation of Matter	When baking soda and vinegar are mixed in a bottle a change occurs, and the system weighs less.	Matter is conserved, so one of the components of the system is leaving and going into a different system, the air, and the mass is not being measured.
Conservation of Energy	A golf ball is dropped onto a surface and does not bounce back to the original height.	Energy is conserved, so the ball must be transferring and/or transforming some of the energy to other systems or it would return to the original height.
Patterns	When a Hereford cow (red with white face) is bred with an Angus bull (black) the calves are black with white faces.	The frequency of traits in a population can be determined by analyzing the patterns of the appearance of that trait over the previous generations of a population. The color, size, or birth weight of hybrid cattle in a herd can be predicted based on the patterns of inheritance of a specific color, size, or birth weight of the previous generations of cattle.

The crosscutting concepts provide an effective tool for focusing student reasoning. The crosscutting concepts are a way to help students understand the expectations for constructing explanations for causes of phenomena and framing the components of the system to investigate in terms of matter, energy, scale, quantity, change, stability, and proportions of components in the system. When teachers use crosscutting concepts to structure questions it helps focus student thinking on specific aspects of a phenomenon (e.g., causes of changes in the system, patterns of change over time, structure of an organism that functions to meet the needs of the organism).

Students are empowered to explain causes of novel phenomena when they deeply understand a small set of core ideas that are regularly used to make sense of a wide variety of phenomena. Whether a student is wondering why the moon sometimes appears orange in the sky or why they can clearly see the bottom of a mountain lake, their understanding of core ideas about how light interacts with matter supports the reasoning necessary to construct an explanation of causes of the phenomena. When students are able to use core ideas to accurately make sense of novel phenomena we know that they understand the core idea. It is not enough for students to know the core ideas; they must apply the core ideas to make sense of phenomenon and meet performance expectations of science learning.

In science, everything has a cause— that is why it is science and not magic!

~Brett Moulding

Crosscutting Concepts

Crosscutting concepts are useful for making sense of phenomena and hence are critical for effective science teaching and learning. The crosscutting concepts provide a language for teachers to effectively communicate with students. Students' attention is directed to specific aspects of phenomena when teachers use crosscutting concepts to prompt students' thinking and reasoning. When teachers use questions that utilize the crosscutting concepts, a consistent language is establish to aid the dialogue between the teacher and students. This dialogue helps students use crosscutting concepts to focus on causes of science phenomena, develop understanding of the systems, and recognize and use patterns as evidence to support explanations. In turn, students will begin using the same language of crosscutting concepts both in their responses to the teacher and for their own internal reasoning.

Although crosscutting concepts are fundamental to an understanding of science and engineering, students are generally expected to build knowledge of these concepts without explicit instruction. In the new vision for science education, crosscutting concepts are expected to be common and familiar touchstones across the science disciplines, grade-levels, and sometimes in other school subjects.

Explicit reference to the concepts, as well as their emergence in multiple disciplinary contexts, helps students develop a cumulative, coherent, and usable understanding of science and engineering. The *Framework* identifies seven crosscutting concepts, shown in Figure 6-2.

Figure 6-2. Crosscutting Concepts from the Framework

1. ***Patterns*** – Observed patterns of forms and events guide organization and classification. Patterns prompt questions about the factors that influence cause and effect relationships. Patterns are useful as evidence to support explanations and arguments.

2. ***Cause and Effect*** – Mechanism and explanation. Events have causes, sometimes simple, sometimes multifaceted and complex. A major activity of science is investigating and explaining causal relationships and the mechanisms by which they are mediated. Such mechanisms can then be tested across given contexts and used to predict and explain events in new contexts.

3. ***Scale, Proportion, and Quantity*** – In considering phenomena, it is critical to recognize what is relevant at different measures of size, time, and energy and to recognize how changes in scale, proportion, or quantity affect a system's structure or performance.

4. ***Systems and System Models*** – Defining the system under study—specifying its boundaries and making explicit a model of that system—provides tools for understanding and testing ideas that are applicable throughout science and engineering.

5. ***Energy and Matter*** – Flows, cycles, and conservation. Tracking fluxes of energy and matter into, out of, and within systems helps one understand the system's possibilities and limitations.

6. ***Structure and Function*** – An object's structure and shape determine many of its properties and functions. The structures, shapes, and substructure of living organisms determine how the organism functions to meet its needs within an environment.

7. ***Stability and Change*** – For natural and built systems alike, conditions of stability and rates of change provide the focus for understanding how the system operates and the causes of changes in systems.

Crosscutting concepts can be organized into three broad groups: causality, systems, and patterns (See Figure 6-3). Each group of concepts functions differently to support student thinking about phenomena. First, scientists seek to establish causality; without the expectation for causality, all phenomena could be explained with, "It's magic." Secondly, scientists use systems to define the parameters of phenomena being investigated. Finally, patterns are useful evidence to support explanations, arguments, and make predictions. Additionally, patterns in phenomena can initiate questions to be investigated. It is important for students to clearly understand that science seeks to establish explanations for causes of phenomena (effects) within and among systems. Unfortunately, science instruction frequently ignores this basic expectation of science.

Using the crosscutting concepts organized around causality, systems, and patterns, is useful in helping students organize questions to make sense of phenomena. For example, when a student notices ice forming on a river, questions in physical science and earth sciences based on crosscutting concepts might include: What caused the ice to form near the edge of the river first? How do inputs and outputs of energy to the system cause changes to the matter to in the system? How does the flow of water in the middle of the river affect the water on the edges? Does this same pattern occur in other rivers? Does the pattern occur each year?

When students encounter natural phenomena in life science and earth science they can use the crosscutting concepts in similar ways to focus questions. For example, when students see changes in an ecosystem such as an increase in the number of Tamarisk on the banks of the Colorado River, questions organized around the crosscutting concepts may include: How does this plant species affect the energy reaching the other species in the system? How do Tamarisk cause changes in the movement of matter (sand) down the river? How does the proportion of Tamarisk on the banks change during flooding episode?

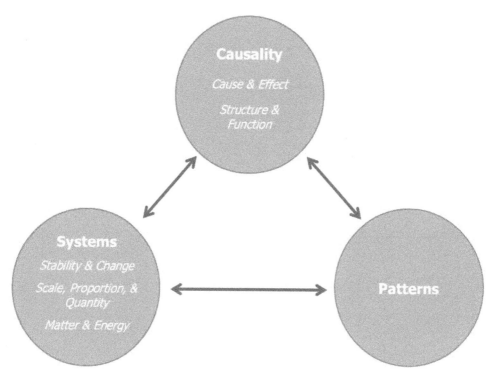

Figure 6-3. Organizing the Crosscutting Concepts. Organization into causality, systems, and patterns is useful for classroom instruction and for students to make sense of phenomena. Reproduced from Moulding, Bybee, & Paulson (2015)

Using the structure of causality, systems, and patterns to organize the crosscutting concepts focuses students on important aspects of phenomena. This structure provides students with a consistent approach for exploring any phenomena by seeking **causal** relationships of the interacting components within and among **systems** and using **patterns** as evidence to support explanations for causes of phenomena. Students are better able to collect relevant evidence needed to support an explanation when they engage in questions such as:

Teaching Science is Phenomenal

- *How does the* system change *when more* energy *is added to the* system?

- *Why does adding heat* energy *to the* system cause *the observed* changes in the system?

- *How does the* portion *of the population with a specific trait* affect changes *in the population over time?*

- *What* caused *the* change *in the* system?

Teachers are responsible for helping students develop a structure to make sense of phenomena. Crosscutting concepts help to focus student thinking in productive ways on specific aspects of the phenomenon (e.g., proportion of salt in water, scale of thickness of crust compared to diameter of Earth, flow of energy in or out of the system during a chemical reaction). Crosscutting concepts become powerful tools when they are consistent touchstones of teachers' and students' language.

Teachers are in the "thinking business," both in supporting students in learning how to think and analyzing students' learning progress. Understanding student thinking requires ways to make thinking visible. The structure of prompts has a significant impact on the degree to which student thinking is focused and becomes visible. The responses inform the teacher for adjusting instruction and students for reflecting on and improving learning. In science education, we establish structures to focus students' reasoning for using evidence to support explanations.

Prompting students with crosscutting sentence stems can focus students' attention on specific aspects of phenomena. These prompts should have follow-up inquiry about how the evidence supports the student's reasoning. It is important to use the crosscutting concepts to develop and support a structure of student reasoning. This structure becomes the way students respond to teacher prompts.

A few sample prompts organized with crosscutting concepts:

- The cause(s) of _____ was/were _____.
  Evidence to support my explanation is _____.

- The changes in the system were caused by _____.
  Evidence to support my explanation is _____.

- The phenomenon of _____ is caused by _____.
  Evidence to support this explanation (claim/explanation) is _____.

Communication is more effective when students understand they are expected to communicate causes of phenomena and provide evidence supporting explanations. Never underestimate the importance of clear expectations for student performances.

Utilizing the consistent language of crosscutting concepts results in students having a structure for reasoning. This language increases the accuracy and consistency of their reasoning. Students use the language teachers consistently and accurately use in the classroom to respond to the teachers' inquiries.

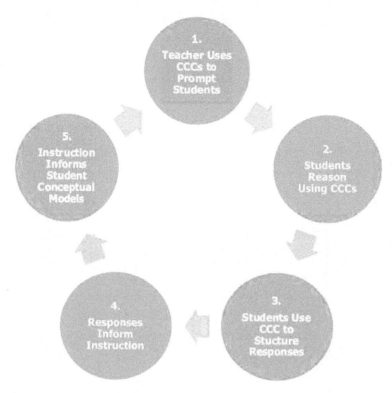

Figure 6-4. Teacher Prompts Using Crosscutting Concepts. Such prompts lead to student responses using crosscutting concepts.

The following is a class discussion that shows a sequence of interactions consistent with the idea of using crosscutting concepts to prompt student responses.

Vignette 2: Using Crosscutting Concepts in Class Discussion

A fourth-grade teacher is beginning a unit on weather and starts with the water cycle. The instruction begins with an informal discussion to elicit students' thinking about the role of energy in the water cycle.

Teacher:	"This morning I noticed water on the playground from the rain, but this afternoon most of the water is gone."
Malia:	"It evaporated!"
Teacher:	"What do you mean 'it evaporated'?"
Malia:	"You know, it evaporated, the water went into the air."
Teacher:	"Can anyone add to Malia's idea?"
Xi:	"Yes, the water changed from a liquid to a gas."
Teacher:	"What caused the water to change from a liquid to a gas?"

Teacher:	"So, let's take a minute to think and write a response to the question – What caused the water to change from a liquid to a gas?" After a few minutes, the teacher calls on Lani.
Lani:	"The sun caused the water to change."
Teacher:	"Can anyone share evidence that the sun was the cause?"
Roberto	"I can. When the sun is shining the puddles on the playground dry up faster than when it is cloudy."
Teacher:	"So, what is causing the water to evaporate?"
Roberto:	"Heat causes the water to evaporate."
Teacher:	"You seem to like this word 'evaporate,' what does it mean?"
Roberto:	"Water, you know, changes from a liquid into a gas and becomes clouds."
Teacher:	"When I look out onto the playground I cannot see any clouds coming off the water…. I want everyone to turn to their shoulder partner and discuss what causes the water to change from a liquid into a gas and why can't we see it."

~Students turn to shoulder partners and talk for a minute.
Then the teacher brings the class to order and calls on Malia~

Malia:	"Things do not just happen, something is causing it to change and I think heat is causing the water to change from a liquid to a gas."
Teacher:	"Why can't I see the water after it evaporates?"
Jacob:	"It is because it is not made of anything, just like air."
Teacher:	"So, let's talk about this. What are the properties of air? What causes a piece of paper to move when I blow on it?"

For the first time in the discussion the students do not raise their hands immediately, and when they do, they struggle with describing the property of air that transfers forces. The teacher begins to formulate from their responses a problem with their understanding that matter is made of particles that have mass and take up space. The teacher decides to change the instruction and engage the students in a performance the next day to focus on the idea that matter has mass and takes up space.

The next day the teacher engages students in a performance of using a 60ml syringe to push Ping-Pong balls across the table. The students then plan and carry out an investigation to use various volumes of air to move racquet balls and foil boats across tables to determine the relationship between the volume of air and the distance the objects move.

Following the investigation, the teacher engages students in a class discussion.

Teacher:	"So, what evidence do we have from the investigation that air has mass and causes a force to transfer from one object to another object?"
Roberto:	"Air has mass and when it is moving it causes other things to move. It is like when I opened the door and the wind blew it out of my hand. The wind caused the door to be pulled out of my hand. The wind is really moving air and air has weight (mass) and when an object with weight is moving, it causes a force. I could feel it and it pulled hard."
Xi:	"The water is there, but we cannot see the water any more. It's like when you blow on a piece of paper, we cannot see the air, but the air causes the paper to move."
Teacher:	"Do all objects have weight? By the way, in science we refer this weight as mass."
Malia:	"Yes!"

Teacher:	"What evidence do you have to support the assertion that the air has mass and can cause an object to move?"
Malia:	"Well, objects cause other things to move because they transfer a force, and a force is something moving that has weight, you know mass. We found that out in the investigation and the more mass the more the ball moved, you know was caused to move."
Stephen:	"And the faster it is moving the more mass, when we pushed the air out of the syringe faster it pushed the ball further. It takes more force to move the ball further. It is just like when the wind is blowing hard it can cause the leaves to move, but when it is blowing soft the leaves on the ground do not move, but you can feel the air on your face. Air has weight – it is really made of matter, you know like sand or the racquet ball or me! Air is really something even though it looks like nothing!"
Teacher:	"So, let's go back to the investigation, what evidence do you have that the air had mass?"
Lani:	"The air moved the ball, so if the air moves the ball it must have mass to transfer a force. Force and mass are related: the more mass the more force."
Teacher:	"Use a page in your notebook to write three pieces of evidence you have to support Malia's idea that air has mass because it can transfer a force."

The teacher walks around the room looking over shoulders and reading students' reasoning. While students were talking, the bell to end the school day rang and students remained in their seats but quit talking and turned to the teacher.

| Teacher: | "Thank you for an excellent discussion and the good examples of writing supported by evidence that air has mass. We will return to these ideas tomorrow, but this afternoon and evening try to find other phenomena that are caused by moving air." |

The discussion following the two investigations provided an opportunity for the teacher to engage students in reasoning. The reasoning seems simple but is predicated on the reasoning of science, specifically, how your evidence supports your explanation. The teacher at one point in the discussion decided to revise instruction to address what was, clearly, an inaccurate conception: that air does not have mass. The teacher could have shifted to tell mode but understood that the experience of air movement would create a better platform for meaningful instruction. The payoff came at a later point in the discussion when the students began confirming their conceptual understanding for how air has mass, therefore it causes objects to move. The causal relationship was the focus of the science investigation.

Does the Concept of Force Meet the Criteria for Crosscutting Concept Status?

One way to better understand the crosscutting concepts is to make an argument for why something that was not included by the NRC as a crosscutting concept should be included. Imagine a concept such as force. What criteria must this concept meet in order to reach the status of crosscutting concept? Let's examine the criteria used by the NRC to include a crosscutting concept in the *Framework*.

1. *Has utility in developing explanation of many phenomena* – from the motion of a particle of air causing feathers to fall slower than golf balls, to the movement of continental plates, to the movement of blood in veins, phenomena operate in systems that are affected by forces.

2. *Provides students with an organizational framework for connecting knowledge across the various science disciplines* – intermolecular forces cause clouds to form, water to move through a plant by capillary action, salts to dissolve in water, and clouds to form, and influences the shape of cells.

3. *Selected for their value across the sciences and in engineering* - understanding of the role of forces in holding matter together is essential to making sense of the shape of planets, solar systems, and stars, the structure of DNA and process of protein synthesis, the movement of objects in a collision, and the structure of molecules.

The *Framework* (2012), emphasized the inclusion of crosscutting concepts, stating

> Hence the purpose of highlighting Crosscutting Concepts as Dimension 2 of the framework is to elevate their role in the development of standards, curricula, instruction, and assessments. These concepts should become common and familiar touchstones across the disciplines and grade levels. Explicit reference to the concepts, as well as their emergence in multiple disciplinary contexts, can help students develop a cumulative, coherent, and usable understanding of science and engineering. (p. 83)

So, how were some of the ideas that help students to structure thinking about phenomena selected and others were not? How does thinking about the nature of the crosscutting concept of forces support our understanding of the crosscutting concepts? First of all, it is not the types of forces (e.g., electromagnetic or gravitational), and especially not the many terms we have to identify specific cases of forces (e.g., hydrogen bonding, adhesion, cohesion, pushes and pulls, buoyancy, air pressure/force, osmotic pressure), but rather the properties that affect systems (e.g., effect of forces on matter, forces act at a distance, conservation of momentum) that have the attributes of other crosscutting concepts.

Thinking about the organizational structure for crosscutting concepts presented in this chapter of Causality, Systems, and Patterns, where would "force, the crosscutting concept" best serve the learner in making sense of phenomena? Perhaps placing it within a role for systems – "matter, energy, and forces." How do forces help us make sense of phenomena in systems? Well, we could first consider an example phenomenon, any phenomenon. For example, clouds form with puffy, rounded shapes. I do not remember seeing many square clouds. So, why do clouds form in billowy, puffy, roundish shapes?

One more consideration, the crosscutting concepts of energy and matter are limited to flows, cycles, and conservation, specific to making sense of systems by tracing the flow of energy into, out of, and within a system as well as the cycling of matter into, out of, and among systems to support explaining causes of change in the system. Energy and matter conservation are why the tracing and accounting for the changes in systems is important. When students investigate, describe, and model the flow and cycling of energy and matter, the causes of these changes are much more accessible. This is a type of accounting tool used across every discipline of science and engineering. How could we use force in a similar manner to support making sense of changes in systems? Forces affecting systems? Although forces are not considered a crosscutting concept in the *Framework*, we hope this little "bird walk" helps deepen your understanding of the crosscutting concepts.

The crosscutting concepts are used to make sense of phenomena. When teachers use the crosscutting concepts frequently, intentionally, consistently, and accurately, students will use them to help make sense of phenomena. These concepts should be a familiar and useful tool across all grade-levels and disciplines of science.

If you are out to describe the truth, leave elegance to the tailor.

~Albert Einstein

Disciplinary Core Ideas

An effective way for students to think about science phenomena is in terms of matter, energy, forces, space, and time. It is important for students to understand that most phenomena can be explained in terms of the interactions among matter, energy, and forces. If students notice that wet sand is easier to walk on than dry sand, they may recognize this as a science phenomenon, so it has a cause. Students may focus on ideas about forces between grains of sand making the surface firmer, or the idea that sand is matter and has mass which requires energy to move (whether the sand is moved by a shovel or with each footstep). They link their ideas to causes and/or structures that cause dry sand to move differently than wet sand. They should draw on science core ideas about interactions among matter, energy, and forces to construct explanations for why it is easier to walk on wet sand than dry sand. Conceptual knowledge of core ideas about forces, matter, and energy are essential for constructing explanations for causes of phenomena. This becomes critical as students engage in making sense of novel phenomena.

A significant instructional innovation for *Framework*-based standards is the expectation that students use core ideas to make sense of phenomena. This is a shift from previous standards focused on students simply knowing core ideas. Core ideas are tools for students to use to support explanations. It is not enough for students to know core ideas (e.g., matter is made of particles, young organisms look very much but not exactly like their parents, objects and organisms are made of matter, radioactive decay of unstable isotopes within the Earth generates heat energy), they must use them. The shift from *knowing* core ideas to *using* core ideas changes how teaching and learning occurs, how assessments are designed, and the outcome of learning.

The disciplinary core ideas described in the *Framework* and NGSS are a set of science concepts, laws, theories, and principles selected to represent a useful set of tools to make sense of science phenomena and engineering design. The core ideas were selected from previous science standards (e.g., NSES, Benchmarks, NAEP Framework). The *Framework* describes manageable sets of disciplinary core ideas, logically organized across a progression, to provide states with coherence upon which to develop performance expectation that describe student learning "… in order to avoid the shallow coverage of a large number of topics and to allow more time for teachers and students to explore each idea in greater depth" (*Framework*, p. 11).

The work of reducing the number of core ideas was carried forth as the *NGSS* were developed, resulting in the distillation of the *Framework's* core ideas into a more potent set of assessment standards. Limiting the number of core ideas across grade-levels provides opportunities for instruction that engage students in deeper understanding of core ideas. This deeper understanding equips students with the tools to make sense of phenomena using the practices and crosscutting concepts.

The new vision for science teaching and learning from the *Framework* includes a clear expectation of fewer core ideas that (a) can be used to support explanations of many phenomena; (b) are useful across multiple science and engineering disciplines; (c) have utility for making sense of more complete science ideas; (d) are useful in making sense of phenomena in our lives; and (e) are conceptually accessible and teachable across many grades. There is a smaller subset of core ideas that are regularly used to make sense of a large number of phenomena. Students are more proficient at science when they conceptualize ideas and accurately apply them to make sense of phenomena. Figure 6-7 on page 87, provides a focused list of core ideas (conceptualized) that are regularly used to make sense of a large number of phenomena.

How Are Core Ideas Used to Make Sense of Phenomena?

Core ideas are the science principles, laws, and theories that have significant and meaningful utility and high explanatory value for making sense of phenomena. The underlying science principles of the core ideas are common to multiple disciplines, but generally written with sufficient detail to tie them to one of the four science disciplines (i.e., life, physical, engineering, earth and space). Using the same core ideas across multiple grade-levels with increasing sophistication contributes to students' abilities to use these ideas to make sense of phenomena. The hope is our students will use these ideas throughout their lives to better understand social and political issues, make personal decisions (e.g., decisions on medical procedures, nutritional choices, environmental action, home site selection) and add to their enjoyment of the natural world.

The core ideas included in the *Framework* were written in a way that makes them useful in supporting explanations for multiple phenomena. The core idea "cycling of matter and associated transfers of energy in a system, of any scale, depends on physical and chemical processes" might be translated by students into the *conceptual model of* "energy is involved when matter changes." This conceptual model is useful for making sense of many phenomena (e.g. melting of snow in spring, growth of a plant, uplift of mountains, canyon winds). Students should learn core ideas in ways that provide sufficient breadth to build sophisticated conceptual models to use beyond the classroom.

How are Conceptual Models Used to Make Sense of Phenomena?

Conceptual models are our students' cognitive understandings of important relationships between the components of systems and/or processes (e.g., energy from the sun causes water to evaporate in the water cycle, rocks weather and erode over time due to forces applied to or within the rock material). Science conceptual models are a set of general properties and interactions of matter, energy, and/or forces (e.g., matter is made of particles; heat flows through matter from warmer to cooler; gravity pulls objects down). Our own conceptual models may be simplifications of complex core ideas, laws, or theories that we have translated into general ideas, models, or concepts (e.g., genetic variation facilitates natural selection, newer layers of rock are found on top of older layers of rock,

energy changes occur when chemical bonds form) that we can apply to make sense of phenomena. Discipline-specific conceptual models (e.g., photosynthesis in biology, uniformitarianism in Earth science, equilibrium in chemistry, objects within a gravitational field fall at the same rate in physics) have greater utility when approached holistically (e.g., photosynthesis is the cycling of matter and flow of energy that causes matter to be rearranged, equilibrium applies to chemical reactions in a test tube as well as homeostasis at the cell, system, and organism level in biology). We argue that discipline-specific conceptual models (e.g., bacteria in the cows' rumen digests cellulose; and Earth's atmosphere is 78% nitrogen, 21% oxygen, 0.4% water, .039% carbon dioxide) have less utility for making sense of a broad range of phenomena. We contend that conceptual models applied to many phenomena across multiple disciplines are more useful and memorable for students.

> Conceptual models are the initial steps that lead to more complex explanations of phenomena. Conceptual models allow scientists, engineers, and students to establish a cognitive understanding of phenomena and/or develop a possible solution to a design problem. Conceptual models may be used to support our explanations of a myriad of phenomena we encounter. The level of complexity of these models changes over time as we use them to make sense of new phenomena. (*Framework*, p. 57)

Most conceptual models can be simplified and represented as physical models (e.g., diagrams, descriptions, physical replicas, mathematical representations, analogies, computer simulations). Physical models may become so integral to our conceptual model that we can only explain the cognitive aspects of the model by using a physical model. Although these physical models do not correspond exactly to the conceptual model and/or phenomenon, the physical model may bring specific aspects of the phenomenon into focus while minimizing and/or obscuring other aspects. It is important to recognize the limitations of models, since all models contain approximations and assumptions, which limit the range of their validity, precision, application, and predictive power.

Conceptual models provide a way to connect shared attributes across many phenomena and are useful for constructing explanations. Students' conceptual models are sometimes tied to a few familiar phenomena and not used to make sense of analogous phenomena. For example, students may connect the conceptual model "matter is made of particles" to how the smell of bread baking in the oven

Teaching Science is Phenomenal

moves from one room to another, or they may recognize the transfer of forces when billiard balls collide, but they may not be able to connect these two conceptual models to explain how a sailboat moves (air is made of particles that transfer a force to the sail, causing the boat to move). Accurate cognitive/mental models are identified as conceptual models; unfortunately, not all mental models are accurate. Helping students to develop their own conceptual models through speaking, writing, and drawing supports meaningful reflection about their own thinking. Student metacognition (thinking about one's own reasoning) improves the accuracy and utility of their cognitive/mental models.

> Taken together, the DCIs and CCCs create a conceptual toolkit that students can use to construct explanations for causes of phenomena. The focus on explaining phenomena represents an important shift in the goals of instruction. Rather than teaching ideas in the abstract or in isolation the new aim is to engage students in using these ideas to explain interesting phenomena. (Duncan & Cavera, 2015, p. 68)

Progression of Core Ideas

The *Framework* and *NGSS* present core ideas in progressions across multiple grade-levels to support students in building and revising increasingly more sophisticated science knowledge. The learning progressions scaffold student knowledge toward a more scientifically-based and coherent view of the natural sciences and engineering, and the ways students can use and learn core ideas. Ideas like natural selection and photosynthesis develop across the grade-bands from simple preliminary ideas to increasingly more sophisticated ideas in the higher grade-bands.

The core ideas empower students with flexibility to make sense of many phenomena, not just ones presented in the classroom. Students should "own" core ideas, not just rent them from the teacher to be recited or presented in explaining a few classroom phenomena.

The *Framework* emphasizes that learning science and engineering involves students using accepted "scientific explanations (i.e., content knowledge) and the practices needed to engage in scientific inquiry and engineering design" (*Framework*, p. 11). The *Framework, NGSS,* and state science standards consistent with the *Framework* are designed to provide a scaffold upon which knowledge and practice are used as needed in science performances.

Figure 6-5. GRC and the Use of Crosscutting Concepts and Core Ideas

The progression of core ideas provides an instructional guide to encourage grade-level appropriate conceptual learning. Instruction that features specific ideas within one grade-level should be linked to core ideas across earlier grade-levels. Making sense of a phenomenon generally requires multiple core ideas. Figure 6-6 is an example of two progressions taken from Appendix E of *NGSS* and shown in Appendix E of this text. These two core ideas can be taught together, related in many meaningful ways, and used to make sense of many phenomena. The analogous phenomena below require understanding of both natural selection and photosynthesis to construct an explanation for causes of the described adaptations.

- Phenomenon: Many plants in tropical rain forests have very large leaves.
- Phenomenon: Desert plants typically have waxy leaves.
- Phenomenon: In the Fall, leaves change color and fall off many types of trees.
- Phenomenon: The majority of trees in rain forests have leaves near their tops.

Other core ideas may also be useful in making sense of the listed phenomena. We recommend that you use *NGSS* Appendix E, found at http://www.nextgenscience.org/ or Appendix E of this book, to find other progressions of core ideas related to these examples.

Figure 6-6. Grade-level Progression of Core Ideas

PROGRESSION OF CORE IDEAS

	K-2*	3-5	6-8	9-12
LS4.B Natural Selection	There are differences in the appearance of organisms of the same kind.	Differences in characteristics between individuals of the same species provide advantages in survival and reproduction.	Both natural and artificial selection result from certain traits giving some individuals an advantage in survival and reproduction, leading to predominance of certain traits in a population.	Natural selection occurs only if there is variation in the genes and traits of organisms in a population. Traits that positively affect survival can become more common in a population.
PS3.D Energy in Chemical Processes and Everyday Life	Sunlight warms Earth's surface.	Energy can be "produced," "used," or "released" by converting stored energy. Plants capture energy from sunlight, which can later be used as fuel or food.	Sunlight is captured by plants and used in a reaction to produce sugar molecules, which can be reversed by burning those molecules to release energy.	Photosynthesis is the primary biological means of capturing radiation from the sun. Energy cannot be destroyed; it can be changed to less useful forms.

Note. We added K-2 to these NGSS progressions and think the progression begins before K.

Students Using Core Ideas in Science Performances

In Vignette 3, students respond to prompts in a number of ways, most of which reveal each student's level of understanding of conservation of matter. The discussion by the students is typical of middle school and/or high school students in making sense of chemical changes in a system.

Vignette 3: Using Core Ideas in Science Performances

The teacher uses a demonstration to present the phenomenon and initiate the classroom discussion. The teacher places a ¼ full beaker of vinegar and a small cup of baking soda on an electron balance. Students use core ideas to make sense of the phenomenon.

Teacher: "Students please think to yourself, without saying anything out loud, your prediction for the changes to the system of baking soda and vinegar when mixed in the beaker while on an electronic massing balance."

            ~Teacher allows two minutes of silent wait time while students think~

Teacher: "Would anyone like to share a prediction and the reasoning behind this prediction."

~Hands go up around the room and the teacher begins to invite students to share~

Ricky:	"The mass will stay the same because matter is conserved."
Rachel:	"It cannot stay the same because bubbles will bubble off."
Peter:	"The inside of a bubble doesn't weigh anything because they are nothing but air, you know air bubbles."
Juan-Carlos:	"The inside of the bubble is made of a gas and gas is matter and all matter has mass. Even if we cannot see them they are still there. It was like when we dropped pieces of paper and they floated down, we could not see what made them float, but it was air molecules causing the paper to fall slower. Molecules are matter, and matter has mass!"
Tiffany:	"The bubbles are made of matter and matter does not disappear, so it is somewhere. I think it is going from the system of the bottle to the system of the air."
Ricky:	"Yeah, matter is conserved."
Teacher:	"Ricky, you keep saying that – matter is conserved. What do you mean by that?"
Ricky:	"You know matter is conserved. It is matter and it is conserved."
Teacher:	"How is the matter being conserved? Does it make the bottle weigh less?"
Ricky:	"The matter must go somewhere, it doesn't disappear. You know, matter is conserved, it can be accounted for and if it weighs less, well, that means the gas matter is not on the weighing scale. The matter is in the air, you know the bubbles."
Teacher:	"Can anyone add to what Richard has said?"
Scott:	"I think Ricky is right. It's kind of like it is still there. It has moved from, you know the system of the beaker, vinegar, and soda to the air, so it weighs less but the same."
Rachel:	"Let me try to interpret what Scott said. The matter in the baking soda and vinegar has become a gas that is in the air now, so we are not weighing the part that became a gas. So this is why the system of beaker, vinegar, and soda weighs less. Some of the matter is now in the system of the air."
Juan-Carlos:	"Yes, because matter is conserved, we can account for all of it. The matter is someplace, moved from one system to another, I think it went from the beaker to the air system."
Teacher:	"So, let me see if I can summarize what you have been telling me. Since matter is conserved we know that all the matter can be accounted for in the beaker system, by identifying that the matter went to the air system. Since the law of conservation of matter is a law, we can use it to account for the changes in all systems."

~ Teacher places the baking soda into the vinegar while all components are on the electronic scale~

Peter:	"The mass is going down!"
Rachel:	"Yeah, exactly, that is what it means by a law, it is always true! We just use it to help us make sense of phenomena like this, it is always true, any place, any time."
Teacher:	"So, the nature of science is that we have natural laws that can always be used to help us make sense of how the world operates."
Peter:	"Even the universe sometimes."
Teacher:	"Sometimes?"

Teaching Science is Phenomenal

Rachel:	"Always, laws are the same everywhere and at any time."
Teacher:	"So, we have a change in this system. Can anyone help us better understand the cause of the changes of the system?"
Maria:	"The cause of the change is a chemical change."
Rachel:	"When that happens one of the things that is produced are the molecules of gas that are in the bubbles."
Maria:	"May I add to what Rachel just said?"
Teacher:	"Tell me more about the change."
Maria:	"There is a chemical change, the atoms are rearranged to new substances made by rearranging the atoms into new molecules."
Teacher:	"Do the new substances have the same properties as the vinegar and baking soda?"
Ricky:	"Heck no, the new stuff is different! I just looked it up on my phone and we made carbon dioxide from the baking soda!"
Teacher:	"OK, this is interesting."
Juan-Carlos:	"The investigation we did in October, you know, we put acid on those rocks and gas bubbles were given off. I remember the gas was carbon dioxide, a chemical reaction caused the gas to be made and a gas is very different than a rock or the acid."
Teacher:	"So, the change is a chemical change and the atoms that were there before are still there, just rearranged into new substances with new properties. Since all of the atoms are still there and like Rachel said, matter is conserved, so the new substances have the same mass, just rearranged into new substances."
Juan-Carlos:	"I like it that these ideas always work and there are other chemical changes like when we eat food it is changed by chemical reactions in our body, the food is different before and after we use it in our body but is made of the same atoms."
Teacher:	"Very interesting, and interestingly enough one of the products of the chemical reactions in our bodies is also carbon dioxide we exhale. Tomorrow we will develop a model to represent chemical change. See if you can observe other phenomena at your home that are caused by chemical change."

~Bell rings and students remain in their seats~

Teacher:	"Very good discussion, and remember, if you are very curious and work very hard, someday you too may be fortunate enough to be a science teacher! Looking forward to seeing you tomorrow!"

The teacher has developed a lesson plan for this performance with a clear focus on specific core ideas students will use to make sense of the phenomenon. When the discussion does not go toward these ideas about the changes in the properties of substances before and after a chemical reaction, she solicits these ideas from students by extending their thinking. She is beginning the unit of instruction by focusing on the two standards below.

- MS-PS1-2. Analyze and interpret data on the properties of substances before and after the substances interact to determine if a chemical reaction has occurred.

- MS- PS1- 5. Develop and use a model to describe how the total number of atoms does not change in a chemical reaction and thus mass is conserved.

The teacher synthesizes student reasoning about conservation of matter and adds a discussion about the nature of science. She is able to initiate an important conversation on how the properties of substances generally change when a chemical reaction occurs. There are a number of ideas and concepts from the conversation to inform future instruction:

1. Ricky and Rachel are relying on the concept that matter is conserved and seem to understand how to use this idea to make sense of the movement of matter from one system to another;

2. Peter is still struggling with the idea that gases have mass, but is learning through the discussion;

3. The students are beginning to understand the nature of science and universality of natural laws;

4. Juan-Carlos is accurately making connections to other phenomena from earlier instruction and phenomena outside of the classroom.

The teacher understands that additional work is needed to engage all of the students and provides additional opportunities for the students to apply their learning. The vignette describes teaching and learning during an Engage phase of instruction. Students will use the same two core ideas as learning progresses through the other phases of instruction.

Using Bundles of Core Ideas

Core ideas are more coherent when bundled. Instruction should embrace the use of multiple core ideas to make sense of a phenomenon. Phenomena are complex and typically require multiple core ideas and a few crosscutting concepts to construct accurate explanations for causes of them. An important reason for bundling core ideas in lessons is for students to gain sufficient insights and depth of understand to apply these ideas in making sense of new and/or analogous phenomena.

The goal is not only for students to know core ideas, but to use core ideas to make sense of phenomena. This means the core ideas must be conceptualized and used to make sense of multiple phenomena. A series of analogous phenomena, such as the ones presented in a typical 5E instructional model, provides students with opportunities to apply bundles of core ideas to make sense of multiple analogous phenomena. When students can accurately apply core ideas, they take ownership of the core ideas - *Students should own their learning, not just rent it from the teacher*. The following table provides examples of conceptually written core ideas students find useful when constructing explanation for phenomena.

Figure 6-7. Examples of Conceptually Written Core Ideas

Basic Science Ideas	• Matter is made of particles. • Matter is conserved. • Matter cycles. • Energy is involved when matter changes. • Energy is conserved. • Energy flows, heat energy moves from high to low. • Energy is transferred and transformed. • Natural laws operate consistently throughout the universe.
Life Science	• Living organisms are different than non-living things. • Cells are the basic unit of life. • Genetic material provides the information for reproduction of cells and organisms. • Genetic information is passed from parent to offspring. • Organisms best adapted for the environment in which they live will survive, grow, and reproduce over less well adapted organisms. • Species of living organisms evolve through natural selection. • Organisms interact with the environment to obtain things they need to live. • Ecosystems describe the interactions among living and non-living parts of the environment.
Earth Science	• The size of the universe and distance between stars is nearly inconceivable. • Light and heat are produced in stars including the sun. • Gravitational force shapes the planets, stars, solar systems, galaxies, and universe. • Uneven heating of the Earth by the sun cycles water and causes weather on Earth. • Radioactive decay of heavy elements in the interior of the Earth provides the energy that causes the cycling of Earth materials and provides energy to move tectonic plates.

Physical Science	• Newton's three laws:
	  o Objects at rest tend to stay at rest and objects in motion tend to stay in motion unless acted upon by a force.
	  o Force of a moving object is directly proportional to the mass of the object and the acceleration of the object $F=ma$.
	  o For every action, there is an equal and opposite reaction.
	• Gravitational and electromagnetic forces act on objects at a distance.
	  o Gravitational force – the closer and more massive a pair of objects, the greater the gravitational force between the objects.
	  o Electromagnetic force – the closer and greater the charge on a pair of objects, the greater the electromagnetic force between the objects.
	• Energy changes when atoms are rearranged into new substances.
	• Rearranging the bonding of atoms in a substance produces a new substance with different properties.
	• Physical changes take in or give off energy.

The *Framework* and *NGSS* call for instruction to engage students in using core ideas and crosscutting concepts in science and engineering performances. The way students use core ideas is similar to how students use empirical evidence to support explanations and arguments. Proficiency at using anything requires applying the acquired knowledge and/or skill to new contexts. This means both the student and teacher become adept at observing phenomena and applying core ideas to make sense of the phenomena.

Summary

Focusing on using disciplinary core ideas in performances to support explanations and arguments is an innovation or shift for science education. In the past, core ideas were the outcome of instruction; in the new vision, the outcome of instruction is student science performance at the intersection of the three dimensions. Proficiency at using core ideas to support explanations and arguments requires students to have a clear understanding of the core ideas and apply them to make sense of many phenomena.

Reflecting on Science Core Ideas

1. Select a phenomenon that you have encountered or an example of a phenomenon from this book.
   a. Which crosscutting concepts focus students' attention on causes of the phenomenon?
   b. Which core ideas can students use to make sense of this science phenomenon?

2. Place a racket ball on top of a basketball and drop them together. The racket ball will bounce higher than when dropped from the same height by itself. Construct an explanation for causes of the racket ball bouncing higher when dropped resting on top of a basketball.
   a. What core ideas do you use to make sense of the observed phenomenon?
   b. How is the crosscutting concept of "energy is conserved" helpful in focusing your attention on causes of the changes between the two ways the ball is dropped?

3. Consider your own personal list of core ideas that you know well and use regularly. Describe three examples of phenomena that you can explain using your personal core ideas (focus on causes of the phenomena)?

4. Vignette 2 was followed by a few reflections on the students' reasoning. Reflect on the nature of this classroom discourse and the ways this teacher has established a classroom where productive dialogue is an effective instructional tool.

5. How did the teacher in Vignette 3 use the crosscutting concepts to focus and/or shift the discussion about the phenomenon?

6. Why is it important for students to use (apply) core ideas in new contexts?

7. Why is it important to teach the nature of science (NOS)? Can you think of an example when you taught NOS?

Bibliography

Bybee, R. (2015). *The BSCS 5E Instructional Model: Creating Teachable Moments*. Washington, DC: NSTA Press.

Moulding, B., Bybee, R., & Paulson, N. (2015). *Vision and Plan for Science Teaching and Learning*. Salt Lake City, UT: Essential Teaching and Learning.

National Research Council. (1999). *NRC Report How People Learn*. Washington, DC: The National Academies Press.

National Research Council. (2012). *A Framework for K-12 Science Education: Practices, Crosscutting Concepts, and Core Ideas*. Washington, DC: The National Academies Press.

National Research Council. (2015). *NRC Report Guide to Implementing the Next Generation Science Standards*. Washington, DC: The National Academies Press.

NGSS Lead States. (2013). *Next Generation Science Standards: For States, By States*. Washington, DC: The National Academies Press.

CHAPTER 7

STRUCTURE, SEQUENCE, AND STRATEGIES OF INSTRUCTION

How can we best organize science instruction?

Chapters 7 and 8 describe how to use the Gather, Reason, Communicate (GRC) instructional sequence within the structure of the 5E instructional model. These instructional sequences provide educators with useful ways to modify existing lessons toward instruction that engage students in three-dimensional performances. The examples focus on teaching and learning that are consistent with developing conceptual understanding.

We have worked with a number of states, state science teachers' associations, universities, informal science organizations, schools, and most importantly districts, to put in place a web site where additional GRC and 5E lessons may be found. The site is https://sites.google.com/3d-grcscience.org/going3d. If for any reason this web site is not available when you read this book, please search the web for "Phenomenal GRC Lessons" or #Going3D w/GRC. As a last resort, you can always text or email one of the grumpy old men who wrote this book and if we are still alive, we can give you the web site. If we are not alive and send you the web site, we recommend you save that email!

Not all lessons and instructional techniques available on the web or in print resources are consistent with the *Framework's* vision of teaching and learning. Lessons should be selected that focus on conceptual understanding of core ideas and crosscutting concepts that develop students' flexibility with applying these ideas to make sense of phenomena. They should include performance sequences that engage students in science and engineering practices in ways that develop skills to gather information, reason about causes of phenomena, and communicate their reasoning through speaking, writing, and/or models.

The good news is most of the best lessons teachers currently use can be redesigned into effective three-dimensional sequences using the tools provided in this book. Some lessons, however, do not have sufficient merit (e.g., not engaging, not relevant for students, focused on memorization, poor standards alignment) and should be summarily discarded. Some instructional techniques within lessons focus only on developing vocabulary or memorizing answers (e.g., mnemonic devices, science songs, word association drills) to regurgitate when prompted. These approaches should be eliminated from your repertoire and replaced with tools and research-supported techniques that aid students in conceptualizing science ideas and concepts. These recommendations echo those of the *Framework* and *NGSS.* Decisions about the structure and sequencing of instruction should be guided by the insights expressed in the following quote.

The Framework and the NGSS focus on developing fundamental science ideas at a deep conceptual level, which likely will involve pruning some of the details that teachers have frequently covered. Some science teachers have developed a wide variety of mnemonics and other creative solutions to support students in learning some of the specific facts that are not in the NGSS. It may be especially difficult for some teachers to leave out part of the curriculum that they have previously thought to be essential in favor of more time for deeper engagement in the core ideas and crosscutting concepts in the NGSS. (NRC Report *Guide to Implementing the Next Generation Science Standards*, 2015, p. 36)

Developing Gather, Reason, and Communicate Sequences for Lessons

The lesson we present here was developed with a group of elementary teachers. It has a GRC sequence describing a series of coherent student performances. These sequences are most effective when presented in the larger structure of the 5E model. Each student performance in the sequence includes a core idea, practice, and crosscutting concept. The teaching suggestions within the lessons provide details on important areas to emphasize during instruction. These suggestions may include readings, websites, simulations, safety considerations, materials, and instructional strategies for the teacher. You will see the suggestions in parentheses and italics below the student performances. Student performances are numbered to more easily follow the instructional sequence.

A hallmark of 5E-GRC lesson sequences is to begin the lesson by engaging students with a phenomenon before presenting information to support explanations. This is a change from traditional lessons that typically begin with explanations and information provided by the teacher followed by students verifying what was presented.

Steps for Developing a GRC Instructional Sequence

Step 1. Select a phenomenon and link it to a performance expectation (PE/standard) or bundle of PEs.

The phenomenon is critical to engaging students and should be presented as an observation, fact, or event. The presentation should be done in ways that elicit student curiosity and questions about the phenomenon. A GRC sequence should present a series of performances that support students in gathering and interpreting evidence to support an explanation for causes of the phenomenon.

Figure 7-1. Defining a Phenomenon

> *Phenomenon: An ice cube melts faster when placed directly on the countertop than if placed on a towel.*
>
> NGSS: **4-PS3-2.** Make observations to provide evidence that energy can be transferred from place to place by ~~sound, light~~, heat, ~~and electric currents~~. *[Assessment Boundary: Assessment does not include quantitative measurements of energy.]*

Next, think of analogous phenomena. The ice cube phenomenon has many analogous phenomena. For example, (1) it is warmer to sleep on top of a sleeping bag than to sleep directly on the ground; (2)

a metal leg on a table feels colder than the drapery in the same room at the same temperature; or (3) a skiff of newly fallen snow melts on the sidewalk but accumulates on the lawn. If you decide to use this ice cube phenomenon in a 5E instructional model, analogous phenomena are essential for the various phases of the 5E model. The example lesson is linked to an NGSS standard, and likely could be linked to state specific standards. Here the excluded portion of the standard is struck out, with additional guidance provided in the assessment boundary.

Step 2. Select a logical series of science and engineering practices (SEP) for the GRC.

The teachers developing this GRC performance sequence used Figure 2-1 and professional judgment to make decisions on the order of the practices. The practice of asking questions about the phenomenon is critical to build students' curiosity and motivation. When using the practice of asking questions, it should be for a purpose. In this case, students are asking questions to plan and carry out an investigation rather than to obtain information from reliable sources, although either option would be appropriate. In this lesson, this decision links the initial prompt of "asking questions" to "plan and carry out an investigation." We will discuss the teaching suggestions in Step 5.

The teachers writing this lesson want students to construct an explanation and communicate the explanation using models. These decisions are based on the practices in the selected standard as well as where the GRC sequence is within the 5E instructional model. If this were a performance within the Engage phase, students would be developing tentative or initial explanations. The teachers instead used this lesson in the Explore and Explain phases. Other practices will be used throughout the lesson to help students build deeper understanding of the flow of heat energy between systems. This understanding can then be applied later in the Elaborate and Evaluate phases.

Figure 7-2. Selecting Science and Engineering Practices for an Instructional Sequence

Phenomenon: An ice cube melts faster when placed directly on the countertop than if placed on a towel.

Gather

1. Students *ask questions* about the phenomenon

2. Students *plan and carry out an investigation* or ~~obtain information~~

(*Teaching Suggestion: This is a good place for students to focus on* questions *about the phenomenon. If the* investigation *is an experiment,* questions *should focus on* designing a fair test *for difference in the melting rates. If students are using the practice* "obtaining information," questions *should focus on* finding the information *they are seeking and searchable terms to* obtain valid and reliable sources of information).

Reason

3. Students *construct an explanation* supported by evidence

Class Discussion

Communicate

4. Students *use a model* to communicate

Step 3. Selecting crosscutting concepts to focus student engagement with the phenomenon.

The teachers decided to emphasize the crosscutting concept of cause and effect. In this performance, the effect is the phenomenon for which students find causes. Teachers know that helping students focus on the change of energy between two systems is critical to making sense of this phenomenon. Teachers decided it was important to scaffold the prompts by indicating "between two systems." The teachers considered other crosscutting concepts such as scale and proportion, and decided these may distract students from the central performances. Each of the four performances featured in the lesson are instructional decisions the professional teacher made during the development and subsequent revision of the lesson.

Figure 7-3. Selecting Crosscutting Concepts for an Instructional Sequence

---

Phenomenon: An ice cube melts faster when placed directly on the countertop than if placed on a towel.

Gather

1. Students ask questions about *causes* of the phenomenon

2. Students plan and carry out an investigation to obtain evidence for *causes* of differences in the rates of *change* of the two *systems*

(Teaching Suggestion: This is a good place for students to focus questions on causes of the phenomenon. If the investigation is an experiment, questions should focus on designing a fair test of causes of difference in the melting rates. Students should focus on changes in the system. Be sure to have students define and describe the systems).

Reason

3. Students construct an explanation supported by evidence from their investigation for *causes* of the phenomenon

Class Discussion

Communicate

4. Students use a model to communicate differences in the transfer of heat *energy* between two *systems* (ice cube and countertop)

Step 4. Determining the core ideas needed to make sense of the phenomenon.

The "rate two ice cubes melt" is not a core idea; however, the core ideas of (1) energy flows from objects with more heat energy to objects with less heat energy, (2) matter changes state when sufficient energy is added or removed, and (3) heat conductivity is a property of substances, can be used by students to make sense of the phenomenon. Often the core ideas are implied rather than explicitly written in the performance expectations, yet students are still expected to apply the appropriate core ideas in the performance. We suggest including how the core ideas, crosscutting concepts, and practices are used by the student in the teaching suggestions that follow the Gather performance.

Student performances should be connected with appropriate core ideas and crosscutting concepts. The crosscutting concepts may be changed to emphasize specific aspects of the phenomenon (e.g., scale in a geologic phenomenon, change in systems in an ecological phenomenon). An example of this change in emphasis can be seen below between performance 3 and 4 when systems are emphasized.

Figure 7-4. Selecting Core Ideas for an Instructional Sequence

---

Phenomenon: An ice cube melts faster when placed directly on the countertop than if placed on a towel.

Gather

1. Students ask questions about causes of the difference in the rate that two ice cubes melt.

2. Students plan and carry out an investigation to obtain evidence for causes of difference in the rate heat energy is transferred between two systems causing ice to change from a solid to a liquid.

(Teaching Suggestion: This is a good place for students to focus questions on causes of the phenomenon. If the investigation is an experiment, questions should focus on designing a fair test for causes of difference in the melting rates. Students should focus on changes in the system. Be sure to have students define the systems. Students use core ideas related to: (1) energy flows from objects with more heat energy to objects with less heat energy, (2) matter changes state when sufficient energy is added or removed, and (3) heat conductivity is a property of substances and determines the rate heat moves through a substance).

Reason

3. Students construct an explanation supported by evidence from their investigation for causes of the differences in the rate heat energy is transferred though different substances to cause ice to change from solid to a liquid.

Class Discussion

Communicate Reasoning

4. Students use a model to communicate differences in the transfer of heat energy between two systems (countertop and ice cube) causing ice to change from a solid to a liquid.

Step 5: Plan class discussions and teaching suggestions.

These two instructional supports are where the authors of this lesson are talking to the teachers who want to use it. These are suggestions for the lessons based upon actual classroom experiences. The teaching suggestions are **not** teacher directions, but rather hints, suggestions, and recommendations. Typically, a teacher using the lesson will make modifications based on professional judgment and the need of the students.

The class discussion is an opportunity for teachers to synthesize students' understanding of practices, core ideas, and crosscutting concepts into an accepted scientific explanation. This is the location within instruction where teachers may redirect student thinking to develop understanding of causes of the phenomenon, more accurate explanations, and more precise language, (e.g., things become objects, stuff becomes substances, survival of the fittest becomes natural selection, and proof becomes evidence to support an explanation). Students will bring much of this language to the discussion from the Gather component of the GRC or from prior phases in a 5E sequence. However, it is equally important for the teacher to formatively assess students' understanding of the words that the students use to communicate their reasoning (see Chapter 4, Vignette 1 and Chapter 6, Vignette 2). Skilled teachers are able to synthesize students' ideas with accepted science principles to focus the discussion toward a scientifically accurate explanation of the phenomenon based upon students' reasoning.

Teaching suggestions after the class discussion focus on the core ideas and crosscutting concepts students apply to make sense of this phenomenon. The performances in the lesson provide opportunities for students to develop deeper understanding of each of the three-dimensions of science.

This lesson is identified as an Explore lesson students use to obtain information for use as evidence. A transition to the Explain phase of the 5E model occurs within this lesson during the class discussion. Class discussion is important for the teaching and learning process and most of the GRC lessons provide multiple opportunities for class discussions to synthesize and clarify student reasoning.

Figure 7-5. Inserting Teaching Suggestions into a GRC Sequence

---

Phenomenon: An ice cube melts faster when placed directly on the countertop than if placed on a towel.

Gather

1. Students *ask questions* about *causes* of the difference in the rate that two ice cubes melt.

2. Students *plan and carry out an investigation* to obtain data to use as evidence for *causes* of the difference in the rate heat energy is transferred between two *systems* causing ice to *change* from a solid to a liquid.

(Teaching Suggestion: This is a good place for students to focus questions on causes of the phenomenon. If the investigation is an experiment, questions should focus on designing a fair test for causes of difference in the melting rates. Students should focus on changes in the system. Be sure to have students define the systems. Students use the core ideas of: (1) energy flows from objects with more heat energy to objects with less heat energy, (2) matter changes state when sufficient energy is added or removed, and (3) heat conductivity is a property of substances and determines the rate heat moves through a substance).

Reason

3. Students *construct an explanation* supported by evidence from the *investigation* of *causes* for differences in the rate that heat energy is transferred though different substances *causing* ice to *change* from a solid to a liquid.

   Class Discussion

   Q: How does heat energy move between two systems?
   Q: Why does the ice cube melt faster when placed directly on countertop than on the towel?
   Q: Which variables need to be controlled in the experiment to have a fair test?
   Q: Why does it take energy to change an ice cube into liquid water?
   Q: How does the towel between the ice cube and countertop affect the rate heat moves?
   Q: How does the evidence you collected support your explanation of causes of the phenomenon?

   (Teaching Suggestions: The discussion should focus on students making sense of the transfer of heat energy between two systems. The ice cube is one system and counter top is the other system. They will compare this change to the rate of transfer of heat between the ice cube and the towel on the countertop which are two new systems. Students should call on evidence from their experiment and discuss transfer of energy at different rates based on the number of layers of towels, or the type of material being used. There will be some discussion of "cold" moving. Work to help students to understand heat moves, what we perceive as cold is the rate heat moves from our body to objects at lower temperatures).

4. Students revise their explanations in light of new evidence from the discussion of *causes* of different rates the two ice cubes *change* from a solid to a liquid.

Communicate Reasoning

5. Students *use two models to communicate* differences in transfer of heat *energy* between two *systems* (countertop and ice cube) *causing* ice to change from a solid to a liquid.

   (Teaching Suggestions: Ask students to individually draw and label the model. The movement of energy is key to the performance. This Communicate performance may be used as a formal formative assessment. Students should show energy moving from the countertop to the ice more quickly for the ice directly on the countertop and more slowly when on the towel. Student models should capture the idea that heat moves from where there is more to where there is less and that heat moves more quickly through some substances than others depending on properties of the substance).

Step 6 – Use the Communicate Reasoning performance as an assessment for student learning.

Formative assessment should always be conducted within instruction and consistent with student performances. Formative assessment provides both the teacher and student with information about learning and opportunities to reflect on learning. The GRC lessons provide many opportunities for informal formative assessment because each of the performances can be assessed. The classroom discussion is also an excellent point in the lesson for formative assessment. Each lesson has "Communicate Reasoning" performances that may be used for effective formal formative assessment. The model we use for formative assessment is from the CCSSO publication "Formative Assessment for Student Learning" (2013). Figure 7-6 shows this model of formative assessment for the Communicate Reasoning performance.

Figure 7-6. Structure of Assessment for Student Learning during Communicate Reasoning

Formative Assessment for Student Learning		
Elicit Evidence of Learning: *Use a model to communicate* differences in the transfer of heat *energy* between two *systems* to cause the ice to melt.		
Evidence of Student Proficiency	**Range of Typical Student Responses**	**Acting on Evidence of Learning**
Student models show the movement of heat energy from the countertop to the ice cube being greater than the movement of heat from the countertop through the towel and into the ice cube. Students describe in the model that heat energy causes the ice to melt. Students indicate the towel slows (insulates) the movement of heat to the ice.	**Full Understanding** – Model shows heat moving from the countertop to the ice cube faster than from the countertop though the towel and into the ice. Model shows ice melting faster when directly on the countertop. Student model addresses conduction and/or insulation of heat. **Partial Understanding** – Model shows movement of energy from the countertop to the ice cube as well as energy moving slower through the towel. **Limited Understanding** – Model shows movement of energy from many places, does not distinguish the differences in the two systems, or shows cold moving.	Engage students in a second series of performances in which heat is moving from their hands into a cold object and then from a warm object into their hand. Student develop a model to show the energy moving from hotter to colder objects. Put a snack size Ziploc bag of cold tap water in one hand and a snack size bag of hot tap water in the other hand. Students draw models of the movement of heat in each hand.

Step 7– Develop grade-level appropriate student prompts for the GRC sequence.

Student prompts require writing a series of performances that students can understand. There is a fine line between giving directions and describing performances. The prompts are not directions for the student to follow, but rather a sequence of performances. The performances come directly from the lesson and are written in grade-level appropriate language. Teachers present the prompts with verbal clarification.

Teachers could use the following sequence of performances to prompt students in the GRC sequence "As Cold as Ice." Many teachers project this slide on the screen, some share it in a Google document, and some use handouts. Teachers may choose to reveal only one performance at a time and wait for students to engage in that performance before revealing the next prompt. These prompts communicate the expectations for students' performances. Prior to the class discussion, students spend time during the Individual Performance synthesizing their own understanding of the phenomenon. During this sustained silent writing (SSW), students may write and/or develop a model of the interaction between the components of a system. This provides students with time to think and organize ideas prior to the class discussion.

Figure 7-7. Student Prompt for the Instructional Sequence "Cold as Ice"

Phenomenon: An ice cube melts faster when placed directly on the countertop than if placed on a towel.

Group Performance

1. *Ask questions* about *causes* of ice cubes on a towel melting slower than directly on counter top.
2. *Plan and carry out an investigation* to obtain evidence for *causes* of difference in how fast the ice cubes melt.
   (Materials: ice cubes, various types of paper towels, plastic bags, timers, and other things if available)
3. *Construct an explanation* supported by evidence for *causes* of the ice cubes melting slower on the towel.

Individual Performance (SSW)*

4. *Use models* to communicate differences in the transfer of heat energy between the *systems* to cause the phenomenon.

Group Discussion

Reflection on Science Learning (Individual)

5. Revise your *explanation* for *causes* of the differences in the *rate* the two ice cubes *change* from a solid to a liquid in light of new evidence from the discussion.

*Sustained Silent Writing

Developing Performance Sequences into Lessons

Developing an extended unit of instruction can be accomplished by linking a series of GRC lessons aligned to one or more standards. Extended units of study provide opportunities for students to apply their learning. Applying learning helps students to conceptualize and retain the skills and knowledge over time. More extensive units of study make the learning experience more memorable and help students make sense of the natural and engineered world beyond the classroom.

In education, the word "lesson" is used to refer to many things. Sometimes it is used as the "daily lesson," the instruction for the day. These lessons tend to be used when a teacher is being observed or a way for teachers to organize the instructional tasks each day. More often the word "Lesson" is used as a way to teach a complete concept or principle within the topic. Sometimes several lessons are linked together to form a unit of instruction. The approach we advocate is to use a lesson to present a series of student performances that help students use the practices, crosscutting concepts, and core ideas to make sense of a set of multiple analogous phenomena. Since we advocate that the student build science knowledge based on previous learning and by consistently and frequently applying a set of core ideas and crosscutting concepts, we believe it is critical to revisit the same core ideas and crosscutting concepts in a variety of contexts and with multiple phenomena over the entire year. In essence, a lesson has no beginning and no end. It is a way to organize a set of performances to make sense of phenomena within a larger learning context.

The following is a summary of the sequence that teachers can use to think through GRC lesson plan development. Developing a lesson is a useful way to deepen your understanding of how to use existing lessons. We encourage you to try adapting your favorite lesson into a lesson with a GRC lesson structure.

It is not the product that is important, but rather the process that provides you with insights into the interactions of the three dimensions of science and the GRC performance sequence in a lesson. We also recommend that you use one of the lessons at the *#Going 3D w/GRC Phenomenal Lessons* website as a guide for your lesson plan development. Remember, the performances are three-dimensional descriptions of what students are doing. The lesson is for professional teachers, so you will not need to write a script for instruction. If you wish to share a few insights and/or strategies (e.g., core idea focus, crosscutting concept insights, reading jigsaw, details of a good experiment, using class debate, guided reading, web searches) place these into the *Teaching Suggestions* section of the lesson.

General Steps for Developing a GRC Sequence in a Lesson

1. Select a phenomenon and connect it to an NGSS or state standard.
2. Establish a clear causal relationship for the phenomenon (e.g., heat energy moves into system causing the system to change, the object is affected by forces acting on the object).
3. Determine a *sequence of practices* that lead from *observing* the phenomenon to *explanations* supported by evidence for *causes* of the phenomenon.
   a. ***Gather***
      i. Ask questions to plan an investigation **OR** obtain information
      ii. Use models to organize **OR** collect data
   b. ***Reason***
      i. Use practices to change data and/or information into evidence
      ii. Construct an explanation supported by evidence and/or develop an argument
   c. ***Communicate Reasoning***
      i. Communicate the argument for how the evidence supports an explanation
      ii. Use models, writing, or speaking to communicate
4. Select *crosscutting concepts* that help students focus on interactions in the system.
5. Determine the *evidence* students need to use to support an *explanation* for *causes* of the phenomenon and <u>how students will obtain the evidence to support their explanations.</u>
   a. *Core ideas*
   b. *Data and observations*
   c. *Crosscutting concepts, e.g. conservation of matter and/or energy*
6. Use the Communicate Reasoning performance as an assessment for student learning.
7. Translate the lesson into *student prompts* using grade-level appropriate language.

Lesson Plan on an Envelope

Lesson plans are not usually as extensive as has been described in this chapter. Once teachers have developed a few good lessons using the GRC, they may be prepared to write lesson ideas as notes to themselves. Some teachers use the back of an envelope or a note pad to develop a few important components of the lesson to engage students in effective science learning. Below is a template for writing a lesson plan on an envelope, which includes the essential ideas needed for a GRC lesson. Note: the lesson on an envelope approach is not for everyone and may leave important ideas out of the lesson.

Figure 7-8. Structure of a Lesson on an Envelope

ENVELOPE LESSON PLAN

1. Find and write the **phenomenon** as an observation, fact, or event.

2. Design ways to present the phenomenon and **strategies to engage students in asking questions** to make sense of the phenomenon.

3. Select **core ideas and crosscutting concepts** students use to support explanations for causes of the phenomenon.

4. Determine a **sequence of practices** to:

   - *Gather and organize information/data,*

   - *Reason causes of the phenomenon, and*

   - *Communicate reason within an explanation and/or argue for causes of the phenomenon*

5. Write **key 3-dimensional student performance** written with SEPs/CCCs/DCIs.

6. Develop **two questions** using **crosscutting concepts** to focus students on the core ideas and crosscutting concepts to elicit student thinking in **class discussion**.

7. Determine the criteria to **assess students' ability to apply learning** to make sense of analogous phenomena.

Envelope Lesson Example

Phenomenon – Duckweed floats on the surface of ponds and has a short root that does not reach the bottom of the pond and does not take in water the plant needs.

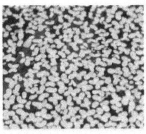

1. Show the duck week in the aquarium and give each group a clear plastic cup with 10-20 plants floating in water.

2. Structure and function as the crosscutting concept, and core ideas that organisms get what they need from the environment, photosynthesis.

3. G. Obtain information, *R.* Analyze data, construct explanations, develop an argument, *C.* Use models to communicate.

4. Plan an investigation (experiment) to provide evidence for how the structure of the duckweed functions to meet the needs of the plant to grow and reproduce.

http://www.mobot.org/jwcross/duckweed/duckweed-root.htm

5. A) How does the structure of the duckweed root function to help the plant survive?

B) How does the duckweed interact with the system in which it lives to survive, reproduce, and grow?

6. The structure of the root keeps the plant upright to keep the best orientation for photosynthesis.

We recommend you use the envelope strategy only after becoming proficient at developing and using a few GRC lessons. Most lessons are not as formal as the type principals require and/or lesson plan models describe. Some teachers need only the "student prompt" such as the example found in Figure 7-7 at the end of the GRC lesson and in the lesson plans at the *#Going3D w/GRC* lesson site. These prompts are an excellent way to deliver lessons, and we highly recommend teachers reflect on and carefully plan questions to use in the class discussion component of lessons.

Summary

Quality science lessons, regardless of the format, provide teachers with tools to engage students in three-dimensional science performances (i.e., practices, crosscutting concepts and core ideas) to make sense of phenomena. Most importantly, these lessons support research-based instruction that engage students in meaningful and enjoyable learning experiences they apply beyond the classroom.

This book provides a way to center instruction on engaging students in making sense of science phenomena and describes ways to integrate the GRC performance sequence into the 5E instructional model. This approach focuses much of the GRC sequence on the science and engineering practices and how core ideas and crosscutting concepts are used by students to reason and develop explanations. The motivation for structuring instruction this way is centered on implementing the vision for instruction presented in the *Framework;* however, good science instruction, regardless of the standards or the subject area, needs structure.

The GRC sequence is most effective when placed in instructional unit that moves students from exploring phenomena to constructing explanations for causes of the phenomena to applying their learning as they make sense of new analogous phenomena. The 5E instructional model moves students through this learning sequence. Many lessons that use GRC sequences include multiple components of the 5E model. The 5E-GRC template presented in Chapter 8 adapts a series of GRC lessons with analogous phenomena to follow the 5E instructional model accomplishes this goal. Each of the lessons in the sequence should address the outcomes of the specific phase of the 5E model.

Building a GRC performance within one phase of the 5E is an important step toward a coherent instructional sequence. Both GRC and 5E-GRC templates are available at the *"Going3D with GRC Phenomenal Lessons"* found at https://sites.google.com/3d-grcscience.org/going3d. Search under the Lesson "Resources Tab."

Reflecting on the Structure of Instruction

1. Why is instruction improved when it has a well developed structure?

2. What benefit does presenting the phenomenon as a statement of an observation or event have in helping students engage in asking questions?

3. Why should formative assessment be continuous during instruction?

4. How does the GRC sequence move students beyond simple recall of facts or information?

5. Why does "communicate reasoning" provide a good opportunity for assessment *for* student learning?

6. Why is the class discussion much more than the teacher explaining?

Bibliography

Bybee, R. (2015). *The BSCS 5E Instructional Model: Creating Teachable Moments*. Washington, DC: NSTA Press.

Council of Chief State School Officers. (2013). *Using the Formative Assessment Rubrics, Reflection and Observation Tools to Support Professional Reflection on Practice*. Washington, DC: CCSSO. Available at https://center.ncsu.edu/ncfalcon/pluginfile.php/2/course/section/57/Formative%20Assessment%20Rubrics%20and%20Observation%20Tools%20Document.pdf

Moulding, B., Bybee, R., & Paulson, N. (2015). *Vision and Plan for Science Teaching and Learning*. Salt Lake City, UT: Essential Teaching and Learning.

National Research Council. (1999). *NRC Report How People Learn*. Washington, DC: The National Academies Press.

National Research Council. (2012). *A Framework for K-12 Science Education: Practices, Crosscutting Concepts, and Core Ideas*. Washington, DC: The National Academies Press.

National Research Council. (2015). *NRC Report Guide to Implementing the Next Generation Science Standards*. Washington, DC: The National Academies Press.

NGSS Lead States. (2013). *Next Generation Science Standards: For States, By States*. Washington, DC: The National Academies Press.

Teaching of science should include the development of students' understanding of inquiry and the nature of science.

~Rodger W. Bybee

CHAPTER 8

5E INSTRUCTIONAL MODEL USING GRC STUDENT PERFORMANCES

How does the 5E instructional model accommodate a GRC performance sequence?

Integration of the 5E and GRC models helps classroom teachers achieve two important goals: (1) the 5E model presents a structure and sequence based on contemporary learning theory; and (2) the GRC model helps teachers realize the three dimensions of NGSS and most state science standards. Most teachers agree with these two aims of science instruction. They do ask us very practical questions, "What does the integration of the 5E and GRC models look like?" And "Do we have an example?" Yes, we have an example, and this chapter presents an example that answers the first question.

In this chapter we present a general 5E-GRC template followed by an example of a lesson that includes a series of GRC performance sequences embedded within each of the 5E phases. This lesson may be thought of as a unit of instruction. The lesson addresses natural selection and is aligned to the NGSS. The lesson moves students from engaging in asking questions about the flying squirrel phenomenon in the Engage phase to application of their learning to make sense of an analogous phenomenon about prairie dogs in the Elaboration and Evaluation phases. These GRC sequences in the lesson have been used by teachers in classrooms and are aligned to NGSS performance expectations. This example may not match your grade-level; however, the lessons provide the rationale for an extended instructional sequence. Additional tools to develop lessons may be found in the appendices. If you wish to try a lesson at your grade-level, you can find examples at each grade-level on the #Going 3D w/GRC website.

Figure 8-1. Template to Integrate GRC Performances into 5E Model

Instructional Sequence **Authors:**		
Grade-level		**Title**
Topic –		
Performance Expectations (Standard) from State Standards or NGSS:		
Lesson Performance Expectations:		

		Student Science Performances
Engage	Students are presented with a phenomenon that engages them in thinking about an explanation for causes of the phenomenon.	***Phenomenon*** *– Presentation of a phenomenon initiates students in the performances. This may be accomplished through a demonstration, video, reading, and/or observation event.* ***Gather*** –Describes 3-D student performances to direct gathering information, making observations, carrying out investigations, or using models to organize data and information. ***Reason*** –Describes 3-D student performances to evaluate information, analyze data, construct explanations, and/or develop arguments for how the evidence supports the explanation. ***Communicate*** – Describes 3-D student performances to communicate current reasoning. Students communicate their current conceptual models and informal explanations for causes of the phenomenon with other students and/or the teacher. Students utilize models to support their communication of preliminary ideas. Teachers use student initial explanations to inform instruction.
Explore	Students explore multiple lines of evidence to support explanations for causes of the phenomenon.	***Phenomenon*** *– Use the same phenomenon from the Engage phase or use an analogous phenomenon (similar context and same causes) to initiate student explanations for causes of the phenomenon.* ***Gather*** –Describes 3-D student performances to direct gathering information, making observations, carrying out investigations, or using models to organize data and information. ***Reason*** –Describes 3-D student performances to evaluate new information, analyze data collected during the Explore phase, construct explanations, and/or develop arguments for how the evidence supports the explanation.
Explain	Student explanations for the phenomenon are synthesized by the teacher through class discussions and/or introducing of formal explanation from text or video.	***Phenomenon*** *– Using the phenomenon from the Explore or Engage phase, engage student with more formal and scientifically accurate explanations to initiate student explanations for causes of the phenomenon.* ***Reason*** –Describes 3-D student performances to construct explanations and/or develop arguments for how the evidence supports the explanation of causes of the phenomenon. This reasoning may occur in student writing, discussion with small groups, or the entire class. Models can be used as tools to reason about relationships and components of systems. The class discussion should synthesize students' reasoning into a scientifically accurate explanation with appropriate science language and key terms added by the teacher. ***Communicate*** – Describes 3-D student performances to communicate individual student reasoning through writing and/or speaking. This communication may be used by the student to evaluate their own understanding of causes of the phenomenon and by the teacher to monitor progress in a formative manner.

Teaching Science is Phenomenal

Elaborate Students are given an analogous phenomenon and asked to apply what they have learned.	*Phenomenon – This should be an analogous phenomenon that requires students to apply their learning from the engaging, exploring, and explaining reasoning to make sense of this phenomenon. This should be an opportunity for student to extend their knowledge by generalizing conceptual models.* **Gather** – Describes 3-D student performances to direct gathering information, making observations, carrying out investigations, or using models to organize data and information. **Reason** – Students use core ideas and crosscutting concepts to develop a model showing the relationship of components within a system, reason about an explanation, and/or develop an argument for how the evidence supports the explanation.	
Evaluate An analogous phenomenon or the phenomenon from the Elaborate phase is used to evaluate student learning.	*Phenomenon – The phenomenon from the Elaborate phase or an analogous phenomenon can be used to engage students in applying their learning from the engaging, exploring, and explaining reasoning, to making sense of this phenomenon.* **Reason** – Students individually construct an explanation, develop a model, and/or develop an argument for how the evidence supports an explanation of causes of the phenomenon. **Communicate** – Students individually communicate their reasoning via an explanation for causes of the phenomenon, using a model and/or written explanations **OR** communicate their argument for how the evidence supports the explanation of causes of the phenomenon.	

Formative Assessment for Student Learning

Elicit Evidence of Learning: *This box is the individual communication performance from the student prompt in the lesson found within Lesson Appendix A.*

Evidence of Student Proficiency Description of the evidence of learning expected for the three-dimensional performance.	**Range of Typical Student Responses** This has examples of student responses from full to limited student understanding. Descriptors of grade-level appropriate student responses: • **Full understanding** • **Partial understanding** • **Limited understanding**	**Acting on Evidence of Learning** This is a brief description of the instructional actions to take based on the students' performance. When the action includes extensive descriptors and/or materials, place them in **Lesson Appendix C.** Description of instruction actions and responses to support student learning. • Action for student who displays partial or limited understanding • Extensions of learning for student who displays full understanding

SEP, CCC, DCI Featured in Lesson	**Science Essentials** *(Student Performance Expectations from Book Appendix C, D, E)*
Science Practices	
Crosscutting Concepts	
Disciplinary Core Ideas	

Lesson template developed by B. Moulding (2012)

Gather, Reason, and Communicate Performances within a 5E Instructional Sequence

We worked with teachers to develop and test this example as a model for integrating GRC performances within a 5E instructional model. The phenomenon for this instructional sequence centers on the flying squirrels that are primarily found in the northeastern United States and southeastern Canada. The example could have focused on any species of organism (e.g., ruby throated hummingbird, diamondback rattlesnake, quaking aspen) that have a limited range due to environmental factors. This instructional sequence explicitly emphasizes three-dimensional performances.

The practice of "constructing an explanation" and crosscutting concept of "structure and function" are featured in this instructional sequence. Students' learning from this instructional sequence can be applied to analogous phenomena (e.g., paddlefish use their beak to find food; grasses grow back after a fire; yeast dries out and then, when water is added, comes to life) and depends on students' ability to use the practices, apply core ideas, and crosscutting concepts. As you review the instructional sequence we suggest you note the following features:

- Use of evidence in the Reasoning and Communicate sections;
- Opportunity for students to progress from current conceptions to the formal introduction of accurate scientific concepts;
- Variation in the emphasis of Gather, Reason, and Communicate;
- Recognition of the SEPs, CCCs, and DCIs from NGSS;
- Inclusion of a sequence of engineering design; and
- Significance of analogous phenomena.

Integrated 5E-GRC Instructional Sequence

The following is an integrated 5E-GRC lesson with multiple GRC performance sequences. It aligns to NGSS, as well as *Framework*-aligned state standards. Remember, standards are not a solution, only an opportunity. The student prompts and the student information for the *Understanding How Natural Selection Resulted in Flying Squirrels* lesson are available in Appendix H of this text.

Figure 8-2. 5E—GRC Instructional Sequence: Flying Squirrels

5E-GRC Instructional Sequence	
Authors: Kenneth Huff, Williamsville Central School District, New York	
Grade Level – MS	**Title: Understanding how Natural Selection Resulted in Flying Squirrels**
Topic - Natural Selection and Adaptation	

NGSS Performance Expectations (Standards):

MS-LS4-4. Construct an explanation based on evidence that describes how genetic variations of traits in a population increase some individuals' probability of surviving and reproducing in a specific environment. *[Clarification Statement: Emphasis is on using simple probability statements and proportional reasoning to construct explanations].*

MS-LS4-6. Use mathematical representations to support explanations of how natural selection may lead to increases and decreases of specific traits in populations over time. *[Clarification Statement: Emphasis is on using mathematical models, probability statements, and proportional reasoning to support explanations of* *trends in changes to populations over time. Assessment Boundary: Assessment does not include Hardy Weinberg calculations].*

MS-ETS1-2. Evaluate competing design solutions using a systematic process to determine how well they meet the criteria and constraints of the problem.

Other Student Performances *Specific to this Lesson:*
- Construct an explanation for why differences in an organism's structures function to cause some individuals to have an advantage for survival.
- Develop a mathematical model to communicate the effects of environmental conditions on survival rates of organisms.
- Develop an argument for how the collected evidence supports the explanation, "changes in the structure of organisms over time occurs in response to the environmental conditions."

Engage Learners	**Student Science Performances**
The goal of Engage is to capture students' attention, interest, and focus on the phenomenon and specific aspects of the phenomenon that lead to the standard. The goal is for students to engage in making sense of the phenomenon using their own conceptual models and core ideas. Create opportunities to informally determine misconceptions expressed by the students. This is a good place in the lesson for informal formative assessment. In the Engage phase students develop preliminary explanations. These explanations may reveal students' current or early understanding of the core ideas.	*Phenomenon: Some, but not all, squirrels can fly from tree to tree.* Northern Flying Squirrel, Dept. of the Interior & NY DEC    **Gather:** 1. Students obtain information by watching the flying squirrels video and developing questions about causes of some, but not all squirrels being able to fly from tree to tree. 2. Students obtain information from reliable sources for how specific body structures function to enable some squirrels to fly. Use link: http://www.dec.ny.gov/docs/administration_pdf/squirrels.pdf *(Teaching Suggestions: Use the video from the URL below to present the phenomenon. Students can watch video on their own devices or project the video for the class. Prompt students to ask questions about how flying helps these squirrels. http://video.nationalgeographic.com/video/weirdest-flying-squirrel. Additional information about flying squirrels is available in Lesson Appendix B found in Appendix H of this book).* **Reason:** 3. Students construct a preliminary explanation for how the body structures of the flying squirrel functions to enable them to survive in forest ecosystems. **Communicate:** 4. Students communicate their preliminary explanations for causes of variation among squirrel species in New York State. *(Teaching Suggestions: For purposes of informal formative assessment, walk around the room and read over students' shoulders or review students' written explanations. The class discussion is another place in the Engage phase where informal formative assessment provides the student and teacher with information on learning).*

| **Explore Phenomenon I**
Students engage in gathering information and data to use as evidence to support preliminary explanations of the phenomenon from the engagement experience and/or analogous phenomena.

The exploration performances provide concrete experiences to extend students' current understanding and demonstrate their ability to make sense of science phenomena.

Students should have experience formulating explanations, investigating phenomena, observing patterns, and developing cognitive and physical abilities. The teacher's role is listening, observing, and guiding students in using core ideas and crosscutting concepts to make sense of phenomena. | *Phenomenon: The wing flaps of flying squirrels are not all the same.*

Gather:
1. Students obtain information from reliable resources for how changes over time have led to some squirrels being able to fly.

(Teaching Suggestions: This website is a reliable resource for students to obtain information: http://evolution.berkeley.edu/evolibrary/article/0_0_0/evo_25*)*

2. Students develop models using paper to investigate the attributes of wing-like structures that have the best proportions of wing dimensions and function to maximize the glide distance.
   Engineering challenge – design and build a paper glider from a single sheet of paper with a structure that allows the glider to fly 2X when dropped from a height of 1X.

*(Teaching Suggestions: Provide each group of students with a sheet of copy paper. Students use the paper to design and build 4 paper gliders capable of flying a horizontal distance of 2x when dropped from a height of x. Emphasize students may **not** throw, but only drop the glider. This modeling exercise is best done in a group of 2-3 so measurements can occur. Some students may wish to gather information about forces, air, and gravity while conducting the investigation).*

Reason:
3. Students analyze and interpret data from the testing of the glider designs to determine which proportions are the most effective at maximizing the glide distance.
4. Students construct an explanation supported by their evidence for why certain structures function to provide an advantage for organisms in a specific environment.
   Class Discussion:
   Q: How does the structure of the paper airplane function to help the glider go further?
   Q: Which specific traits in the flying squirrel provide the best structure for flying?
   Q: How did what you have learned about the paper airplane relate to the advantages and disadvantage of the wings of flying squirrels.
   Q: Why doesn't the flying squirrel species just evolve huge wings that help them glide even further?

(Teaching Suggestions: Focus class discussion on structure and function of body parts of the flying squirrels. Return students' discussion to engineering design as it relates to the flying squirrels but include sufficient discussion on the interactions of the glider with air to ensure students understand the physics of a glider).

5. Students develop an argument for how the evidence they gathered during the investigation supports the explanation that specific structures function to provide an advantage for some individuals in the forest ecosystem. |

Explore 2 This Explore is OPTIONAL if students need greater understanding of natural selection and variation of traits in a population. In a 5E lesson sequence additional Explore phases are added to develop students' conceptual understanding of complex science ideas or concepts.	*Phenomenon: Some students can jump higher than others.* **Gather:** 1. Students ask questions to obtain information about causes of some organisms being better adapted to survive in a specific environment in which they live but not well adapted to survive in other environments. 2. Students plan and carry out an investigation to obtain data on the proportion of individuals in a population with specific traits that allow these individuals to jump high enough to gather food needed to survive. *(Teaching Suggestions: Create a simulation by hanging "food" from the classroom ceiling at various heights where only a percentage of students are tall enough to reach. We suggest salt water taffy. Students who can reach and collect two objects will survive and reproduce, students who can reach one object will survive but not reproduce, and students who cannot reach any of the objects will not survive. Emphasize the idea that resources are limited and there is a competition among organisms for resources but manage movement in the classroom. Create a class chart on the board and have students record their data on a common chart).* **Reason:** 3. Students analyze and interpret data to determine the proportion of individuals that survive in the simulation activity environment. 4. Students construct an explanation for how variations in the physical structures of organisms (students) affect an individual's ability to reach food needed to survive.
Explore 3 This is an optional explore to support students' understanding of the how the environment and ecosystem affects the organism best able to survive in an environment. Classroom discussions are opportunities for the teacher to support instruction on the nature of the practices, crosscutting concepts and essential core idea. It is important to synthesize students' understanding.	*Phenomenon: Flying squirrels can escape predators by flying.* **Gather:** 1. Students obtain information from reliable sources about the ecosystem and behavior of the flying squirrels. *(Teaching Suggestions: Students examine data resources from the list below to determine preferred habitat components such as: foraging, winter survival, predators, and den sites).* List of resources that include data: https://ecos.fws.gov/docs/five_year_review/doc4177.pdf https://www.fs.fed.us/ne/newtown_square/publications/other_publishers/OCR/ne_2006_menzel001.pdf http://www.esf.edu/efb/lomolino/courses/mammaldiversity/labs/nys4.pdf http://www.esf.edu/aec/adks/mammals/southern_flying_squirrel.htm **Reason** 2. Students develop a new argument for how evidence they have gathered supports an explanation for how changes to an environment cause changes in the numbers of organisms able to survive in that environment. **Class Discussion:** Q: If your species survives this environment, does it mean the species has adapted to the change in the environment? Q: Do individuals adapt to changes in their environment or do populations adapt? Q: How might the proportion of organisms with a specific trait change for future generations if the environment changes?

	(Teaching Suggestions: The class discussion helps students begin to understand that populations of organisms (not individuals) adapt to the environment in which they live. It is important to focus on time scale for changes).
	3. Students revise explanations for why variation of traits in a population is necessary for organisms to change over time when the environment changes.

Explain Phenomena
The scientific explanation for causes of phenomena are prominent in this phase. Students engage in 3D performances.
 	
The focus is on accurate use of Core Ideas and Crosscutting Concepts to make sense of the phenomena featured in the Engage and Explore phases.
 	
The teacher directs students' attention to key aspects of the prior phases and first asks students for their explanations. Both the teacher and students formatively assess the learning progress.
 	
The class discussion is essential to the Explain Phase.
 	
The communication performance is a good place to provide a formative assessment of learning.
 	
Teachers may wish to revisit these ideas through a reading or lecture based on student understanding.
	Phenomenon: Some squirrels are better adapted to forest ecosystems.
	
	Reason:
	1. Students construct an explanation for causes of why some individuals in a population are more likely than others to survive and reproduce in forest ecosystems.
	
	    Class Discussion:
	    Q: Why do some species survive and others do not when the environment changes?
	    Q: Why is variation of traits in a population necessary for structural changes in a species to occur over many generations?
	    Q: How might genetic makeup of the population change with every generation?
	    Q: What happens to a population of organisms if only a few individuals of the species survive natural changes to the environment?
	
	(Teaching suggestions: Focus questions on how natural selection operates to cause changes in the distribution of traits in a population. Student explanations should convey species with an advantage in the environment are the most likely to survive. Organisms that do not possess adequate characteristics are less likely to survive).
	
	2. Students develop an argument for how evidence they have gathered supports their explanation for why specific structures function to help the flying squirrel be successful in the forest ecosystem.
	
	Communicate:
	3. Students individually revise their explanation for why changes over time in the physical structures of organisms are evidence of natural selection.
	
	(Teaching Suggestions: During the Explain phase, listen to the discussion and read students' written explanations to determine scientific accuracy, knowing and recognizing that students do not yet fully understand the core ideas. Introduce scientifically accurate core ideas and science language. You may wish to use readings, videos, or websites that use scientifically accurate explanations to support learning).

Formative Assessment for Student Learning

Elicit Evidence of Learning: Revise your explanation for why changes over time in the physical structures of organisms are evidence of natural selection.

Evidence of Student Proficiency	Range of Typical Student Responses	Acting on Evidence of Learning
Students explain that organisms best adapted for the environment in which they live survive and reproduce. The traits that helps them survive remains in the squirrel population and over time is exhibited in more squirrels. Students should describe that these changes happen over many, many generations and an individual does not adapt but a population adapts. Students should describe that some individuals are slightly better at jumping from tree to tree because their body structures allow them to survive and pass this trait to future generation. Students should recognize that adaptations are evidence for natural selection leading to the evolution of organisms through structural changes over time.	**Full understanding** – The flying squirrels that have better structures for jumping and gliding from tree to tree get food, avoid predators, and find mates to reproduce; their offspring have good traits for survival. This is natural selection. **Partial understanding** – Natural selection favors squirrels that fly best, get away from predators, and live to have offspring. **Limited understanding** – It is survival of the fittest.	Students with limited understanding should engage in a reading and discussion on the peppered moth Students with partial or full understanding should continue to the Elaborate phase of the lesson.

Elaborating Scientific Concepts and Abilities	*Phenomenon: There are no flying squirrels native to Montana, Idaho, Wyoming, or Utah, where Uinta Ground Squirrel are common.*
The students are involved in learning experiences that extend, expand, and enrich the concepts and abilities developed in the prior phases. The intention is to facilitate the transfer of concepts and abilities to related, but new situations.	 *Uinta Ground Squirrel from the Utah DWR.* **Gather:** 1. Students ask questions to obtain information about what causes the Uinta Ground Squirrel to be better adapted to survive in Utah and Wyoming than Flying Squirrels. 2. Students obtain information from reliable sources about body structures and how these structures function to enable Uinta Ground Squirrel to survive.
In the elaboration phase, the teacher challenges students with a new phenomenon and encourages interactions among students and with other sources such as written material, databases, simulations, and web-based searches.	*(Teaching Suggestions: State Division of Natural Resources and National Parks are good resources for information with MS reading levels.* *https://dwrcdc.nr.utah.gov/rsgis2/search/Display.asp?FlNm=sperarma)*

Reason:
3. Students use a model (T-Chart) to compare body structures and function of the Uinta Ground Squirrel to the New York Flying Squirrel.
4. Students construct an explanation supported by evidence for causes of differences in the structure of the two species and habitats.

(Teaching Suggestions: Students examine data resources to determine preferred habitat components such as foraging, predators, and den sites).

Class Discussion
Q: How are Uinta Ground Squirrel and flying squirrel body structures different?
Q: How do the structures of the ground squirrel help them survive?
Q: How has natural selection caused differences in these squirrel species?
Q: How might the proportion of organisms with a specific trait change, if the environment changes (e.g., logging of trees in New York or more rainfall in Wyoming causing many more trees to grow)?

5. Students revise their explanations for why variation of traits in a population led to squirrels in one environment having body structures for burrowing and in another environment body structures for flying.

(Teaching Suggestions: The Elaborate phase provides students with an opportunity to apply their understanding of natural selection and adaptation to an analogous phenomenon. This discussion provides an opportunity for students to consider the idea that if some organisms are not well adapted to a specific environment, they may not immediately go extinct, but there is suppression in the number of individuals in the population with specific traits).

Communicate
6. Students communicate their explanation for why variation of traits in a population led to squirrels in one environment with body structures for burrowing and in another environment structures for flying.

Evaluate Learners
At this point, students receive feedback on their explanations and abilities. Informal formative evaluations have been occurring from the initial phase of the instructional sequence. In the Evaluate phase, the teacher should involve students in experiences that are understandable and consistent and congruent with explanations from prior phases.

Phenomena: Prairie dogs live in colonies of underground dens in the American prairie.

Credit: Lee Winnike, USFWS

Gather
1. Students obtain information about how the structures of the American Prairie Dog makes this squirrel well adapted for living on the western prairies of North America.
https://naturalhistory.si.edu/mna/image_info.cfm?species_id=54

Students apply their learning from previous phases to make sense of why ground squirrels have different structures that help them survive in environments with few trees. Students should use evidence from readings and describe how the structure of claws, small tails, and/or other structures help ground squirrels to burrow and avoid predators by living underground. There are other structures students may describe including body shape, digestive system, etc.	**Reason** 2. Students develop an argument for how specific structures prairie dogs possess function to enable this species to survive and reproduce in the plains and grasslands of North America but not in the forests of the northeastern United States and Canada. **Communicate** 3. Students construct an explanation based on evidence for why genetic variations of traits in the prairie dog population increased the probability of some individuals' surviving and reproducing in response to environmental changes over time.

Formative Assessment for Student Learning

Elicit Evidence of Learning: Construct an explanation based on evidence for how genetic variations of traits in the Prairie Dog population increased the probability of some individuals' surviving and reproducing in response to environmental changes over time.

Evidence of Student Proficiency	Range of Typical Student Responses	Acting on Evidence of Learning
Student explanations provide the reasons why some organisms with traits that help them survive in an environment are more likely than others to survive and reproduce. The traits of these offspring continue to be more prevalent in the population, while traits that do not increase the chances of survival become less prevalent in the population. Organism well adapted for one environment may not be well adapted for another environment. In all environments, organisms with similar needs may compete with one another for resources (food, shelter, mates). In any particular environment, the growth and survival of organisms depend on physical condition. Offspring of individuals with favorable traits are more likely to survive and reproduce. The proportion of individuals that have advantageous characteristics will increase. Natural selection leads to organisms best suited to survive in a particular environment.	**Full understanding** – The prairie dogs that have good claws for digging deep burrows to get away from predators and the ones that are able to alert the family when hawks and coyotes come around are the ones that survive. The claws, loud voices, and good eyesight are traits that give these individuals a better chance to survive. When the environment changes, for example a new predator or a climate change, the population with more genetic variation may adapt to the change. This all takes many generations. **Partial understanding** – The prairie dogs that are the smartest survive and the ones that are not as smart do not. However, if things change, maybe the ones that are smaller and need less food can survive and big fat ones starve. **Limited understanding** – The prairie dogs that are best adapted to one environment are able to survive in new environments as well.	Students with partial and limited understanding can be provided with an opportunity to watch the free online PBS Video, "How does evolution really work?" After the video, they can engage in a group discussion with other students about how changes in the species shown in the video are similar to the evolution of flying squirrels in how they change over time.

Featured in Lesson	Science Essentials *(From Book Appendix C, D, E)*
Science Practices Construct an explanation Develop arguments from evidence Analyze data	Revise causal explanations that are supported by data and relate these explanations to current knowledge. Use patterns as evidence to support explanations. Use evidence to support arguments about science explanations for phenomena.
Crosscutting Concepts Cause and effect Structure and function	Identify causes of observed patterns in natural systems. Develop explanations for phenomena based on structure and function relationships.
Disciplinary Core Ideas LS 4.B Natural Selection LS4.C Adaptation ETS 1. B Developing Possible Solutions	Natural selection leads to the predominance of certain traits in a population and the suppression of others. Adaptation by natural selection acting over generations is one important process by which species change over time in response to changes in environmental conditions. Traits that support successful survival and reproduction in the new environment become more common and those that do not become less common. Thus, the distribution of traits in a population changes.
Conceptual Models Essential for Student Performances	Heredity is parents passing genetic traits to their offspring.

Lesson template developed by B. Moulding (2012).

Summary

The 5E and GRC models are complementary components of instruction. The former is a major foundation for student learning while the latter is a practical component addressing the vision of the *Framework* and standards.

If you want to explore other examples, the website #Going3D w/GRC provides lessons for each grade-level (K-5), each discipline (6-8), and each subject (9-12) aligned to the NGSS and a number of state standards. The site is organized by NGSS standards; however, most states have a crosswalk from NGSS to their standards. The lessons are three-dimensional, student centered, and were developed and vetted by teachers across many states.

Reflecting on 5E Instructional Model Using GRC Student Performances

1. The 5E-GRC lessons are structured around a series of student performances followed by teaching suggestions. How does writing the lesson as three-dimensional student performances help shift the lessons to be more "student centered?"

2. Why should lessons first engage the student in observing or exploring a phenomenon before obtaining information about the phenomenon?

3. In the Explanation phase of the instructional sequence, the teacher formally synthesizes students' explanations and adds accurate science language and concepts. Why is it important for this to occur after students have engaged in making sense of the phenomenon?

Bibliography

Bybee, R. (2015). *The BSCS 5E Instructional Model: Creating Teachable Moments*. Washington, DC: NSTA Press.

Moulding, B., Bybee, R., & Paulson, N. (2015). *Vision and Plan for Science Teaching and Learning*. Salt Lake City, UT: Essential Teaching and Learning.

NGSS Lead States. (2013). *Next Generation Science Standards: For States, By States*. Washington, DC: The National Academies Press.

CHAPTER 9

ESSAYS ON SCIENCE TEACHING AND LEARNING

How do other aspects of the educational system affect teaching and learning?

This chapter is a collection of essays germane to science teaching and learning: relationships, the nature of science, and educational considerations beyond lessons. While each of these topics could fill a book, we present them to prompt your thinking. We are fortunate that some of our friends and colleagues contributed ideas and insights to this collection.

Part One: Relationships

In this section, we address the impact of strong, trusting relationships on student learning. These relationships should extend beyond the walls of the classroom and into the students' home lives. We round out this section with a call for teaching civil discourse within and beyond the science classroom.

Essay 1   The Importance of a Positive and Intellectually Safe Classroom Environment
Essay 2   Building Partnerships with Parents
Essay 3   Civility and Science Teaching

Part Two: Nature of Science

After establishing scientific reasoning as a powerful way of knowing, we address the role of science in providing stability in the current sociopolitical climate. We also address the increasing presence of engineering within science education, and conclude this section with a discussion of and examples for teaching based on phenomena.

Essay 4   Evidence Distinguishes Science from Other Ways of Knowing
Essay 5   Teaching About Scientific Explanations: An Imperative for Contemporary Education
Essay 6   Engineering in Science Education
Essay 7   Teaching Science Based on Phenomena

Part Three: Educational Practices

Implementing the Framework and the Next Generation Science Standards (NGSS) will require that teachers assess and adjust their current instructional practices. Beginning with a discussion on the role of professional development for guiding implementation of the Framework and NGSS, we use this section to address the shift toward cultivating curiosity in science education, the opportunities presented by the new science standards, the role of homework in teaching, and the need for shifting assessment practices aligned with the Framework.

Essay 8   Professional Development and Professional Learning
Essay 9   Standards are an Opportunity, Not a Solution
Essay 10   Science in K-2 Curiosity and Literacy
Essay 11   Role of Homework in Student Learning
Essay 12   Assessing Student Learning to Inform Instruction

Everyone should be respected as an individual, but no one idolized.

~Albert Einstein

PART 1: RELATIONSHIPS

Essay 1
The Importance of a Positive and Intellectually Safe Classroom Environment

Ken Huff, Science Teacher, Mill Middle School Williamsville, New York

Brett Moulding

The classroom environment significantly affects teaching and learning. The classroom environment may be thought of as an ecosystem with interacting and interdependent living and non-living components. The students and teacher are the living, growing, and learning components; but just like any ecosystem, the non-living components are as important as the living components. Time in class, space and seating arrangements, temperature, standards, instructional resources, class rules, and many other non-living components of the classroom environment constrain and inform the interactions among the living components of the ecosystem.

Safe Learning Environments

The learning environment is an important element of effective science instruction. Learning environments where students feel safe to take intellectual risks provide opportunities for students to advance reasoning through metacognitive analysis of their own and others' ideas.

Such environments begin with the teacher modeling *active listening* of students' reasoning. When the teacher listens intently to students describing their understanding of the relationship of evidence supporting explanations for causes of phenomena, the student learns how to productively engage in civil dialogue, a critical outcome of teaching and learning. Careful listening is an important aspect of science learning and contributes significantly to a positive learning environment by establishing a relationship of respect within the classroom. When teachers model this behavior, students behave in a consistent manner. Listening to students also leads to insightful questions, providing students with think time and providing teachers with time to reflect on student reasoning and to respond in ways that will extend student thinking.

It takes time to get students to understand that more than one explanation for a scientific event is possible and that alternative explanations should always be examined. One way to encourage this thinking is for teachers to frequently introduce and discuss alternative beliefs and explanations or describe the ways scientists disagree and resolve their disagreements. Some researchers, in collaboration with science teachers, have found that argumentation in classrooms is more likely to occur when students are permitted and encouraged to talk directly with each other, rather than having their discussions mediated by the teacher. Other researchers have found that teacher-mediated whole-group discussion is more productive. Most successful teachers use a combination of talk formats to provide opportunities for both of these types of discourse. No matter what the format, teachers need to work actively to support classroom norms that emphasize responsibility, respect, and the construction of arguments based on theory and evidence. (National Research Council [NRC], 2008, p. 96)

When situated within a productive learning environment, science provides a forum for students to engage in argumentation about how or why specific evidence supports or refutes an explanation (Chen, Hand, & Norton-Meier, 2016). Classroom discussion is more productive when students know their teacher and classmates are not evaluating them personally but are engaging with their ideas and evidence (Smart & Marshall, 2013). Science instruction that consistently values the appropriate use of evidence is an important part of establishing a productive classroom environment.

Classroom Discourse

Classroom discussion is an important instructional strategy for engaging students in science reasoning (Smart & Marshal, 2013; Tobin, Ritchie, Oakley, Mergard, & Hudson, 2013). Classroom discussions act as funnels for students to bring together ideas about phenomena, core ideas, and crosscutting concepts and then coalesce these ideas into cogent and accurate explanations. Classroom discussions are most effective when teachers listen carefully to and extend students' reasoning. Opportunities occur during class discussions to add science language to students' concepts and ideas in relevant and meaningful ways. Effective teachers carefully plan what appear to be spontaneous moments within classroom discussions and understand how to empower students to seize the moment and take ownership of their learning. These discussions are the appropriate forum for discussion on a myriad of science ideas (e.g., experiments, fair tests, variables, nature of science, the role of evidence in science).

Joy of Learning

Meaningful learning is enjoyable. Ideally, students will find pleasure in learning relevant and interesting science. Often, the joy of learning comes from students pursuing science around phenomena in which they have a genuine curiosity, or from learning important ideas that they can apply as they discover new phenomena.

> Sigmund Freud described childhood as a period of trying to balance primal urges to find pleasure and avoid pain with the growing need to be part of a group. Every piece of research since that essay has shown that Freud was right. Human lives are governed by the desire to experience joy. Becoming educated should **not** require giving up joy; but rather lead to **finding joy in new kinds of things:** reading novels instead of playing with small figures, **conducting experiments instead of sinking cups in the bathtub,** and debating serious issues rather than stringing together nonsense words. (Engel, 2015, para. 7, emphasis added)

Facilitating science learning in the classroom provides an opportunity for teachers to emphasize increasing students' ability to use the three dimensions of science: science and engineering practices, crosscutting concepts, and disciplinary core ideas. The innovations of the *Framework* have focused teachers on seeking coherent approaches to weave the three dimensions of science together in curriculum, instruction, and assessment. These innovations provide opportunities for various instructional strategies to engage students in science learning when the classroom environment is productive and safe. In positive instructional environments, students are able to produce artifacts that represent meaningful science learning. An important product of science learning is discourse, which provides an impetus for students to reflect on what they do and do not conceptually understand (NRC, 2008).

Science teaching and learning should be centered on everyday experience around science phenomena relevant to the student. Teachers typically find themselves with opportunities to develop insights from a diversity of perspectives and understandings that students bring to the classroom. In planning, implementing, and reflecting on instruction, teachers thoughtfully cultivate learning experiences which engage students with central questions about the natural world.

When students explore questions and share ideas respectfully, they learn from each other as real scientists in a laboratory or in the field might do. Students discover that they disagree and devise ways to test their ideas. This instructional approach takes advantage of the natural curiosity of young people, which research has shown is effective in increasing reasoning and problem-solving skills.

Essay 2
Building Partnerships with Parents

Brett Moulding

Parents are the teacher's best partner for supporting student learning. Parental involvement in the science classroom is linked with increased student engagement and achievement (Castro et al., 2015; Harackiewicz, Rozek, & Hulleman, 2012; Hill & Tyson, 2009). When parents communicate high expectations, and scaffold their students' achievement, student engagement increases (Hill & Tyson, 2009; Jeynes, 2010). Teachers are essential resources for parents to learn how to be involved in their student's education by learning about innovations in science education, how science teaching and learning is structured in their student's classroom, the rationale for the curriculum design, and the goals for pedagogical innovations. It is the responsibility of the teacher to establish multiple lines of communication that provide parents with a picture of science education in the 21st century and how their student benefits from these innovations in science teaching and learning. Parents need to understand how these factors influence their child's experience in the science classroom in order to communicate clear and effective learning expectations (Castro et al., 2015).

Teachers should value opportunities to engage parents with the school and become skilled in the knowledge and dispositions for effectively communicating with the school community. Early positive communication with parents is essential for creating a strong school-home partnership that benefits student's interest and success in school. In the 21st century, teachers have multiple communication opportunities to provide parents with information about student progress. Communication tools range from school-to-home communication books, parent conferences, social media, web pages, phone calls, emails, and online gradebooks.

Teachers should assume that communication is rarely a discrete, individual event, but rather occurs within the context of ongoing exchanges (Adler & Rodman, 1994). Teachers should try to use a variety of effective strategies to make communication with parents as informative and interactive as possible, incorporating new communication methods, while retaining the human touch. Each communication with parents, regardless of format, should reflect interest in their student's learning. Teachers should be thoughtful about planning systematic and strategic parent communications with the goal of developing meaningful partnerships to support student learning.

One important step that teachers can take toward parent advocacy and education is providing a disclosure statement that includes a clear and positive vision of science teaching and learning in their classroom, including the goals and the class procedures that support student learning. This statement should clearly outline why science learning is important, how the research supports the planned approaches to science teaching and learning, and the parents' role in student learning. Finally, teachers should do what is reasonable to ensure parents have read and understand the disclosure statement.

Positive interactions with parents are important to support students' disposition toward learning science in the classroom. When possible, teachers should focus on students' positive accomplishments and learning. Parents generally understand that teachers are in partnership with them and their student, with the common goal of successful and meaningful learning experiences. Parent-teacher alliances benefit student learning in many ways, most importantly the student's sense of belonging to your class and an obligation to work to be successful in science (Castro et al., 2015; Harackiewicz et al., 2012; Hill & Tyson, 2009). These approaches support the student identifying with science.

Teachers should use simple and clear messages when communicating with parents, who are more interested in knowing their student is engaged in doing science than knowing the details of the curriculum. One way to accomplish this is to provide parents with examples of their student's writing and help them understand how science learning is progressing. The lessons shared in this book provide good examples of how to engage students in ways that produce writing that represents student performances. Using notebooks and other artifacts from students to share learning progress at parent teacher conferences or reaching out through the occasional phone call or email to address the student's educational progress are good ways help parents stay invested in their student's science education.

Ultimately, a consistent and well-thought-out message and disposition toward teaching and learning underlies all effective communication with parents and students. A wise principal once told me, "in order to be a good teacher, you must first be a good person. In a world in which you can do anything, choose to be kind."

Essay 3
Civility and Science Teaching

Rodger W. Bybee

What do I mean by civility? How does science teaching uniquely contribute to civility and civil discourse? How can instructional materials and teaching strategies contribute to students' understanding of civility and development of abilities and sensibilities of civil discourse? Why should civility and civil discourse be included in science education? Now more than ever these questions require response.

To the first question, I have found two books particularly insightful regarding the theme of civility: *Civility* by Stephen L. Carter (1998) and *How Civility Works* by Keith J. Bybee (2016). In the former, Stephen Carter first points out the essential virtue of integrity because it helps individuals understand what the right course of action. He goes on to point out that civility follows, as it is a tool for interacting with others. Civility, Carter argues, "is the sum of the many sacrifices we are called to make for the sake of living together" (Carter, 1998, p. 11).

Keith Bybee (yes, we are related) makes the point that "in this most general sense civility is a code of public conduct" (Bybee, 2016, p. 7). He goes on to point out the close connections among politeness, courtesy, manners, and civility. From these general definitions, one can see the need for civility as it relates to social order and specifically to this discussion of science education, routine, and regularity in classrooms and teaching and learning settings.

There is a need for greater civility and its essential role for citizens in a democracy. Civility requires individuals to recognize and accept norms and laws that limit their goals and aspirations. In short, freedom is essential but not limitless. The values, abilities, and sensibilities of civility can develop science experiences, particularly those that include discussions, dialogue, and discourse or that require students to adapt their current ideas based on evidence, support their reasoning, and communicate their new ideas. Extending civility to science education implies teaching students how to conduct themselves individually and in a group. This aim is not new. Teachers implement this aim every day as they establish the norms and behavior expectations for their students.

Civil discourse has to do with the way students interact in groups. For example, listening, responding to other students' ideas, expressing their ideas, disagreeing with others, explaining an idea that differs from another student's idea, and not interrupting or "talking over" another student.

What is the unique contribution of science education? The unique contribution of science education is found in the empirical basis for statements, conclusions, and decisions. The importance of facts and empirical data combined with logic and reasoning in support of explanations and solutions, stand out as the answers to the question.

Answering the third question, "How can instructional materials and teaching strategies contribute to students' understanding of civility and development of abilities and sensibilities of civil discourse?" offers opportunities for teachers to involve students in experiences that develop the abilities and sensibilities of civility and civil discourse. As students are involved in activities with competencies for identifying, acquiring, and applying science knowledge, values, and skills, these experiences should contribute to an understanding of their role as citizens and provide opportunities for teachers to establish norms of civil interactions and the rules of civil discourse as the students work in groups and teams. Teachers may find guidance for civil discourse in classrooms from sources such as Classroom Discussions: Using Math Talk to Help Students Learn (Chopin, O'Connor, & Anderson, 2009) and Teaching for Civic Engagement (Colley, 2016).

Finally, the question—why science? In life, people have to draw conclusions and make decisions based on information they are given, read, hear or find on the Internet. Of the information is a mixture of science-related facts and other proposals grounded in political or economic perspectives, for example. They have to evaluate information presented by others and they have to distinguish personal opinion and beliefs from evidence-based statements. Some of the science practices are cognitive abilities that help people apply information to the decisions they must make.

In conclusion, a note about civility and science teaching may sound like a unique theme. However, teachers continually help students develop the abilities to interact with others in polite ways. This note simply serves as a reminder that group work and classroom discussions provide a context for developing civility and science teaching.

In questions of science, the authority of a thousand is not worth the humble reasoning of a single individual.

~Galileo Galilei

PART TWO: NATURE OF SCIENCE

Essay 4
Evidence Distinguishes Science from Other Ways of Knowing

Brett Moulding

Science is one of many ways of making sense of the world (Brickhouse, Lowery, & Schultz, 2000; von Glasersfeld, 1995). Psychologists and philosophers who study scientific reasoning, not merely as a way to do science but as a way of understanding ideas and issues outside of the classroom, focus on empirical evidence as the defining attribute of science (Bybee, 2015a).

Appendix H of NGSS (NRC, 2012) addresses the central role of evidence in students' understanding of science. This approach to making meaning in the world is predicated on the scientist as a reasoner who actively connects evidence to causes of phenomena, and positions scientific thinking as a set of skills and knowledge that can and should be taught as young learners develop their individual and academic identities (Archer et al., 2010; Brickhouse et al., 2000). Such learning includes honing inquiry and observation skills to gather evidence from reliable sources and logically designed experiments; developing problem-solving strategies that include rectifying theory and evidence; applying conceptual understanding of null hypotheses; determining whether specific evidence supports or does not support an explanation; and establishing logical arguments to communicate how each piece of evidence supports or refutes a specific explanation.

Because evidence plays a key role in making sense of science phenomena it should be central to all discussion within the science classroom. As students pursue explanations for science phenomena, they should continually ask themselves "What evidence do we have to support that assertion?" For science teachers to assess the degree to which their students are engaged with the content, they need look no further than how students are seeking and applying evidence.

Essay 5
Scientific Explanations: An Imperative for Contemporary Education

Rodger W. Bybee

In these times of uncertainty and unconventional ways of explaining observations and events, it is worth a reminder that science can bring certainty and provide order to what may be presented as alternative explanations and the dismissal of science as an evidence-based way of explaining the world. The contemporary situation underscores the need for all teachers of science to introduce and emphasize ideas that form the nature of science and scientific explanations (Duschl, 2000; Flick & Lederman, 2005; Lederman & Lederman, 2004). This brief essay presents background information for teachers and should be viewed as a complement to information in A Framework for K-12 Science Education (NRC, 2012) and Next Generation Science Standards (NGSS Lead States, 2013).

Development of scientific explanations begins with a question about a natural phenomenon. In particular, the question may try to explain the cause for an effect. For children, the scientific question can emerge from curiosity about objects, organisms, or events in their world. For scientists, the question can extend inquiries about the stability and change of populations of organisms due to climate change. Once the question is asked, a process of scientific inquiry begins, and there eventually may be an answer in the form of an evidence-based explanation. Concepts that characterize scientific inquiry and the activities of scientists include defining the system under study, development models to assist in the explanation, and recognizing the scale, proportion, and quantity of phenomena to be studied.

The inquiry process includes planning and conducting investigations, constructing models, and using mathematics. In addition, inquiry includes systematic collecting, analyzing and interpreting data, identifying appropriate variables in investigations, and taking precise, accurate, and reproducible measurements. However, science includes more than collecting, analyzing, and interpreting data. Scientists also engage in important processes such as constructing explanations, elaborating models, and engaging in reasoned arguments, all based on evidence. These processes extend, clarify, and unite the observations and data and, very importantly, develop deeper and broader scientific explanations. Examples include what we know about natural hazards, emerging diseases, antibiotic resistance, and the causes and consequences of changing the Earth's atmosphere.

In this discussion, I have incorporated many practices of inquiry as they are described in the Next Generation Science Standards.

1. Asking questions (for science) and defining problems (for engineering)
2. Developing and using models
3. Planning and carrying out investigations
4. Analyzing and interpreting data
5. Using mathematics and computational thinking
6. Constructing explanations (for science) and designing solutions (for engineering)
7. Engaging in argument from evidence
8. Obtaining, evaluating, and communicating information

There are further ideas that differentiate scientific explanations from other types of explanations. Among those ideas are the following:

- Scientific explanations are based on empirical evidence. The appeal to authority or simply stating a belief, or lack of belief, does not meet the criteria of being scientific. Evidence is based on sense experiences or on an extension of the senses through technology.

- Scientific explanations are public. Scientists make presentations at scientific meetings or publish in professional journals, making knowledge public and available to other scientists.

- Scientific explanations are tentative. Explanations can and do change. Science does not "prove" something for all time. Scientists do not assume there are absolute truths.

- Scientific explanations are historical. Science builds on past explanations and those explanations are in turn the basis for future explanations.

- Scientific explanations are probabilistic. The statistical view of nature is evident implicitly or explicitly when stating scientific predictions of phenomena.

- Scientific explanations assume cause-effect relationships. Much of science is directed toward determining causal relationships and developing explanations for interactions and linkages between and among phenomena. Distinctions among causality, correlation, coincidence, and contingency separate science from other ways of explaining observations.

- Scientific explanations are linked to technologies. Scientific explanations sometimes are limited by technology. New technologies can result in new fields of inquiry or extend current lines of inquiry. Examples include the interactions between technology and advances in molecular biology and the role of technology in planetary explorations.

You likely noticed that several crosscutting concepts of the NGSS appeared in the previous discussions. This is one of the reasons crosscutting concepts are included in contemporary standards. They help identify and clarify the unique characteristic of scientific explanation.

1. Patterns
2. Cause and effect
3. Scale, proportion, and quantity
4. Systems and system models
5. Energy and matter
6. Structure and function
7. Stability and change

I refer you to the Next Generation Science Standards (NGSS Lead States, 2013), in particular Appendix H in Volume II, for further details about the nature of science. The references include other resources that you will find helpful as you teach students about the scientific enterprise.

In conclusion, we are at a time in history when teaching about the nature of science is more than important; it is an imperative. Our students need to understand what science is, what it does, and why it is important for society.

Engineering in Science Education

Rodger W. Bybee

Engineering has gained a presence in science education. A 2012 national survey of science and mathematics education reported 24% of high schools offered engineering courses (Banilower et al., 2013). This percentage has likely increased due to the inclusion of engineering design in *A Framework for K-12 Science Education* (NRC, 2012) and the *Next Generation Science Standards* (NGSS Lead States, 2013.)

The emergence of engineering underscores the need to address basic educational questions that include: What is the primary goal of engineering in K-12 education? What are the core concepts, processes, and habits of mind for K-12 education programs?

One of the first issues that must be addressed is: What is the primary purpose of K-12 engineering education? Answering this question centers on a short list of possibilities: engineering literacy, college and career preparation, and achievement in other disciplines such as science and mathematics.

While these goals are not necessarily mutually exclusive, education in grades K-12 has a long history of emphasis on what, in the context of this discussion, would be referred to as engineering literacy. The goal of K-12 education is not to prepare engineers. In contrast, the goal of engineering literacy emphasizes an understanding, appreciation, and experience with the fundamental concepts, habits of mind, and processes of engineering.

Within the aim of engineering literacy, one can identify general knowledge and skills required for college and careers in the 21st century. For example, engineering literacy includes: recognizing problems and thinking in terms of systems, applying knowledge from other disciplines, using data, evidence, and critical analysis in formulating possible solutions to problems.

Central to the elaboration and application of engineering literacy is an answer to the questions that heads this section—What is engineering? The context for answering this question here is K-12 education. More specifically--What are the core ideas, design practices, and habits of mind that are unique to engineering and that differentiate it from other disciplines?

The basis for this discussion on the structure of engineering in the context of education was established in *The Process of Education* a little book by Jerome Bruner published in 1960. According to Bruner, "...the curriculum of a subject should be determined by the most fundamental understanding that can be achieved of the underlying principles that give structure to that subject" (Bruner, 1960, p. 31). Bruner also made this point: "Mastery of the fundamental ideas of a field involves not only the grasping of general principles, but also the development of an attitude toward learning and inquiry" (Bruner, 1960, p. 20).

So, to use Bruner's terms, there is a need to describe a set of underlying principles that give structure to engineering. Further, fundamental abilities and attitudes relative to problem solving should be described as a part of the curricular structure of engineering. Although published almost 50 years ago, we note that these ideas are consistent with contemporary learning theory (See, e.g. *How People Learn,* NRC, 2000).

Prior work by the National Academy of Engineering (NAE) and published as *Engineering in K-12 Education* (NAE, 2009) defined core ideas and fundamental processes in K-12 engineering education. The following are from that report:

- Design—a purposeful, iterative process with an explicit goal governed by specifications and constraints.
- Analysis—a systematic, detailed examination intended to (1) define or clarify problems, (2) inform design decisions, (3) predict or assess performance, (4) determine economic feasibility, (5) evaluate alternatives, or (6) investigate failures.
- Constraints—the physical, economical, legal, political, social, ethical, aesthetic, and time limitations inherent to or imposed upon the design of a solution to a technical problem.
- Modeling—any graphical, physical, or mathematical representation of the essential features of a system or process that facilitates engineering design.
- Optimization—the pursuit of the best possible solution to a technical problem in which trade-offs are necessary to balance competing or conflicting constraints.
- Trade-offs—decisions made to relinquish or reduce one attribute of a design in order to maximize another attribute.
- System—any organized collection of discrete elements (e.g., parts, processes, people) designed to work together in interdependent ways to fulfill one or more functions.

The curricular structure put forth in the NAE report integrates concepts and processes unique to engineering. The NAE committee recommended an emphasis on engineering design and the incorporation of developmentally appropriate mathematics, science, and technology knowledge and skills.

While the NAE report integrates engineering concepts and processes, the NGSS practices may be more familiar and appropriate for many K-12 educators. This is especially true given the stated emphasis on engineering design. Following are the practices as stated with a priority on engineering:

- Defining Problems
- Developing and using Models
- Planning and Carrying Out Investigations
- Analyzing and interpreting data
- Using Mathematics and Computational Thinking
- Designing Solutions
- Constructing Explanations
- Engaging in Argument from Evidence
- Obtaining, Evaluating, and Communicating Information

Finally, the NAE committee identified engineering habits of mind that include: (1) systems thinking, (2) creativity, (3) optimism, (4) collaboration, (5) communication, and (6) attention to ethical considerations.

In everyday terms the NAE report outlined what students should, know, value, and be able to do as a result of K-12 engineering education. Several things about response to the educational clarification for engineering should be noted. First, the collective priority is on engineering design, clarifying a problem and applying knowledge from other disciplines, data, and reasoning to propose the best solution. Second, the implication of emphasizing design is that education programs use the context of problem solving as a means to introduce and "teach" the core ideas, practices, and habits of mind. Third, there is a need for those teaching K-12 engineering to recognize that the core ideas and design practices are *both* learning outcomes. That is, students should know about constraints and be able to recognize and address them as they pursue the solution to an engineering problem. Finally, the shared values, attitudes, and skills of engineering, i.e. habits of mind, can also be developed within the context of engineering design.

I will conclude this discussion by summarizing the following priorities for K-12 engineering education:

- Engineering literacy should be the primary goal of policies, programs and practices of K-12 engineering education.

- Core ideas, design practices, and habits of mind have been described for engineering literacy.

- K-12 engineering education programs should emphasize engineering design. By programs we are referring to instructional materials and assessments for K-12 grades; programs for initial preparation of elementary, middle and high school teachers; and professional development programs for K-12 classroom teachers.

Essay 7

Teaching Science Based on Phenomena

Rodger W. Bybee

"Yeap! Finland Will Become the First Country in the World to Get Rid of All School Subjects" Upon reading this title, I, like most educators, was amazed. My first reaction was "Really? What about science? What will be the basis of the school curriculum?"

Answers to these questions center on phenomena-based learning. This contemporary idea brings new clarity to studying "the real world." Teaching begins with phenomena and progresses to the information, concepts, processes and skills needed to make sense of the phenomena. Yes, this approach requires crossing the boundaries of traditional disciplines. Instead of beginning with the life sciences and studying cells, ecosystems, and biomes, students have the opportunity to choose from what they see and experience in their world—phenomena.

Phenomena are studied using an interdisciplinary approach. Think, for example, of studying environmental phenomena that present a problem and require a solution. Disciplines for this study might include biology, engineering, and math. In the process of phenomena-based learning, students collaborate by sharing results of gathering information, investigating solutions, and proposing solutions to problems.

Teaching science moves beyond traditional disciplinary approaches with phenomena-based education. Originating with natural phenomena, the teacher's role includes facilitating the gathering of information by students, helping students design investigations, working with students as they analyze data, and finally providing feedback as students use the evidence from their investigations to formulate explanations for natural phenomena or propose solutions to problems.

In Helsinki Finland, 70% of teachers are participating in preparatory work as they implement phenomena-based education. Subject specialists cooperate and contribute to student learning experiences.

We are now at a point where we must educate our children in what no one knew yesterday, and prepare our schools for what no one knows yet.

~Margaret Mead

PART THREE: EDUCATIONAL PRACTICES

Essay 8
Professional Development and Professional Learning

Sam Shaw, Team Leader, Division of Learning & Instruction, South Dakota Department of Education
Brett Moulding

The interactions between teachers and students in individual classrooms determines the success of student learning. Teachers are the linchpins in any effort to improve science education, so it stands to reason that implementing the *Framework* (NRC, 2012) and *Next Generation Science Standards* (NGSS Lead States, 2013) requires significant and ongoing preparation and professional development. As Hawley and Rosenholtz (1984) concluded,

> In virtually every instance in which researchers have examined the factors that account for student performance, teachers prove to have a greater impact than programs. This is true for average students and exceptional students, for normal classrooms and special classrooms. (p. x)

Just as teachers should engage students in doing science performances, so too should professional development engage teachers in science performances that feature and reflect on effective instructional strategies. Successful professional development should immerse teachers, like students, in investigation of science phenomena. Science professional development should model for teachers the three-dimensional science performances that also lead to student engagement in science. Sustained and effective instructional changes result from professional development that models good instruction, engages teachers in instructional planning and adaptation, includes opportunities for teachers to implement planned approaches to instruction, and provides opportunities for reflection on teaching and learning. In this way, professional development holds potential for inspiring teachers to shift toward a learner-centered model of teaching, wherein students discover and make new connections for themselves, rather than the traditional lecture-based approach to education (Weimer, 2013). Teachers should experience the wonder of discovery and engage in three-dimensional science performances to model the reasoning they expect of their students.

Engaging teachers in making sense of phenomena is a powerful way to model good science teaching and learning. Parents will jokingly say 'Do as I say, not as I do,' knowing full well that their children will model their behavior on the parents' actions. Professional development cannot be effective if the primary delivery mechanism only involves "telling" about good teaching.

Quality professional development has a clear set of criteria. Explicit standards for teaching, professional development, education programs, and the education system were included in the original National Science Education Standards (NSES) published by the NRC in 1996 (Bybee, 2015b). The *Framework* (NRC, 2012) and *Next Generation Science Standards* (NGSS Lead States, 2013) did not provide an update to the NSES professional development guidance. However, in 2015 the Council of State Science Supervisors (CSSS), a group of state-level science supervisors representing each of the states, developed a set of standards specific to and in line with the vision for teaching and learning presented in the *Framework*, and the resulting NGSS. This book also made a specific attempt to align the description of teaching and learning to be consistent with the CSSS *Science Professional Learning Standards* and the *Framework*. We encourage you to use these standards to establish a clear expectation for quality professional development and professional learning. This recommendation is directed to both the providers of professional development as well as educators participating in professional learning. The CSSS *Science Professional Learning Standards* are available at: http://cosss.org/Professional-Learning.

We recommend that all educators of science engage in ongoing and sustained professional learning experiences consistent with the nature of the science performances they plan to use in their classroom (e.g., three-dimensional, phenomena based, engaging and interesting). We further recommend that professional development providers establish and model a professional and respectful collegial learning culture during all professional development so that teachers and principals are respected as valued professional educators.

SPLS are now on the new CSSS website: http://cosss.org/Professional-Learning. We recommend that educators review these standards and establish an expectation for how professional development should be structured, the values and dispositions you should expect from providers, peers, and yourself in professional learning environments. We recommend that providers of professional development should carefully review the standards and consider both the deliverables and the responses of educators to your professional development and respond appropriately and professionally to make changes to meet the standards for research-based professional learning opportunities.

Essay 9

Standards are an Opportunity, Not a Solution

Brett Moulding

The goal of educational reform is to improve student learning. Student learning occurs when teachers work day by day to help students learn the dispositions, knowledge, and skills to engage in doing science. Standards do not improve teaching and learning, they only provide an opportunity for teaching and learning to improve. The opportunity comes in the form of thinking about the outcomes of science education in different ways, engaging in aligned professional development, and rethinking the teaching and learning interactions occurring every day in the classroom.

The NGSS and state standards inspired by the *Framework* provide a structure for thinking about how students engage in science and how they approach explanations of phenomena. In this regard, standards provide opportunities for educators to rethink the expectations for science. The structure of the new standards is inherent in the crosscutting concepts and practices, but it also resides in the acceptance that we must teach fewer core ideas, more deeply, and have student use these ideas to make sense of phenomena.

Standards are not enough to improve students' learning of science; change requires shifting instruction to focus on asking students to reason about causes of phenomena and use evidence to support their reasoning. This shift comes in three parts: (1) engaging students in science performances during which they use each of the three dimensions to make sense of phenomena; (2) valuing and cultivating students' curiosity about science phenomena; and (3) students valuing and using science as a process of obtaining knowledge supported by empirical evidence. The *Framework*-inspired standards are consistent with each of these shifts for science teaching and learning (NGSS Lead States, 2012).

Implementing the innovations called for in the *Framework* will require a monumental effort on the part of all professional educators. This is an opportunity for professional teachers to embrace new instructional approaches and strategies for science teaching and learning. As a part of ongoing professional development, it will require teachers to reflect on their own learning. It will require hard work, patience, and courage to change in ways that make a difference in student learning and ultimately in students' lives beyond school. The hope is for the professional development to create opportunities for professional learning that is consistent with the goals of the framework to meet the needs of all children. It will require that we make equity in opportunity to learn a priority and moral responsibility for every educator in every school and classroom. It will require building and leveraging networks, partnerships, and collaborations within and across districts and states. It will require coherence in educational programs, curriculums, and professional development.

Finally, we must attend to communication and vision for the changes in teaching necessary to support changes in learning. We continue to hear the lament that these new standards will be a challenge to implement or the declaration that these standards are a solution. We see the new standards as an opportunity for professional teachers to continue to improve their craft and do what all professional teachers do: informed by research and knowing our students better than anyone, we do what is best for our students.

Essay 10

Science in K-2: Curiosity and Literacy

Brett Moulding

Science teaching and learning in the early grades helps students make personal relevance with science content. The goals at the early grades should be to use science to make sense of phenomena, but more importantly, to support and direct natural curiosity (NRC, 2012). Cultivating curiosity with K-2 students seems like a simple task since young children are so naturally curious; unfortunately, instruction is too often about telling rather than wondering.

The goal for science education is to engage students with experiences that make them more curious. Curiosity is seen in the questions students ask not the questions the teacher asks. When introducing phenomena, it is important to create a situation for students to ask questions and engage their curiosity. Presenting phenomena in ways that engage students in asking questions, even before we say anything, is one of the most effective ways to cultivate curiosity. The key is for the teacher to value good questions more than good answers.

An important strategy for reading comprehension and science learning is to read with questions in mind. Prior to presenting readings on the learning topics, teachers can present a phenomenon, elicit good questions from students, and then synthesize students' questions into a reading guide on the spot. The following is a short vignette with a teacher who uses just such a strategy with her Kindergarten students.

Ms. Lofgren is a Kindergarten teacher and starts off each Thursday and Friday morning with a short discussion of science phenomena. Sometimes, but not always, she maneuvers the discussion toward the topic she is planning to introduce with an investigation, video, and/or read aloud about a phenomenon.

Teacher: Good morning.

~Students in chorus: Good morning Ms. Lofgren!~

Teacher: Did anyone notice something interesting on their way to school?

~Hands go up around the room and Mrs. Lofgren calls on students.~

Kevin: I saw it raining on one side of the road and not the other!

Josh: Yeah, I had to cross the road to get wet!

Maria: It was not raining when I left home, but was raining at school. I think this is a phenomenon.

Teacher: What might have caused this phenomenon?

Miguel: Sometimes clouds are in one place and not another.

Teacher: That is interesting, but what does this have to do with rain?

Miguel: Clouds make rain.

Kevin: Yeah, but sometime there are clouds that do not rain.

Susan: There are two types of clouds, rain clouds and puffy white clouds, not all cause rain.

Teacher: What evidence do you have that not all clouds cause rain.

Maria: Well, like, it rains only when there are clouds.

Sam: I like clouds that look like things.

Teacher: Does it always rain when there are clouds?

Maria: No, I have seen clouds in blue skies and it did not rain.

Kevin: Yes, I have seen the sky full of clouds and it didn't rain.

Sam: Sometimes clouds look like dragons.

Teacher: So, what evidence... you remember this word. (Ms. Lofgren walks over to the "Wall of Science Words" and points to the word" Evidence" which students have talked about with the teacher all year long and has five or six student and teacher drawings of plants, animals, and rocks that show the results of previous discussions about evidence).

Teacher continues: So, what evidence do you have that clouds are needed for rain?

Susan: Clouds cause rain; my evidence is that every time it rains we have clouds.

Sam: Yes, even clouds that look like dragons can rain, if they are big dark dragons.

Maria: Clouds cause rain because if there are no clouds it does not rain.

John: Clouds can change and when you have more clouds it sometimes, but not always rains.

Teacher: Let's take our ideas outside and look at clouds for a while.

Ms. Lofgren asks the students to follow her as always, keeping hands to themselves, and voices off, outside to lay in the shade of a big oak tree and watch clouds. She invites them to watch quietly for changes in the clouds, with their imaginations sometime on and sometimes off, to imagine shapes and see if the clouds get bigger or smaller. The students lay in the shade on the cool grass watching and whispering to one another about clouds. They smile and wonder. After just the right amount of time, which only teachers know, Ms. Lofgren asks the students to listen as she reads the story of *"Little Cloud,"* by Eric Carle, while they continue to watch and think about clouds. Students listen intently and watch for a long time. The students talked about clouds for days, and never stopped wondering.

The way we engage our students in science can have a profound effect on how they view science and learning. The hope of every teacher is that their students become lifelong learners. How would we view science education if our goal is for our students to be more curious in high school then they were in kindergarten? How would instruction change to achieve this goal? How would we view successful teaching and learning? It is important for our students to enjoy learning science. The most important aspect of the joy of learning is in wondering. Curiosity is our emotion that drives our thirst for learning; it is driven by questions and wondering. The effective teaching and learning of science is wonder-filled.

Role of Homework in Student Learning

Brett Moulding

All too often, homework is an over-assigned and under-utilized learning tool. Homework is used to have students memorize information, do worksheets, or complete a set of repetitive drills with little or no connection to the world outside of the classroom. Ideally, science homework is an opportunity to apply the knowledge and skills students have learned in school to make sense of phenomena in their non-school life. Engaging in science outside of class can build student curiosity and interest for science as students apply science learning in a new setting and bring their findings back to the classroom (Sutton & Kreuger, 2001).

Science learning through homework encourages students and parents to engage in science together. This is most true in the elementary years; but can be fostered at the secondary level as well (Fan, Xu, Cai, He, & Fan, 2017). Parents will value and gain insight into the new vision for science teaching and learning, as outlined in the NRC *Framework and NGSS* when assignments are motivating and include clear instructions (NGSS Lead States, 2013).

Teachers should use homework to provide students with authentic and relevant learning experiences at home. Science homework should not be school work done at home; but rather an application of skills and knowledge to a new set of phenomena that can build students conceptual understanding of the application to new phenomena. In order for homework to connect with and build upon in-class learning, the planning phase of the assignments should occur in school and the investigation phase should be carried out at home. This requires investigations that are safe and need little or no equipment (e.g., investigation of the rate of salt water and fresh water freezing; population density studies of organisms such as clover, noxious weeds, or insects; behavior of animals such as squirrels, birds, bats). These types of investigation are best carried out beyond the classroom.

Homework assignments allow space and time for students to engage in long-term, sustained projects that require multiple levels of understanding; for example, observing ecosystems, interviewing multiple scientists in the community, or engineering solutions to protect the local environment. Observing the night sky on one night may be an interesting activity, but observations of the night sky over weeks or months develop deep understanding and interest that leads to a lifelong fascination in astronomy. Maintaining an observation journal for six months or longer can lead to students developing a lifelong interest and identity with science.

Well-designed homework can bring parents and other adults into a student's community of science learners. Well-structured homework assignments should have clear criteria and written rubrics that describe expectations, outline student learning goals, and describe clear expectations and the roles of adults at home in student learning. Assignments should include students discussing their learning and synthesizing their science understanding with others, including older siblings, parents, relatives, and adults in their community.

A homework assignment should be a major event in student learning, but less is more when it comes to homework. A product that has been refined by the student results in more effective learning than a large volume of work completed with little thought. It is important for students to do their best and for teachers to examine student work. The quality of student work is often determined by the standards a teacher sets on the assignment, time spent reviewing the expectations, and suggestions for improvements.

Involving students in current science news (e.g., eclipses, engineering innovations, space exploration events, genetic technology breakthroughs) creates opportunities to learn about the nature of science and contributes to curiosity. Connecting newsworthy science events to the science learning in school helps students take an important step toward science literacy. Curiosity prepares the brain for better learning (Gruber et al., 2014), and can move students from studying science to identifying themselves as scientists and investigators.

Essay 12
Assessing Student Learning to Inform Instruction

Brett Moulding

Perhaps the most important innovation in the *Framework* (2012) and Next Generation Science Standards (NGSS Lead States, 2013) is the idea that student science performances have multiple dimensions. Of course, this presents a significant challenge and opportunity for assessment development. Developing large-scale assessments at the intersection of three dimensions requires an understanding that science assessment has never been done without engaging students across multiple aspects of knowledge and skills (e.g., reading, listening, analyzing). The key is that rather than making assessments more difficult, the three dimensions provide a scaffold to support student performances through: 1) using crosscutting concepts to engage students to define the system, understand that they are seeking a causal relationship of phenomena, and seeking for patterns; 2) engaging in familiar science and engineering practices [e.g., analyzing data, gathering information, communicating information, developing models, and constructing explanations]; and, 3) using fewer core ideas at a larger grain size that have utility across many science performances [e.g., matter is made of particles; thermal energy flows from high to low; for any particular environment some kinds of organisms survive well, some survive less well, and some cannot survive at all]. Engaging students in using the same core ideas to make sense of varied phenomena is one of the innovations of the new standards.

Assessing Science Performances

The *Framework* and *NGSS* describe standards in terms of the performances we expect students to be able to do when they understand science. Performance expectations are best assessed with performance tasks: tasks that student perform, tasks that provide evidence of student performances, and tasks that are aligned to the three dimensions of science as "performance expectations" also known as "the standards." The use of the descriptor "Performance Expectations" in the *Framework* and *NGSS* is intentional. These are the performances expected of students who are proficient in science.

Designing a performance task aligned to the standards should start with first analyzing the standards and then moving to the acceptable evidence, core ideas, and crosscutting concepts that students might use to engage in science and/or engineering practices.

1. What is the best way to write an assessment task that engages students in the practice?
2. What is the core idea and crosscutting concept being assessed?
3. What phenomenon provides a good opportunity for the student to use the core idea and crosscutting concept in a meaningful science performance?
4. How will multiple crosscutting concepts be used to focus students on specific aspects of the phenomenon?
5. What information is provided to the students in the question/prompt and what information must they provide?

Assessment is most effective when embedded within teaching and learning and used to inform both the teacher and student of learning progress. Both the teacher and the student should reflect on performances on assessments and use assessment information to understand and improve student learning. Crosscutting concepts provide a useful structure for prompting student responses. The following assessment examples model role of crosscutting concepts in prompting student performance:

Example One: Students observe a video of fast moving water eroding the banks of a river and are prompted:

"Use a model to show how different parts of the system of the atmosphere, land, and river interact during a storm to cause the observed changes in the system."

The prompt focuses students on causes of change in the system. This helps the student focus on causal relationships for the changes. Students who fully understand the crosscutting concepts have a significant advantage on items like this and provide educators with a clear picture of science learning.

Example Two: In Chapter 2, the phenomenon "the moon appears orange" was presented. Below is an example of a prompt that utilizes the crosscutting concepts to elicit student thinking about causes of this phenomenon. The key to effectively engage students in reasoning in this performance is appropriate use of crosscutting concepts in the prompt and the students' use of crosscutting concepts in the response. This prompt is placed within instruction.

Phenomenon – Sometimes the moon appears to be orange in color.

Group Performance

1. Define the system and formulate questions about causes and patterns of the moon sometimes appearing orange.
2. Construct an explanation for the changes in the system that cause the moon to sometimes appear orange.
3. Develop a model to explain how changes in the system cause the moon to sometimes appear orange.
4. Develop evidence that supports an explanation for causes of the moon sometimes appearing orange.

Individual Performance

5. Construct a written explanation for causes of the patterns of the moon sometimes appearing orange, and develop an argument for how the evidence you collected supports your explanations.

Group Discussion

6. Assessment of Learning: Develop an argument for how the evidence you have gathered supports your explanation for why the quantity of atmosphere sunlight travels through causes the moon light to appear orange (Use the structure below)

    a. Describe the phenomenon of the orange-appearing color of the moon.
    b. Develop a model to show the paths of light that travels from moon to Earth with each color of light.
    c. Construct an explanation supported by evidence for why changes in the system result in patterns of orange moon appearance and cite evidence to support your explanation.
    d. Develop an argument for how your evidence supports your explanation for causes of the color change.
    e. Write a summary that includes examples of similar patterns appearing in this or other systems.

Science Reflection – Consider the importance of credible sources of evidence to support your explanation and how the validity of sources impacts your arguments for a scientific explanation of causes of phenomena.

SAMPLE RESPONSE

> *Occasionally, when the moon begins to rise on any given night it comes with an added flare; it shows itself in an orange/red tint. This can happen at all times of the year and in any city.*
>
> *When the moon is coming up the horizon, we see moonlight through a greater quantity of atmosphere, so the proportion of the light being reflected and/or scattered is greater. By the time the light not reflected reaches our eyes, most of the blue, green, and purple visible light has scattered amongst the atmosphere and the red, yellow, and orange visible light is mostly what we see, causing the orange "harvest" moon phenomenon.*
>
> *We know the atmosphere is thicker closest to the Earth's surface; when light travels through more of this thicker atmosphere, more light is scattered. The pattern generally observed is the moon appears orange when it is near the horizon and white when the moon is high in the sky. This pattern supports the explanations for causes of the phenomenon.*
>
> *The phenomenon can also be observed when the air is polluted with dust or smoke from forest fires. The pattern of the color is consistent and can be observed when different types of particles are in the air. At times, dust, smoke, and pollution can be a cause to this phenomenon, which cause me to wonder, do cities with greater pollution levels have the orange moon phenomenon more often?*

Assessment of student understanding in science is critical for informing teachers for instruction and student for learning. Classroom assessment provides critical information for improving teaching and learning. Assessment is a tool to inform instruction and measure and inform student learning at the intersection of the three dimensions. Formative assessment is an essential component of instruction and belongs in the classroom. Assessment should be a seamless part of instruction, be an engaging and interesting experience for students, and provide information for continuous improvement in teaching and learning.

Bibliography

Adler, R. B., & Rodman, G. (1994). *Understanding Human Communication.* Fort Worth, TX: Harcourt Books.

Archer, L., DeWitt, J., Osborne, J., Dillon., J., Willis, B., & Wong, B. (2010). "Doing" Science versus "Being" a Scientist: Examining 10/22-year-old Schoolchildren's Constructions of Science through the Lens of Identity. *Science Education, 94*(4), 617-639. doi: 10.1002/sce.20399

Banilower, E. R., Smith, P. S., Weiss, I. R., Malzahn, K. A., Campbell, K. M., & Weiss, A. M., (2013). *Report of the 2012 National Survey of Science and Mathematics Education.* Chapel Hill, NC: Horizon Research, Inc.

Brickhouse, N. W., Lowery, P., & Schultz, K. (2000). What Kind of Girl Does Science? The Construction of School Science Identities. *Research in Science Teaching, 37*(5), 441-458.

Bruner, J (1960). *The Process of Education.* New York, NY: Vantage Books.

Bybee, K. (2016). *How Civility Works. Stanford.* CA: Stanford University Press.

Bybee, R. (2015a). Scientific literacy. In R. Gunstone (Ed.), *Encyclopedia of Science Education* (944-947). Dordrecht, NL: Springer.

Bybee, R. (2015b). *The BSCS 5E Instructional Model: Creating Teachable Moments.* Washington, DC: NSTA Press,

Carter, S. (1998). *Civility: Manners, Morals, and the Etiquette of Democracy.* New York: Basic Books.

Castro, M., Exposito-Casa, E., Lopez-Martin, E., Lizasoain, L., Navarro-Asencio, E., & Gaviria, J. L. (2015). Parental Involvement on Student Academic Achievement: A Meta-Analysis. *Educational Research Review, 14*, 33-46. https://doi.org/10.1016/j.edurev.2015.01.002

Chen, Y., Hand, B., & Norton-Meier, L. (2016). Teacher Roles of Questioning in Early Elementary Science Classrooms: A Framework Promoting Student Cognitive Complexities in Argumentation. *Research in Science Education, 47*(2), 373-405. doi: 10.1007/s11165-015-9506-6

Chopin, S. H., O'Conner, C., & Anderson, N. (2009). *Classroom Discussions: Using Math Talk to Help Students Learn.* Sausalito, CA: Math Solutions Publications.

Colley, M. (2016, October 24). *Teaching for Civic Engagement.* [Teachers Voice Web Blog]. Retrieved from https://www.teachingchannel.org/blog/2016/10/24/teaching-for-civic-engagement/

Duschl, R. (2000). Making the nature of science explicit. In R. Millar, J. Leech & J. Osborne (Eds.) *Improving Science Education: The Contribution of Research.* Philadelphia, PA USA: Open University Press.

Engel, S. (2015, January 26). *Joy: A Subject Schools Lack.* The Atlantic.

Fan, H., Xu, J., Cai, Z., He, J., & Fan, X. (2017). Homework and Students' Achievement in Math and Science: A 30-Year Meta-Analysis, 1986-2015. *Educational Research Review, 20*, 35-54. http://dx.doi.org/10.1016/j.edurev.2016.11.003

Flick, L., & Lederman, N. (2004). *Scientific Inquiry and Nature of Science.* Boston, MA: Kluwer Academic Publishers.

Gruber, M. J., Bernard, B. D., Ranganath, C., (2014). States of Curiosity Modulate Hippocampus-Dependent Learning via the Dopaminergic Circuit. *Neuron, 84*(2), 486-496. https://doi.org/10.1016/j.neuron.2014.08.060

Harackiewicz, J. M., Rozek, C. S., Hulleman, C. S., & Hyde, J. S. (2012). Helping Parents to Motivate Adolescents in Mathematics and Science: An Experimental Test of a Utility-Value Intervention. *Association for Psychological Science, 23*(8), 899-906.

Hawley, W. D., & Rosenholtz, S. (1984). Good Schools: A Synthesis of Research on How Schools Influence Student Achievement. *Peabody Journal of Education, 4,* 1-178

Hill, N. E., & Tyson, D. F. (2009). Parental Involvement in Middle School: A Meta-Analytic Assessment of the Strategies that Promote Achievement. *Developmental Psychology, 45*(3), 740-763. doi: 10.1037/a0015362

Jeynes, W. H. (2010). The Salience of the Subtle Aspects of Parental Involvement and Encouraging that Involvement: Implications for School-Based Programs. *Teachers College Record, 112*(3), 747-774. EJ888462

Lederman, N. & Lederman, J. (2004). Revising Instruction to Teach the Nature of Science: Modifying Activities to Enhance Students' Understanding of Science. *Science Teacher, 71*(9), 36-39.

National Academy of Engineering (2009). *Engineering in K-12 Education.* Washington, DC: The National Academy Press.

National Research Council. (1999). *NRC Report How People Learn.* Washington, DC: The National Academies Press.

National Research Council (2008). *Ready, Set, Science!: Putting Research to Work in K-8 Science Classrooms.* Washington: DC. National Academies Press. https://doi.org/10.17226/11882.

National Research Council. (2012). *A Framework for K-12 Science Education: Practices, Crosscutting Concepts, and Core Ideas.* Washington, DC: The National Academies Press.

National Research Council (2015) *NRC Report Guide to Implementing the Next Generation Science Standards.* Washington, DC: The National Academies Press.

NGSS Lead States (2013). *Next Generation Science Standards: For States, by States.* Washington, DC: The National Academies Press.

Smart, J. B., & Marshall, J. C. (2013) Interactions Between Classroom Discourse, Teacher Questioning, and Student Cognitive Engagement in Middle School Science. *Journal of Science Teacher Education, 24*(2), 249-267. doi: 10.1007/s10972-012-9297-9

Sutton, J., & Krueger, A., (Eds.). (2001). *EDThoughts: What We Know about Science Teaching and Learning.* Aurora, CO: Mid-continent Research for Education and Learning.

Tobin, K., Ritchie, S. M., Oakley, J. L., Mergard, V. & Hudson, P. (2013). Relationships Between Emotional Climate and the Fluency of Classroom Interactions. *Learning Environments Research, 16*(71). https://doi.org/10.1007/s10984-013-9125-y

von Glasersfeld, E. (1995). *Radical Constructivism: A Way of Knowing and Learning.* Studies in Mathematics Education Series: 6. Bristol, PA: Taylor & Francis.

Weimer, M. (2013). *Learner-Centered Teaching: Five Key Changes to Practice* (2nd ed.). San Francisco, CA: Jossey-Bass.

CHAPTER 10

PUTTING IT ALL TOGETHER

So, what is the take-away from this book?

First of all, let us tell you right now, the way we have described teaching and learning science is not an easier way to teach; we believe it is a ***better*** way to teach. This approach to teaching and learning requires significantly more effort on the part of the teacher, but is rewarded with meaningful student learning. Secondly, you will never perfect your teaching craft; you will only improve over time. Finally, working harder to become a better teacher is worthwhile; no one may notice, but you and your students will know.

Three-Dimensional Science Performances

Framework-aligned standards are significantly different than past standards and require changes to instruction to meet the goals of these new expectations. The central goal of the standards is for students to use, not just know, the core ideas and crosscutting concepts while engaging in science and engineering practices to make sense of phenomena. We refer to this type of engagement as student performances. These performances generally center around students making sense of phenomena that are relevant and connected to real-world applications. When students are proficient in science they can apply their learning to make sense of science phenomena beyond the classroom.

This book has presented an instructional model that engages students in Gather, Reason, and Communicate performance sequences within the BSCS 5E instructional model. The book advocates for using this instructional model, aligned to standards that are consistent with the *Framework*, and for engaging students in science performances at the intersection of science and engineering practices, crosscutting concepts, and core ideas.

The Structure of Instruction

The structure of instruction is critical for engaging students while also making science teaching and learning efficient and effective. A well-planned instructional sequence can provide better opportunities for students to consider phenomena, ask questions, gather information and data, construct explanations supported by evidence, develop arguments for how the evidence supports the explanation, and communicate their reasoning.

Sequencing instruction is an important aspect of teaching and learning. The 5E model moves students from engaging in one phenomenon to applying the core idea and crosscutting concepts to make sense of analogous phenomena. The GRC performances engage students in gathering data and information to be used in reasoning explanations and arguments that are communicated to oneself and others. The two sequences work well together in presenting structured and coherent student learning performance.

Coherent approaches to implementing new standards requires all parts of the systems to work toward common goals and to evaluate the effectiveness of policies, procedures, teaching experiences, curriculum materials and assessment resources, and professional learning that supports the desired instructional approaches. Minimizing the scope of instructional change necessary to implement new standards with fidelity does a disservice to teachers working hard to improve science teaching and learning. Professional learning opportunities are needed that model the nature and nuance of instruction to support teachers in changing the classroom to meeting the needs of all students.

Phenomena

Learning science begins with curiosity and questions about phenomena. The questions lead students to obtain information, data, and ideas to make sense of the phenomena. Teachers provide students with structures to investigation the natural and engineered world. Phenomena should be presented to students as observation. Students develop and use questions to support the investigation of causes of the phenomenon and analogous phenomena in the instructional sequence and beyond school.

Your reputation is what others think of you, your character is what you know about yourself.
~Dale J. Moulding

Professional Educators

Professionals, by definition, have specialized, research-based knowledge and expertise. Knowing how students learn science is as important as knowing science. Teaching is a wonderful profession. The work of teachers in the classroom makes a difference in the lives of students. The profession we belong to is based on research, which requires continuous improvement of your skills, methodologies, and instructional strategies. The greatest reward we receive as teachers is our students' learning and positive disposition toward learning.

If you have gotten this far in the book, we know you are tenacious and value the nature of the teaching and learning needed to implement the innovations described in the *Framework*. If you are at this point in the book by skipping to the last chapter, we know you are sufficiently curious and resourceful to inspire curiosity in your students, so go back and read the book. In any case we encourage you to consider using the instructional approaches, the structures of three-dimensional teaching and learning, 5E, and GRC to improve your instruction.

The changes we are recommending will not be easy nor will they develop quickly; but if implemented with fidelity and dedication, they can transform the lives of your students. We believe teaching is the most rewarding of all professions; but only if you work hard at it, listen to your students to understand their reasoning, remain tenaciously engaged in doing the best you can for all students, work as a professional, continue to learn and improve throughout your career, and reflect on the difference you make in the lives of your students. Reflecting on the positive impact you have in the lives of your students is part of your compensation package. Enjoy your opportunity to be a teacher, make the most of it for your students.

Reflections on Teaching and Learning

- Learning is fun, and learning science is a blast
- Curiosity is the key to learning science
- Reflecting on teaching and learning is critical for both instructional improvement and job satisfaction
  - Celebrate success
  - Plan for continuous improvement
  - Find solutions to improve less successful instruction
  - Continue to improve throughout your career
- You are a professional teacher and work hard every day to improve the lives of children
- Enjoy your phenomenal career as a professional educator

Bibliography

National Research Council. (2015). *Guide to Implementing the Next Generation Science Standards.* Committee on Guidance on Implementing the Next Generation Science Standards. Board on Science Education, Division of Behavioral and Social Sciences and Education, Washington, DC: The National Academies Press.

Debarger, A. H., Penuel, W. R., Moorthy, S., Beauvineau, Y., Kennedy, C. A., & Boscardin, C. K. (2017). Investigating purposeful science curriculum adaptation as a strategy to improve teaching and learning. *Science Education, 101*(1), 66-98.

APPENDICES

Appendix A – Science and Engineering Practices from the Framework

Appendix B –Crosscutting Concepts from the Framework

Appendix C – Science Essentials: Science and Engineering Practices

Appendix D –Science Essentials: Crosscutting Concepts

Appendix E – Science Essentials: Disciplinary Core Ideas

Appendix F – GRC Lesson Template

Appendix G – 5E and Gather, Reason, Communicate Performance Sequences

Appendix H – Student Prompts for the 5E-GRC Lesson from Chapter 8

APPENDIX A
Science and Engineering Practices from the *Framework*

1. Asking Questions (Science) and Defining Problems (Engineering)
Students asking questions is a fundamental way to gather relevant information in the process of making sense of phenomena. Students should develop questions that can be answered using empirical evidence. In engineering, the process of gathering information begins with defining a problem. Questions are asked by students to help gather information that can be used to make sense of a problem.

Asking questions has a purpose in gathering information to use in constructing explanations and/or finding solutions – asking question to obtain information, asking questions to design an investigation, asking questions to determine the limitations and/or resources for engineering a solution to a problem.

2. Developing and Using Models
Students use models in a number of ways to gather information using charts, graphs, or physical models that generate data (e.g., stream model, weather models). Students use models to reason and make sense of phenomena and make predictions (e.g., model of Earth, moon and sun to make sense of relative position and phases of the moon, equations, bridges with stress on key points), and communicate ideas using models (e.g., graphs, solar system, balanced chemical equations).

Developing and using models have three important purposes. First, models are used to organize gathered information. Secondly, models are used to reason the relationship between variables or determine patterns. Finally, models are used to communicate reasoning. Models include mathematical relationships, equations, diagrams, T-charts, graphs, pictures, physical models, mental models, and representations of all types.

3. Planning and Carrying Out Investigations
Students gather information and data through investigations in the field, laboratory, or mind. Planning an investigation requires significantly more knowledge and skills than carrying out an investigation. In the early grades, students generally carry out investigations planned for them, but often, in the middle grades, the investigations students do are ways to scaffold the tools and abilities to plan future investigations. When students conduct an investigation on population sampling by tossing a ring and counting the number of clover stems in the ring and then calculating the population, they are building tools for planning population studies on their own with other species (e.g., rabbits, deer, fish, oaks) in a larger area. Some investigations require students to plan and carry out experiments requiring identification of variables to control, as well as selection of an independent variable and monitoring of the dependent variables. Students should also be engaged in investigations that test solutions to engineering designs. This process requires students to determine relevant variables, ways to measure and collect data, and the most useful analysis of data to provide evidence of the effectiveness, efficiency, and durability of various designs. This analysis must be done under the criteria and constraints of the problem.

Planning and carrying out investigations is used to obtain information that can be used as evidence to support explanations and/or arguments.

4. Analyzing and Interpreting Data

Investigations provide data that, when analyzed, provide greater insights into cause and effect relationships. Often, until analyzed, data have little meaning. Students may use a number of tools and techniques (e.g., graphs, statistical analysis, charts, tables, models) to make sense of data. Tools may be used to seek patterns in data or determine if a finding is significant or not significant. The ability to analyze data (e.g., determining the accuracy of data, developing visualizations of data) has been greatly enhanced by modern computational tools. Analyzing data from testing engineering designs is useful in determining the best solution to a problem or providing a fair test to compare the efficiencies of multiple engineered systems.

Analyzing and interpreting data is for the purpose of finding patterns to use as evidence and/or refining data in ways that adds to the veracity of the data that is used as evidence.

5. Using Mathematics and Computational Thinking

Mathematics and computational thinking are fundamental tools for representing physical variables and relationships. These tools are useful for a range of processes for reasoning to construct meaning by way of simulations, statistically analyzing data, and recognizing, expressing, and applying quantitative relationships. Statistical techniques are useful tools to analyze data and develop ways to recognize patterns in causal, probabilistic, and correlational relationships. The mathematical models students use are critical for solving problems by engineering solutions or formulating scientific explanations. Often, mathematical reasoning and computational thinking are the skills students use to engage in engineering design solutions.

Mathematical representations of relationships of phenomena are important for students making sense of cause and effect relationships. Consider the relationship between the force and mass of a falling object. Dropping a golf ball and a Ping-Pong ball on the back of your hand from a height of one meter will result in two different forces. The force an object exerts when falling from a height of one meter is described by the equation $F = ma$ (force is equal to mass multiplied by acceleration). Both the golf ball and the Ping-Pong ball have the same acceleration, but the mass of the golf ball is greater so the force exerted by the golf ball on your hand will be greater. The equation provides us with a way to reason about the relationship among force, mass, and acceleration.

Computational thinking for students in the 21st century is a basic skill. Utilizing computers to gather, analyze, and communicate information requires students to think of gathering data using electronic devices (e.g., motion detectors, pressure gauges, pH meters, digital cameras), analyzing data using spreadsheets, and communicating the information via the web and social media tools. Students of the 21st century are quick to access and use these tools. Instruction supporting computational thinking provides students with the strategies to use computational tools in science performances.

Using mathematics and computational thinking provides students with the tools to change data into evidence. Mathematical thinking provides students with the tools to establish the validity and reliability of the data and observations they gather. Computational thinking includes using computers to gather and analyze data from investigations and other sources.

6. Constructing Explanations (Science) and Designing Solutions (Engineering)

The central outcome of science education is for students to develop the abilities to construct explanations supported by evidence for causes of phenomena. The goal of an explanation is to provide an account of the most plausible mechanism for a phenomenon that is simple, logical, and consistent with existing data. Students' explanations of phenomena are based on evidence from a personal set of core ideas, information from observations and/or investigations, and application of crosscutting concepts. Students should be able to construct coherent explanations of phenomena consistent with accepted science laws, models, theories, and/or explanations.

Designing solutions to engineering problems requires students to design a systematic process for considering the problem, determining constraints, and accommodating criteria. "Solutions result from a process of balancing competing criteria of desired functions, technological feasibility, cost, safety, esthetics, and compliance with legal requirements" Engineering solutions to problems should include testing the solution, evaluating the degree to which the solution is successful or unsuccessful, redesigning improvements, and testing the solution again. Engineering solutions is an iterative process.

Constructing explanations and designing solutions are central to all of sciences. The other practices are used to obtain the evidence to support science explanations for causes of phenomena.

7. Engaging in Argument from Evidence

Arguments build from explanations and set forth the reasoning that connects evidence to explanations. Evidence is the basis for argument for a proposed explanation. Arguing in science is very different from the common use of the word. Arguing, in science, requires a systematic line of empirical evidence logically connecting the best scientific explanation for an observed natural phenomenon. Argumentation is an essential tool to reveal the strengths and weaknesses in reasoning that connect available evidence to an explanation. Students proficient in argument are able to produce arguments to defend their own explanations as well as accept reasoned arguments from others that lead to modifying or abandoning their own line of reasoning in light of new evidence or reasoned explanations. Additionally, and perhaps more importantly, there is the need for students to develop the skills and dispositions to offer reasoned and civil comments to others' arguments and remain focused on the explanation, reasoning, and evidence and not the person making the argument. Because argument is a two-way proposition, it should be done in a collaborative environment where everyone is seeking the best explanation for the available evidence. Engineering also uses reasoned argument to determine the best solution to a problem. Argument is one of the tools to find the best solution to a problem given the criteria and constraints. In engineering, it is not about the truth but rather about the best solution to a problem. Argumentation is one of the tools to systematically compare alternative solutions to a problem and support one solution over others.

Engaging in argument is for the purpose of establishing the relationship for how the gathered evidence supports or refutes an explanation for causes of a phenomenon or the solution to an engineering problem.

8. Obtaining, Evaluating, and Communicating Information

Science and engineering depend upon the ability to add to the body of knowledge and to access and use that knowledge when new phenomena or problems arise. The process of obtaining, evaluating, and communicating information requires that students engage in all of the practices in their progression of gathering, reasoning, and communicating. Reading and listening are two ways students obtain information, but they also gather information from asking questions, conducting investigations, making observations, considering mathematical relationships, and using models to gather information on phenomena. In the 21st century, students have devices they can use to gather information quickly and efficiently, but the information must be evaluated carefully before it should be used in science. The evaluation of the scientific validity of information has become an essential skill of the 21st century.

Written and oral communication are critical ways scientists, engineers, and students communicate findings and ideas (models) and engage in argumentation. Writing and speaking are critical ways for students to communicate their thinking.

Obtaining information from reliable sources is an important part of gathering and essential for students to have the raw material they need to reason with as they engage in other practices. Evaluating information is for the express purpose of determining the validity of the information and how the gathered information supports or refutes an explanation. Communicating information as an explanation is presented is essential to students being able to support explanations with arguments for how the evidence and information they have gathered supports or refutes a specific explanation.

APPENDIX B
Crosscutting Concepts from the *Framework*

1. *Patterns* – Observed patterns of forms and events guide organization and classification. Patterns prompt questions about the factors that influence cause and effect relationships. Patterns are useful as evidence to support explanations and arguments.

2. *Cause and Effect* – Mechanism and explanation. Events have causes, sometimes simple, sometimes multifaceted and complex. A major activity of science is investigating and explaining causal relationships and the mechanisms by which they are mediated. Such mechanisms can then be tested across given contexts and used to predict and explain events in new contexts.

3. *Scale, Proportion, and Quantity* – In considering phenomena, it is critical to recognize what is relevant at different measures of size, time, and energy and to recognize how changes in scale, proportion, or quantity affect a system's structure or performance.

4. *Systems and System Models* – Defining the system under study—specifying its boundaries and making explicit a model of that system—provides tools for understanding and testing ideas that are applicable throughout science and engineering.

5. *Energy and Matter* – Flows, cycles, and conservation. Tracking fluxes of energy and matter into, out of, and within systems helps one understand the system's possibilities and limitations.

6. *Structure and Function* – An object's structure and shape determine many of its properties and functions. The structures, shapes, and substructure of living organisms determine how the organism functions to meet its needs within an environment.

7. *Stability and Change* – For natural and built systems alike, conditions of stability and rates of change provide the focus for understanding how the system operates and the causes of changes in systems.

APPENDIX C
Science Essentials: Science and Engineering Practices

Grade K-5			
Understanding Scientific Explanations	**Generating Scientific Evidence**	**Reflecting on Scientific Knowledge**	**Participating Productively in Science**
1. Asking Questions (Science) and Defining problems (Engineering)			
A. Identify questions relevant to science or engineering problems. B. Distinguish between science questions and non-science questions	C. Pose questions that are testable. D. Formulate testable hypotheses and pose questions in science that seek evidence relevant to the question.	E. Consider the scope of the questions posed. F. Reflect on the possible domains of questions posed.	G. Ask science questions so others understand the question. H. Gather information from others to help develop relevant questions. I. Ask relevant questions to increase understanding of others. J. Work collaboratively to develop science questions.
2. Developing and Using Models			
A. Distinguish between representation and the actual object and/or phenomena represented in a model. B. Relate useful models to simple phenomena. C. Use representations to describe phenomena.	D. Use representations to generate evidence E. Compare evidence generated to accepted science models.	F. Describe ways to use models to think about science. G. Use representations to reflect on mechanisms of how things work.	H. Share science concepts and understanding with others using representations. I. Share science findings in written and graphic presentations to others.
3. Planning and Carrying Out Investigations			
A. Describe how science investigations contribute to science explanations.	B. Make careful observations that generate evidence. C. Plan and design investigations that generate evidence. D. Control variables to develop a fair test when doing investigations. E. Recognize patterns in observations and data.	F. Consider other ways of making observations. G. Reflect on the way data is collected and consider the accuracy of various methods.	H. Discuss and compare observations with others observing the same events. I. Collaborate with others to develop science investigations. J. Seek information and ideas from others doing similar investigations. K. Work collaboratively in science investigations.

Grade K-5			
Understanding Scientific Explanations	**Generating Scientific Evidence**	**Reflecting on Scientific Knowledge**	**Participating Productively in Science**
4. Analyzing and Interpreting Data			
A. Compare data to make sense of and explain phenomena.	B. Compare data and use comparisons as evidence.	C. Reflect on the data in light of others' data about similar investigations.	E. Analyze and share findings.
5. Using Mathematics and Computational Thinking			
A. Compare data quantitatively. B. Use mathematics to compare explanations and understand scale.	C. Make and use measurements as evidence. D. Compare evidence from measurements.	E. Reflect on the accuracy of measurements. F. Use averages and graphs to compare data.	G. Share findings and data using tables, charts, and graphs.
6. Constructing Explanations (Science) and Designing Solutions (Engineering)			
A. Explain science phenomena. B. Compare multiple explanations of the same science phenomena.	C. Explain science observations using evidence. D. Design a solution to a problem and use evidence to compare the advantages of the design to other solutions.	E. Compare two or more science explanations for an observation. F. Evaluate multiple explanations used to explain science phenomena.	G. Share explanations with others. H. Work collaboratively to construct science explanations and design solutions.
7. Engaging in Argument from Evidence			
A. Describe the role of evidence in science explanations. B. Relate the role of science explanations to science arguments.	C. Use evidence to support ideas. D. Use evidence to generate or support explanations. E. Use evidence to support arguments about science explanations and phenomena.	F. Compare types of evidence. G. Determine the best evidence for a specific argument.	H. Listen to others' explanations. I. Share the sources of information used to support arguments.
8. Obtaining, Evaluating, and Communicating Information			
A. Read and understand science information. B. Read and understand science information from multiple sources.	C. Describe information gathered from multiple sources. D. Use appropriate terminology and descriptions. E. Gather and share information using many forms of communication.	F. Identify multiple sources of information. G. Compare science information from multiple sources.	H. Share science information with others through written, oral, and multi-media reports.

Secondary			
Understanding Scientific Explanations	**Generating Scientific Evidence**	**Reflecting on Scientific Knowledge**	**Participating Productively in Science**
1. Asking Questions (Science) and Defining Problems (Engineering)			
A. Identify questions relevant to science or engineering problems. B. Distinguish between science questions and non-science questions. C. Ask questions that arise from phenomena, models, theory, or unexpected results. D. Pose questions that are testable.	E. Formulate testable hypotheses and pose questions in science that seek evidence relevant to the question. F. Ask questions that require relevant empirical evidence. G. Ask questions to determine relationships between independent and dependent variables. H. Ask questions to clarify or identify the premise(s) of an argument.	I. Consider the scope of the questions posed. J. Ask questions to refine a model, an explanation, or an engineering problem. K. Ask questions that challenge the premise of an argument and/or the interpretation of data.	L. Write science questions that others understand. M. Work collaboratively to develop science questions. N. Ask relevant questions to increase understanding of others.
2. Developing and Using Models			
A. Distinguish between representation and the actual object and/or phenomena represented in a model. B. Relate useful models to simple phenomena. C. Make sense of representations that describe phenomena.	A. Use representations to generate evidence. B. Compare evidence generated to accepted science models. C. Use and/or construct models to predict, explain, and/or collect data to test ideas about phenomena in natural or designed systems. D. Pose models to describe mechanisms at unobservable scales. E. Examine merits and limitations of various models.	F. Describe ways to use models to reflect on science concepts or ideas. G. Use representations to reflect on mechanisms of how things work. H. Reflect on ways to modify models to improve their efficiency. I. Reflect on the components of models of simple systems with uncertain and less predictable factors.	J. Share science concepts and understanding with others using representations. K. Share science findings in written and graphic presentations to others. L. Use multiple types of models to represent and explain phenomena to others.

3. Planning and Carrying Out Investigations

A. Describe how science investigations contribute to science explanations. B. Use questions to make sense of the design of an investigation or experiment.	C. Make careful observations that generate evidence. D. Plan investigations that generate empirical evidence. E. Recognize patterns in observations and data. F. Plan and carry out investigations and/or test design solutions in a safe and ethical manner. G. Select appropriate tools to collect, record, analyze, and evaluate data. H. Collect data to answer scientific questions or test design solutions under a range of conditions.	I. Consider multiple ways of making observations. J. Reflect on the way data are collected and consider the accuracy of data. K. Evaluate various methods of collecting data. L. Consider possible confounding variables or effects and ensure the investigation's design has controlled for them. M. Reflect on the accuracy of various methods for collecting data.	N. Discuss and compare observations with others observing the same events. O. Collaborate with others to develop science investigations. P. Seek information and ideas from others doing similar investigations. Q. Work collaboratively in science investigations.

4. Analyzing and Interpreting Data

A. Compare data to make sense of and explain phenomena. B. Use data to define an operational range for a design solution. C. Make sense of graphical displays (e.g., maps) of large data sets to identify temporal and spatial relationships.	D. Compare data and use comparisons as evidence. E. Use mean, median, mode, and variability to analyze and characterize data. F. Use graphical displays to analyze data in order to identify linear and nonlinear relationships. G. Distinguish between causal and correlational relationships. H. Use tools, technologies, and models (e.g., computational, mathematical) to generate and analyze data to make valid and reliable scientific claims or determine the best design solution for a problem.	I. Reflect on data in light of others' data about similar investigations. J. Consider limitations of data analysis, such as measurement error, and seek to improve precision and accuracy of data with better technological tools and methods such as multiple trials. K. Evaluate the impact of new data on a working explanation of a phenomenon or design solution.	L. Analyze and share findings. M. Consider limitations (e.g., measurement error, sample selection) when analyzing and interpreting data. N. Determine function fits to data, including slope, intercept, and correlation coefficient for linear fits.

5. Using Mathematics and Computational Thinking

A. Use mathematics to compare explanations and understand scale. B. Use mathematical or algorithmic representations of phenomena to make sense of phenomena or solutions to problems.	C. Make and use measurements as evidence. D. Compare evidence from measurements. E. Use mathematical thinking and/or computational outcomes to compare alternative solutions to an engineering problem. F. Use mathematical expressions to represent phenomena to support explanations. G. Use probability and/or statistics to support explanations or arguments.	H. Reflect on the accuracy of measurements. I. Analyze simple data sets for patterns that suggest relationships. J. Use statistical and mathematical techniques, data displays, tables, and/or graphs to find patterns and/or relationships in data.	K. Share findings with others using data presented in tables, charts, and graphs. L. Use simple limit cases to test mathematical expressions, computer programs or algorithms, or simulations to see if a model "makes sense" by comparing the outcomes with what is known about the real world.

6. Constructing Explanations (Science) and Designing Solutions (Engineering)

A. Describe the evidence supporting a valid explanation. B. Compare multiple explanations of the same science phenomenon. C. Evaluate attributes of explanations from models or representations. D. Revise causal explanations that are supported by data and relate these explanations to current knowledge.	E. Explain science observations using evidence. F. Design a solution to a problem and use evidence to compare the advantages of the design to other solutions. G. Use patterns as evidence to support explanations. H. Apply scientific reasoning to link evidence to explanations. I. Base explanations on evidence and the assumption that natural laws operate today as they did in the past and will continue to do so in the future. J. Use qualitative and quantitative relationships between variables to construct explanations for phenomena.	K. Evaluate multiple explanations for a science phenomenon. L. Describe the role of evidence in science explanations. M. Base causal explanations on valid and reliable empirical evidence from multiple sources and the assumption that natural laws operate today as they did in the past and will continue to do so in the future. N. Reflect on the best evidence to support a specific explanation.	O. Share explanations with others. P. Work collaboratively to construct science explanations and design solutions. Q. Communicate quantitative claims regarding the relationship between dependent and independent variables. R. Share explanations and arguments based on evidence obtained from a variety of sources (e.g., scientific principles, models, theories) and peer review.

7. Engaging in Argument from Evidence

A. Determine the best evidence supporting an argument.	E. Use evidence to generate or support explanations.	I. Reflect on the best evidence supporting an explanation.	M. Listen and make sense of others' explanations.
B. Relate the role of science explanation to science arguments.	F. Use evidence to support arguments about science explanations of phenomena.	J. Relate the role of science explanations to arguments.	N. Evaluate and share the sources of information used to support arguments.
C. Use models to understand arguments.	G. Use evidence to support and justify ideas.	K. Respectfully provide and receive critique on scientific arguments.	O. Debate the merits of competing arguments, models, or design solutions.
D. Compare multiple arguments based on the strengths and weaknesses of the evidence supporting the argument.	H. Construct causal explanations of phenomena using evidence and logic.	L. Reflect on and revise arguments and design solutions in light of new evidence.	P. Evaluate the evidence and reasoning for arguments supporting currently accepted explanations.
			Q. Evaluate and share weaknesses in one's own arguments and collaborate to seek better evidence.

8. Obtaining, Evaluating, and Communicating Information

A. Read and understand science information from multiple sources.	D. Describe information gathered from multiple sources.	I. Identify multiple sources of information.	L. Share science information with others through written, oral, and multi-media reports and presentations.
B. Read critically using scientific knowledge and reasoning to evaluate data, hypotheses, conclusions, and competing information.	E. Use appropriate terminology and descriptions.	J. Compare science information from multiple sources.	M. Read critically primary scientific literature adapted for classroom use to identify evidence and evaluate the validity and reliability of the claims, methods, and designs.
C. Obtain information from reliable sources.	F. Gather and share information using many forms of communication.	K. Reflect on the claims, methods, and designs that appear in scientific and technical texts or media reports.	
	G. Generate and communicate ideas using scientific language and reasoning.		N. Produce written texts, models, and/or oral discourse to communicate ideas.
	H. Gather information from appropriate sources and evaluate the credibility and possible bias of the source and methods used.		

APPENDIX D
Science Essentials: Crosscutting Concepts

Grades K-5			
Identify and Describe	**Model and Predict**	**Explain and Solve**	**Compare and Analyze**
1. **Patterns, similarity, and diversity**: Observed patterns in nature guide organization and classification, and prompt questions about relationships and causes underlying the patterns.			
• Identify and describe patterns in the natural world. • Identify and describe patterns of symmetry in nature. • Identify and describe the purpose for patterns in engineered objects.	• Use models to investigate patterns in phenomena. • Use patterns to make predictions. • Use patterns to identify and classify objects, mechanisms, and organisms. • Develop warranted inference from patterns observed in data.	• Use patterns as evidence to support science explanations. • Use patterns as evidence to support arguments. • Develop explanations for causes of patterns. • Use patterns as evidence to support explanations.	• Analyze phenomena for evidence of patterns. • Analyze data to determine patterns. • Analyze patterns that are related to time. • Use graphs and charts to investigate and analyze patterns in data.
2. **Scale, proportion, and quantity**: In considering phenomena, it is critical to recognize what is relevant at different size, time, and energy scales, and to recognize proportional relationships between different quantities as scales change.			
• Use scale, proportion, and quantity to describe systems. • Use measurement to compare objects. • Use mathematical relationships to describe objects. • Describe the movement of objects specific to time scales. (e.g., orbit of planets, movement of tectonic plates).	• Use scale, proportion, and quantity to model systems. • Predict the movement of objects over time. • Use measurement to compare phenomena represented by models. • Develop models of events in terms of time (e.g., volcanic eruptions, weathering, uplift, life cycle of stars, rusting of metal).	• Use scale and quantity to support explanations of how systems operate. • Use ratio to support explanations (e.g., more dense objects sink, force of a moving object increases as speed and mass increase). • Use proportion and quantity to support explanations.	• Use ratio and proportion to analyze systems. • Compare objects and systems that are at the same scale. • Compare microscopic organism to macroscopic scales. • Compare distances at various scales. • Compare the motion of objects across various distances. • Use geologic timelines and scales to compare events in the past.

Grades K-5			
Identify and Describe	**Model and Predict**	**Explain and Solve**	**Compare and Analyze**
3. **Cause and effect**: Mechanism and prediction. Events have causes, sometimes simple, sometime multifaceted. Deciphering causal relationships, and the mechanisms by which they are mediated, is a major activity of science.			
• Identify and describe causes of phenomena. • Describe the conditions necessary for phenomena to occur (e.g., temperature necessary for seeds to germinate, temperature for a chemical reaction to occur). • Identify causes of observed patterns in natural systems. • Identify the components contributing to the cause of an effect.	• Use patterns to determine causes of observed phenomena.	• Use evidence to support explanations for causes of phenomena. • Explain why specific order of events is necessary to cause some phenomena to occur. • Design and build machines capable of performing specified tasks.	• Analyze the relative impacts of various causes contributing to specific phenomena. • Justify predictions using cause effect relationships. • Compare multiple causes contributing to one event.
4. **Systems and system models:** Delimiting and defining the system under study and making a model of it are tools for developing understanding used throughout science and engineering.			
• Describe the interactions of specific components of a system. • Describe the input of energy necessary to cause changes in system. • Describe systems in terms of interactions and components.	• Draw models of things that work together in a system. • Model simple systems. • Use diagrams and representations to model systems. • Use conceptual models to represent systems.	• Explain interactions across multiple systems. • Explain the inputs and outputs of matter, energy, and forces in a system. • Develop explanations for the role of various components of systems.	• Analyze interactions within a system. • Analyze interactions across multiple systems.
5. **Energy and matter**: Flows, cycles and conservation. Tracking energy and matter flows, into, out of, and within systems helps one understand their system's behavior.			
• Distinguish between the common use of the word energy and the way science uses the word. • Describe the transfer of energy. • Describe the role of energy in causing changes (e.g., heat evaporates water, energy lifting an object).	• Use conservation of matter and energy to predict changes in systems. • Use models to describe the flow of energy. • Use the particle model to describe the cycling of matter.	• Use energy flow to explain changes in systems. • Use matter cycles to explain cycles in systems. • Explain matter cycles in terms of the flow of energy in systems. • Explain the relationship of energy to changes in matter.	• Analyze the conservation of energy and matter in complex systems.

Grades K-5			
Identify and Describe	**Model and Predict**	**Explain and Solve**	**Compare and Analyze**
6. Form and function: The way an object is shaped or structured determines many of its properties and functions.			
• Identify the attributes of a structure that contribute to its stability (e.g., diagonal bracing, spherical share). • Relate the structure to the mechanical functioning of a machine or organism.	• Describe how the materials that objects are constructed from affect the function of the object. • Compare the structure of substances in various phases to the way they function.	• Explain the function of microscopic structures on organisms. • Develop an explanation for phenomena based on structure and function relationships.	• Use the structure of substances to design and engineer objects with specific capabilities. • Investigate phenomena and describe the structure/function relationships. • Analyze the design of mechanical systems in terms of structure and function of the system.
7. Stability and change: For both designed and natural systems, conditions of stability and what controls rates of change are critical elements to consider and understand.			
• Distinguish between events that are changing and ones that are stable. • Describe stability and change in terms of time scales. • Describe systems in terms of stability and change. • Identify things that trigger changes to a system that was previously stable.	• Use models to predict changes in systems that are stable to ones that are changing. • Describe systems that are stable over very long periods of time. • Use models to describe opposing forces that result in stability. • Use models of time scales to investigate changes to systems that seem stable.	• Explain changes in a system in terms of inputs and outputs. • Explain the necessary attributes of stable systems. • Explain patterns of change overtime. • Explain phenomena in terms of equilibrium.	• Compare systems that are stable at one scale and not stable on another scale. • Analyze patterns of change and stability. • Analyze the attributes of systems that are engineered for stability or controlled change.

Adapted from Ch. 4 NRC Framework: Dimension 2: Crosscutting Concepts

Secondary			
Identify and Describe	**Model and Predict**	**Explain and Solve**	**Compare and Analyze**
1. **Patterns, Similarity, and Diversity:** Observed patterns in nature guide organization and classification, and prompt questions about relationships and causes underlying the patterns.			
• Identify and describe patterns in the natural world. • Identify and describe patterns of symmetry in nature. • Identify and describe the purpose for patterns in engineered objects.	• Use models to investigate patterns in phenomena. • Use patterns to make predictions. • Use patterns to identify and classify objects, mechanisms, and organisms. • Develop warranted inferences from patterns observed in data. • Use patterns in rates of change and mathematical relationships to develop information about how natural and human designed systems operate.	• Use patterns as evidence to support science explanations. • Use patterns as evidence to support arguments. • Use patterns of performance to analyze design solutions. • Use patterns to explain cause and effect relationships.	• Analyze phenomena for evidence of patterns. • Analyze data to determine patterns. • Analyze patterns that are related to time. • Use graphs and charts to investigate and analyze patterns in data. • Relate macroscopic patterns to the nature of microscopic and atomic-level structure. • Use mathematical representations to analyze patterns.
2. **Cause and Effect:** Events have causes, sometimes simple, sometime multifaceted. Deciphering causal relationships, and the mechanisms by which they are mediated, is a major activity of science.			
• Identify and describe causes of phenomena. • Describe the conditions necessary for phenomena to occur (e.g., temperature necessary for seeds to germinate, temperature for a chemical reaction to occur). • Identify causes of observed patterns in natural systems. • Describe the likelihood of a cause and effect relationship occurring in terms of probability.	• Use patterns to determine causes of observed phenomena. • Examine small-scale systems to predict cause and effect relationships of larger scale phenomena. • Use cause and effect relationships to predict the frequency of a phenomenon. • Justify predictions using cause/effect relationships.	• Use evidence to support explanations for causes of phenomena. • Explain order of events necessary to cause a phenomenon to occur. • Design and build machines capable of performing specified tasks. • Design and/or analyze systems that cause a desired effect.	• Compare multiple causes contributing to one phenomenon. • Analyze the relative impacts of various causes contributing to a change. • Analyze the scale of the effect of changes in systems. • Use empirical evidence to distinguish between causal and correlational relationships. • Analyze data to determine if relationships are causal or correlational.

Secondary			
Identify and Describe	**Model and Predict**	**Explain and Solve**	**Compare and Analyze**
3. **Scale, Proportion, and Quantity:** In considering phenomena, recognize what is relevant at different size, time, and energy scales, recognize proportional relationships between different quantities as scales change.			
• Describe phenomena that can be observed at one scale, but not at another. • Use measurement to compare objects. • Use mathematical relationships to describe objects. • Describe the movement of objects specific to time scales (e.g., orbit of planets, movement of tectonic plates). • Use algebraic thinking to examine data and predict the effect of one variable on another (e.g., linear growth, exponential growth).	• Use scale, proportion, and quantity to model systems. • Predict changes over time. • Use measurement to compare phenomena represented by models. • Develop models of events using accurate time scales. • Use algebraic expressions and equations to explain scientific relationships. • Use models to examine systems that are too small, too large, too fast, or too slow to observe directly. • Use models at one scale to understand phenomena at a different order of magnitude.	• Use patterns that can be observed at one scale to explain phenomena at another scale. • Use ratio to support explanations (e.g., more dense objects sink, force of a moving object increases as speed and mass increase). • Use proportion and quantity to support explanations. • Use quantitative reasoning to compare solutions to problems.	• Use proportional relationships (e.g., density, speed, concentration) to analyze components of a system. • Compare objects and systems that are at the same scale. • Compare microscopic organisms to macroscopic scales. • Compare distances at various scales. • Compare the motion of objects across various distances. • Use geologic timelines and scales to compare events in the past.
4. **Systems and System Models:** Delimiting and defining the system under study and making a model of it are tools for developing understanding used throughout science and engineering.			
• Describe the interactions of specific components of systems. • Describe energy inputs to systems that cause changes. • Describe systems in terms of interactions and components. • Describe systems that interact with other systems and are part of larger more complex systems. • Describe the limitations of models in terms of precision and reliability for predictions.	• Use diagrams and representations to model systems. • Use conceptual models to represent systems. • Use models to represent the inputs, outputs, cycling, and flow of matter and energy in systems. • Use models to predict the behavior of a system.	• Explain interactions across multiple systems. • Explain the inputs and outputs of matter, energy, and forces in a system. • Develop explanations for the role of various components of systems. • Design systems to do specific tasks.	• Analyze interactions within a system and across multiple systems. • Analyze the limitations of models that are used to represent specific aspects of systems. • Evaluate limitations of an investigation of complex systems. • Evaluate the degree to which an investigation defines the boundaries of a system.

Secondary			
Identify and Describe	**Model and Predict**	**Explain and Solve**	**Compare and Analyze**
5. **Energy and Matter:** Flows, Cycles and Conservation. Tracking energy and matter flows, into, out of, and within systems helps one understand their system's behavior.			
• Distinguish between the common use of the word energy and the way science uses the word. • Describe the transfer of energy. • Describe the role of energy in causing changes (e.g., heat evaporates water, energy lifting an object). • Account for the conservation of energy in a system. • Account for the conservation of matter in a system.	• Use principles of conservation of matter and energy to predict changes in systems. • Use models to describe the flow of energy. • Use the particle model to describe matter cycling. • Use models to trace the flow of energy in systems.	• Use energy flow to explain changes in systems. • Use matter cycles to explain cycles in systems. • Explain matter cycles in terms of the flow of energy in systems. • Explain the relationship of energy to changes in matter. • Explain how energy is involved when matter changes. • Explain the transformation of energy in systems.	• Analyze the conservation of energy and matter in complex systems. • Analyze the flow of energy and cycling of matter into, out of, and within a system. • Analyze nuclear processes in terms of the conservation of the total number of protons and neutrons.
6. **Structure and Function:** The way an object is shaped or structured determines many of its properties and functions.			
• Identify the attributes of a structure that contribute to stability (e.g., diagonal bracing, spherical shape). • Relate the structure to the mechanical functioning of a machine or organism. • Investigate phenomena and describe the structure/function relationships.	• Describe how the materials that objects are constructed from affect the function of the object. • Investigate or design new systems or structures for the properties of material and the structure of different components to reveal function. • Use models to visualize and describe how a system's function depends on the shapes, composition, and relationships among parts.	• Explain the function of microscopic structures on organisms. • Develop explanations for phenomena based on structure and function relationships. • Design structures that utilize specific properties of materials to best serve a specific function. • Explain how the structures of an organism function to help it live.	• Analyze the design of mechanical systems in terms of structure and function. • Infer the properties and function of a natural or designed system based on overall structure, components, and molecular properties. • Compare the structure of substances in various phases to the way they function. • Analyze complex and microscopic structures and systems by using models to determine how they operate.

Secondary			
Identify and Describe	**Model and Predict**	**Explain and Solve**	**Compare and Analyze**
7. **Stability and Change:** For both designed and natural systems, conditions of stability and what controls rates of change are critical elements to consider and understand.			
• Distinguish between events that are changing and ones that are stable. • Describe stability and change in terms of time scales. • Describe systems in terms of stability and change. • Identify things that trigger changes to a system that was previously stable. • Describe changes to stability in terms of sudden events or gradual changes over time. • Describe systems that are stable over very long periods of time.	• Use models to predict changes in stable systems to changes in unstable systems. • Use models to describe opposing forces that result in stability. • Model systems in dynamic equilibrium. • Use mathematical relationships to model change and rates of change over short and very long periods.	• Explain changes in a system in terms of inputs and outputs. • Explain the necessary attributes of stable systems. • Explain patterns of change overtime. • Explain phenomena in terms of equilibrium. • Explain the stability and change in natural systems over time and at multiple scales. • Explain how feedback mechanisms keep systems in equilibrium. • Design systems for greater or lesser stability.	• Compare systems that are stable at one scale and not stable on another scale. • Analyze patterns of change and stability. • Analyze the attributes of systems engineered for stability or controlled change. • Analyze how small changes in a system may lead to large changes in parts of the system. • Evaluate systems in terms of how specific components of the system change and/or remain stable.

APPENDIX E
Science Essentials: Disciplinary Core Ideas

Earth Space Science Progression			
K-2	**3-5**	**6-8**	**9-12**
ESS1.A The universe and its stars			
Patterns of movement of the sun, moon, and stars as seen from Earth can be observed, described, and predicted.	Stars range greatly in size and distance from Earth and this can explain their relative brightness.	The solar system is part of the Milky Way, which is one of many billions of galaxies.	Light spectra from stars are used to determine their characteristics, processes, and lifecycles. Solar activity creates elements through nuclear fusion. Development of technologies improve astronomical data that provide empirical evidence for the Big Bang theory.
ESS1.B Earth and the solar system			
Patterns of movement of the sun, moon, and stars as seen from Earth can be observed, described, and predicted.	The Earth's orbit and rotation, and the orbit of the moon around the Earth cause observable patterns.	The solar system contains many varied objects held together by gravity. Solar system models explain and predict eclipses, lunar phases, and seasons.	Kepler's laws describe common features of the motions of orbiting objects. Observations from astronomy and space probes provide evidence for explanations of solar system formation. Changes in Earth's tilt and orbit cause climate changes such as Ice Ages.
ESS1.C The history of planet Earth			
Some events on Earth occur very quickly; others can occur very slowly.	Certain features on Earth can be used to order events that have occurred in a landscape.	Rock strata and the fossil record can be used as evidence to organize the relative occurrence of major historical events in Earth's history.	The rock record resulting from tectonic and other geoscience processes as well as objects from the solar system can provide evidence of Earth's early history and the relative ages of major geologic formations.
ESS2.A Earth materials and systems			
Wind and water change the shape of the land.	Four major Earth systems interact. Rainfall helps shape the land and affects the types of living things found in a region. Water, ice, wind, gravity and organisms break rocks, soils and sediments into smaller pieces and move them around.	Energy flows and matter cycles within and among Earth's systems, including the sun and Earth's interior as primary energy sources. Plate tectonics is one result of these processes.	Feedback effects exist within and among Earth's systems.

Earth Space Science Progression			
K-2	**3-5**	**6-8**	**9-12**
ESS2.B Plate tectonics and large-scale system interactions			
Maps show where things are located. One can map the shapes and kinds of land and water in any area.	Earth's physical features occur in patterns, as do earthquakes and volcanoes. Maps can be used to locate features and determine patterns in those events.	Plate tectonics is the unifying theory that explains movements of rocks at Earth's surface and geological history. Maps are used to display evidence of plate movement.	Radioactive decay within Earth's interior contributes to thermal convection in the mantle.
ESS2.C The roles of water in Earth's surface processes			
Water is found in many types of places and in different forms on Earth.	Most of Earth's water is in the ocean and much of the Earth's fresh water is in glaciers or underground.	Water cycles among land, ocean, and atmosphere, and is propelled by sunlight and gravity. Density variations of sea water drive interconnected ocean currents. Water movement causes weathering and erosion, changing landscape features.	The planet's dynamics are greatly influenced by water's unique chemical and physical properties.
ESS2.D Weather and climate			
Weather is the combination of sunlight, wind, snow or rain, and temperature in a particular region and time. People record weather patterns over time.	Climate describes patterns of typical weather conditions over different scales and variations. Historical weather patterns can be analyzed.	Complex interactions determine local weather patterns and influence climate, including the role of the ocean.	The role of radiation from the sun and its interactions with the atmosphere, ocean, and land are the foundation for the global climate system. Global climate models are used to predict future changes, including changes influenced by human behavior and natural factors.
ESS2.E Biogeology			
Plants and animals can change their local environment.	Living things can affect the physical characteristics of their environment.	See Content in LS4.A and LS4.D	The biosphere and Earth's other systems have many interconnections that cause a continual co-evolution of Earth's surface and life on it

Teaching Science is Phenomenal

Earth Space Science Progression			
K-2	**3-5**	**6-8**	**9-12**
ESS3.A Natural resources			
Living things need water, air, and resources from the land, and they live in places that have the things they need. Humans use natural resources for everything they do.	Energy and fuels humans use are derived from natural sources and their use affects the environment. Some resources are renewable over time, others are not.	Humans depend on Earth's land, ocean, atmosphere, and biosphere for different resources, many of which are limited or not renewable. Resources are distributed unevenly around the planet as a result of past geologic processes.	Resource availability has guided the development of human society and use of natural resources has associated costs, risks, and benefits.
ESS3.B Natural hazards			
In a region, some kinds of severe weather are more likely than others. Forecasts allow communities to prepare for severe weather.	A variety of hazards result from natural processes; humans cannot eliminate hazards but can reduce their impacts.	Mapping the history of natural hazards in a region can increase understanding of related geological forces.	Natural hazards and other geological events have shaped the course of human history at local, regional, and global scales.
ESS3.C Human impacts on Earth systems			
Things people do can affect the environment but they can make choices to reduce their impacts.	Societal activities have had major effects on the land, ocean, atmosphere, and even outer space. Societal activities can also help protect Earth's resources and environments.	Human activities have altered the biosphere, sometimes damaging it, although changes to environments can have different impacts for different living things. Activities and technologies can be engineered to reduce people's impacts on Earth.	Sustainability of human societies and the biodiversity that supports them requires responsible management of natural resources, including the development of technologies.
ESS3.D Global climate change			
N/A	N/A	Human activities affect global warming. Decisions to reduce the impact of global warming depend on understanding climate science, engineering capabilities, and social dynamics.	Global climate models used to predict changes continue to be improved, although discoveries about the global climate system are ongoing and continually needed.

Life Science Progression			
K-2	**3-5**	**6-8**	**9-12**
LS1.A Structure and function			
All organisms have external parts that they use to perform daily functions.	Organisms have both internal and external macroscopic structures that allow for growth, survival, behavior, and reproduction.	All living things are made up of cells. In organisms, cells work together to form tissues and organs that are specialized for particular body functions.	Systems of specialized cells within organisms help perform essential functions of life. Any one system in an organism is made up of numerous parts. Feedback mechanisms maintain an organism's internal conditions within certain limits and mediate behaviors.
LS1.B Growth and development of organisms			
Parents and offspring engage in behaviors that help the offspring survive.	Reproduction is essential to every kind of organism. Organisms have unique and diverse life cycles.	Animals engage in behaviors that increase the odds of reproduction. An organism's growth is affected by genetic and environmental factors.	Growth and division of cells in organisms occurs by mitosis and differentiation for specific cell types.
LS1.C Organization for matter and energy flow in organisms			
Animals obtain food they need from plants or other animals. Plants need water and light.	Food provides animals with the materials and energy needed for body repair, growth, warmth, and motion. Plants acquire material for growth chiefly from air and water, and process matter and obtain energy from sunlight, which is used to maintain conditions necessary for survival.	Plants use the energy from light to make sugars through photosynthesis. Within individual organisms, food is broken down through a series of chemical reactions that rearrange molecules and release energy.	The hydrocarbon backbones of sugars produced through photosynthesis are used to make amino acids and other molecules that can be assembled into proteins or DNA. Through cellular respiration, matter and energy flow through different organizational levels of an organism as elements are recombined to form different products and transfer energy.
LS1.D Information Processing			
Animals sense & communicate information and respond to inputs with behaviors that help them grow and survive.	Different sense receptors are specialized for particular kinds of information; Animals use their perceptions and memories to guide their actions.	Each sense receptor responds to different inputs, transmitting them as signals that travel along nerve cells to the brain; The signals are then processed in the brain, resulting in immediate behavior or memories.	N/A
LS2.A Interdependent relationships in ecosystems			
Plants depend on water and light to grow, and also depend on animals for pollination or to move their seeds around.	The food of almost any animal can be traced back to plants. Organisms are related in food webs in which some animals eat plants for food and other animals eat the animals that eat plants, while decomposers restore some materials back to the soil.	Organisms and populations are dependent on their environmental interactions with other living things and with nonliving factors, any of which can limit growth. Competitive, predatory, and mutually beneficial interactions vary across ecosystems but the patterns are shared.	Ecosystems have carrying capacities resulting from biotic and abiotic factors. The fundamental tension between resource availability and organism populations affects the abundance of species in any given ecosystem.

Teaching Science is Phenomenal

Life Science Progression			
K-2	**3-5**	**6-8**	**9-12**
LS2.B Cycles of matter and energy transfer in ecosystems			
This content is included in LS1.C and ESS3.A.	Matter cycles between the air and soil and among organisms as they live and die.	The atoms that make up the organisms in an ecosystem are cycled repeatedly between the living and nonliving parts of the ecosystem. Food webs model how matter and energy are transferred among producers, consumers, and decomposers as the three groups interact within an ecosystem.	Photosynthesis and cellular respiration provide most of the energy for life processes. Only a fraction of matter consumed at the lower level of a food web is transferred up, resulting in fewer organisms at higher levels. At each link in an ecosystem, elements are combined in different ways and matter and energy are conserved. Photosynthesis and cellular respiration are key components of the global carbon cycle.
LS2.C Ecosystem dynamics, functioning, and resilience			
N/A	When the environment changes some organisms survive and reproduce, some move to new locations, some move into the transformed environment, and some die.	Ecosystem characteristics vary over time. Disruptions to any part of an ecosystem can lead to shifts in all of its populations. The completeness or integrity of an ecosystem's biodiversity is often used as a measure of its health.	If a biological or physical disturbance to an ecosystem occurs, including one induced by human activity, the ecosystem may return to its more or less original state or become a very different ecosystem, depending on the complex set of interactions within the ecosystem.
LS2.D Social interactions and group behavior			
N/A	Being part of a group helps animals obtain food, defend themselves, and cope with changes.	N/A	Group behavior has evolved because membership can increase the chances of survival for individuals and their genetic relatives.
LS3.A Inheritance of traits			
Young organisms are very much, but not exactly, like their parents and also resemble other organisms of the same kind.	Different organisms vary in how they look and function because they have different inherited information; the environment also affects the traits that an organism develops.	Genes chiefly regulate a specific protein, which affect an individual's traits.	DNA carries instructions for forming species' characteristics. Each cell in an organism has the same genetic content, but genes expressed by cells can differ.
LS3.B Variation of traits			
N/A	N/A	In sexual reproduction, each parent contributes half of the genetic material acquired by the offspring, resulting in variation between parent and offspring. Genetic information can be altered due to mutations, which may result in beneficial, negative, or no change to proteins in or traits of an organism.	The variation and distribution of traits in a population depend on genetic and environmental factors. Genetic variation can result from mutations caused by environmental factors or errors in DNA replication, or from chromosomes swapping sections during meiosis.

Life Science Progression			
K-2	**3-5**	**6-8**	**9-12**
LS4.A Evidence of common ancestry and diversity			
N/A	Some living organisms resemble organisms that once lived on Earth. Fossils provide evidence about the types of organisms and environments that existed long ago.	The fossil record documents the existence, diversity, extinction, and change of many life forms and their environments through Earth's history. The fossil record and comparisons of anatomical similarities between organisms enables the inference of lines of evolutionary descent.	The ongoing branching that produces multiple lines of descent can be inferred by comparing DNA sequences, amino acid sequences, and anatomical and embryological evidence of different organisms.
LS4.B Natural selection			
N/A	Differences in characteristics between individuals of the same species provide advantages in surviving and reproducing.	Both natural and artificial selection result from certain traits giving some individuals an advantage in surviving and reproducing, leading to predominance of certain traits in a population.	Natural selection occurs only if there is variation in the genes and traits between organisms in a population. Traits that positively affect survival can become more common in a population.
LS4.C Adaptation			
N/A	Particular organisms can only survive in particular environments. Populations of organisms live in a variety of habitats. Change in those habitats affects the organisms living there.	Species can change over time in response to changes in environmental conditions through adaptation by natural selection acting over generations. Traits that support successful survival and reproduction in the new environment become more common.	Evolution results primarily from genetic variation of individuals in a species, competition for resources, and proliferation of organisms better able to survive and reproduce. Adaptation means that the distribution of traits in a population, as well as species expansion, emergence or extinction, can change when conditions change.
LS4.D Biodiversity and humans			
A range of different organisms lives in different places.	N/A	Changes in biodiversity can influence humans' resources and ecosystem services they rely on.	Biodiversity is increased by formation of new species and reduced by extinction. Humans depend on biodiversity but also have adverse impacts on it. Sustaining biodiversity is essential to supporting life on Earth.

Teaching Science is Phenomenal

Physical Science Progression			
K-2	**3-5**	**6-8**	**9-12**
PS1.A Structure of matter (includes PS1.C Nuclear processes)			
Matter exists as different substances that have observable different properties. Different properties are suited to different purposes. Objects can be built up from smaller parts.	Matter exists as particles that are too small to see, and so matter is always conserved even if it seems to disappear. Measurements of a variety of observable properties can be used to identify particular materials.	The fact that matter is composed of atoms and molecules can be used to explain the properties of substances, diversity of materials, states of matter, phase changes, and conservation of matter.	The sub-atomic structural model and interactions between electric charges at the atomic scale can be used to explain the structure and interactions of matter, including chemical reactions and nuclear processes. Repeating patterns of the periodic table reflect patterns of outer electrons. A stable molecule has less energy than the same set of atoms separated; one must provide at least this energy to take the molecule apart.
PS1.B Chemical reactions			
Heating and cooling substances cause changes that are sometimes reversible and sometimes not.	Chemical reactions that occur when substances are mixed can be identified by the emergence of substances with different properties; the total mass remains the same.	Reacting substances rearrange to form different molecules, but the number of atoms is conserved. Some reactions release energy and others absorb energy.	Chemical processes are understood in terms of collisions of molecules, rearrangement of atoms, and changes in energy as determined by properties of elements involved.
PS2.A Forces and motion			
Pushes and pulls can have different strengths and directions, and can change the speed or direction of its motion or start or stop it.	The effect of unbalanced forces on an object results in a change of motion. Patterns of motion can be used to predict future motion. Some forces act through contact, some forces act even when the objects are not in contact. The gravitational force of Earth acting on an object near Earth's surface pulls that object toward the planet's center.	The role of the mass of an object must be qualitatively accounted for in any change of motion due to the application of a force.	Newton's 2nd law ($F=ma$) and the conservation of momentum can be used to predict changes in the motion of macroscopic objects.

Physical Science Progression			
K-2	**3-5**	**6-8**	**9-12**
PS2.B Types of interactions			
N/A	N/A	Forces that act at a distance involve fields that can be mapped by their relative strength and effect on an object.	Forces at a distance are explained by fields that can transfer energy and can be described in terms of the arrangement and properties of the interacting objects and the distance between them. These forces can be used to describe the relationship between electrical and magnetic fields.
PS2.C Stability & instability in physical systems			
N/A	N/A	N/A	N/A
PS3.A Definitions of energy			
N/A	Moving objects contain energy. The faster the object moves, the more energy it has. Energy can be moved from place to place by moving objects, or through sound, light, or electrical currents. Energy can be converted from one form to another form.	Kinetic energy can be distinguished from the various forms of potential energy. Energy changes to and from each type can be tracked through physical or chemical interactions. The relationship between the temperature and the total energy of a system depends on the types, states, and amounts of matter.	The total energy within a system is conserved. Energy transfer within and between systems can be described and predicted in terms of energy associated with the motion or configuration of particles (objects). Systems move toward stable states.
PS3.B Conservation of energy and energy transfer			
Content is found in PS3.D			
PS3.C Relationship between energy and forces			
Bigger pushes and pulls cause bigger changes in an object's motion or shape.	When objects collide, contact forces transfer energy so as to change the objects' motions.	When two objects interact, each one exerts a force on the other, and these forces can transfer energy between them.	Fields contain energy that depends on the arrangement of the objects in the field.

Physical Science Progression			
K-2	**3-5**	**6-8**	**9-12**
PS3.D Energy in chemical processes and everyday life			
Sunlight warms Earth's surface.	Energy can be "produced," "used," or "released" by converting stored energy. Plants capture energy from sunlight, which can later be used as fuel or food.	Sunlight is captured by plants and used in a reaction to produce sugar molecules, which can be reversed by burning those molecules to release energy.	Photosynthesis is the primary biological means of capturing radiation from the sun; energy cannot be destroyed, it can be converted to less useful forms.
PS4.A Wave properties			
Sound can make matter vibrate, and vibrating matter can make sound.	Waves are regular patterns of motion, which can be made in water by disturbing the surface. Waves of the same type can differ in amplitude and wavelength. Waves can make objects move.	A simple wave model has a repeating pattern with a specific wavelength, frequency, and amplitude, and mechanical waves need a medium through which they are transmitted. This model can explain many phenomena including sound and light. Waves can transmit energy.	The wavelength and frequency of a wave are related to one another by the speed of the wave, which depends on the type of wave and the medium through which it is passing. Waves can be used to transmit information and energy.
PS4.B Electromagnetic radiation			
Objects can be seen only when light is available to illuminate them.	Objects can be seen when light reflected from their surface enters our eyes.	The construct of a wave is used to model how light interacts with objects.	Both an electromagnetic wave model and a photon model explain features of electromagnetic radiation broadly and describe common applications of electromagnetic radiation.
PS4.C Information technologies and instrumentation			
People use devices to send and receive information.	Patterns can encode, send, receive and decode information.	Waves can be used to transmit digital information. Digitized information is comprised of a pattern of 1s and 0s.	Large amounts of information can be stored and shipped around as a result of being digitized.

APPENDIX F
GRC Lesson Template

Lessons consistent with this template and electronic templates are available at the #Going3Dw/GRC website: https://sites.google.com/3d-grcscience.org/going3d

3D-Student Science Performance *Author(s):*		
Grade		**Lesson Title**
Lesson Topic		

Performance Expectations (Standard) from State Standards or NGSS:

Lesson Performance Expectations:
-
-

Describe the phase(s) of the 5E instructional sequence this lesson addresses:
Engage
Explore
Explain
Elaborate
Evaluate
 	
In this box provide insight into how the GRC sequence is used within a phase of the 5E instructional model.
 	
Sometimes the sequence crosses two or three of the phases. Most GRC performance sequences address two of the phases
 	
Describe here the **core ideas** that are addressed in this lesson and the degree to which they will be addressed by this lesson. "For this lesson, the central core idea is..."
	Student Science Performance
	Phenomenon:
	Gather In this section students are asking questions, obtaining information, planning and carrying out an investigation, using mathematical and computational thinking, or using models to gather and organize data and/or information.
	
	  1. Students ....
	  2. Students ....
	
	(Teaching Suggestions: This section should contain a brief overview of information teachers will need to facilitate the lesson - this may include links to video clips, links to readings, crosscutting concepts and core ideas to emphasize. Safety advice and other insights about the gathering portion of the lesson. When materials for the investigation are needed we recommend that you include them here or place them in the lesson appendix and reference them here.)
	
	Reason In this section students are evaluating information, analyzing data, using mathematical/computational thinking, constructing explanations, developing arguments, and/or using models to reason, predict, and develop evidence.
	
	  3. Students ....
	  4. Students ....
	
	Class Discussion:
	
	Q: How does ...
	Q: What caused changes in the system of ...
	Q: Why does the input of energy cause ...
	
	(Teaching Suggestions: The questions to initiate class discussion need to be developed before this phase of the sequence. The questions are typically "how, why, or what causes...". This is a good place to prompt with crosscutting concepts.)
	
	  5. Students .... *(if needed)*
	
	Communicate (In this section students are communicating information, communicating arguments, written and oral, for how their evidence supports or refutes an explanation, and using models to communicate their reasoning and make their thinking visible.)
	
	  6. Students ......
	
	(Teaching Suggestions: if needed)

Formative Assessment for Student Learning		
Elicit Evidence of Learning: This box is the individual communication performance from the student prompts in Lesson Appendix A		
Evidence of Student Proficiency Description of the evidence of learning expected for the three-dimensional performance.	**Range of Typical Student Responses** This section provides a range of typical student responses. Often uses a three- point scale. Descriptors of grade-level appropriate student responses: • *Full understanding* • *Partial understanding* • *Limited understanding*	**Acting on Evidence of Learning** This is a brief description of the instructional actions to take based on the students' performance. When the action includes extensive descriptors and/or materials you may wish use Lesson Appendix C. Description of instruction action and response to support student learning. • action for student who displays partial or limited understanding • extensions of learning for student who displays full understanding

SEP, CCC, DCI Featured in Lesson	Science Essentials *(Student Performance Expectations from Book Appendix C, D, E)*
Science Practices	
Crosscutting Concepts	
Disciplinary Core Ideas	

Lesson Appendices

Lessons contain appendixes with prompts for students to see during the lesson, examples of student work, readings, and other supporting information. Generally, each lesson has Appendix A and B, but sometimes Appendix C is needed. Each is described below.

Lesson Appendix A - Student Prompts The student prompt can be used to engage students in science performances and typically have 3-5 group performances and one individual performance. The individual performance usually lies within the communicate reasoning part of the sequence and can serve as a formal formative assessment. Often teachers add opportunities for class discussion into the instructional sequence to discuss things like "Good Questions to Find Resources" or "Class Debate" or "Discussion of Science Language Student Should Use"

Student Prompt for the Lesson

Phenomenon: .....

Group Performances:
1. Ask questions to plan an investigation...... for the causes of changes in the system ...
2. Plan and an investigation to gather evidence for.... causes of changes in the system ...
3. Construct an explanation .... for the causes of changes in the system ......
4. Use a model to ....

Class Discussion

Individual Performances:
5. Develop an argument for how the evidence you collected supports or refutes your explanation for the causes of the phenomenon.

Appendix B - Typically readings, websites, or other tools to help students obtain information are put into this appendix. This is a good place for pictures of models (diagrams or charts students use) or pictures of students engaged in the performances. You may also place pictures of the phenomenon here.

Appendix C - Place descriptions and resources for "acting on evidence of learning" from the "Formative Assessment for Student Learning". Typically, this is an additional reading with class discussion questions or other resource students use to meet the learning expectation.

APPENDIX G
5E and Gather, Reason, Communicate Performance Sequences

5E Instructional Sequence	Gather, Reason, and Communicate Performances (GRC)
Engaging - Engages students in using the **practices** to make sense of a phenomenon to increase curiosity and interest. Making visible student conceptual understanding of **core ideas** and **crosscutting concepts** needed to make sense of the phenomenon.	**Gathering –** Students obtain and organize information by investigating, reading, listening, using models, and writing about causes of an analogous phenomenon. **Reasoning –** Students analyze data, use models to determine causality relationships, and evaluate gathered information. Students construct explanations supported by evidence and develop arguments for how the evidence supports the explanations. **Communicating Reasoning –** Students communicate their reasoning though writing, models, and/or speaking their explanations supported by evidence, and/or argument for how the evidence supports the explanations students have developed through reasoning.
Exploring - Engages students in making sense of an analogous phenomenon by gathering additional information from various valid sources to add to the core ideas and explanation of the analogous phenomenon.	**Gathering –** Students obtain and organize information by investigating, reading, listening, using models/simulations, and writing. The gathering is focused on the analogous phenomenon and using the core idea to make sense of the phenomenon. **Reasoning –** Students analyze data, use models to determine causal relationships, and evaluate gathered information. Students construct explanations supported by evidence and develop arguments for how the evidence supports the explanations.
Explaining Phenomena - Engages students in constructing scientific explanations for causes of phenomena. The teacher focuses students' attention though discussion or evaluation of individual student work on accurate use of core ideas and crosscutting concepts to synthesize a common class-wide understanding of cause of the phenomenon.	**Reasoning –** Students focus on both the "engaging" and "exploring" phenomena to construct explanations supported by evidence and develop arguments for how the evidence supports the explanations. Students engage in a class discussion, round table, or poster session that is synthesized by the teacher to bring a common understanding of causes of the two phenomena and how the core ideas and crosscutting concepts are used. **Communicating –** Students communicate explanations, models, and arguments after the discussion that are used by the teacher to formatively assess student learning that both the teacher and student develop greater understanding of the learning specific to practices, crosscutting concepts, and core ideas.
Elaborating - Engages students in applying the knowledge and abilities learned across the engage, explore, and explanation phases to make sense of a novel but analogous phenomenon.	**Gathering –** Students obtain and organize information by investigating, reading, listening, using models, and writing about causes of an analogous phenomenon. **Reasoning –** Students analyze data, use models to determine causality relationships, and evaluate gathered information. Students construct explanations supported by evidence and develop arguments for how the evidence supports the explanations. **Communicating Reasoning –** Students communicate their reasoning though writing, models, and/or speaking the explanations supported by evidence and/or argument for how the evidence supports the explanations.

5E Instructional Sequence	Gather, Reason, and Communicate Performances (GRC)
Evaluating Learners Students receive feedback on the adequacy of their models, explanations, arguments, and abilities to use crosscutting concepts and core ideas. Formative assessment has been occurring from the beginning of the instructional sequence; but at this point assessments are more formal. The Evaluate phase involves students in making sense of a novel phenomenon that is analogous other phases.	**Reasoning** — Students focus on both the "engaging" and "exploring" phenomena to construct explanations supported by evidence and develop arguments for how the evidence supports the explanations. Students engage in a class discussion, round table, or poster session that is synthesized by the teacher to bring a common understanding of causes of the two phenomena and how the core ideas and crosscutting concepts are used. **Communicating** — Students communicate explanations, models, and arguments that are used by the teacher for summative evaluation of student ability to use of the practices, crosscutting concepts, and core ideas to make sense of phenomena.

APPENDIX H
Student Prompts for 5E-GRC Lesson from Chapter 8

These prompts are used with students. They can be projected on the screen or shared using a Google document or a printed handout. Early grade teachers may only show one performance at a time and read through the prompt with the students.

Engage
Phenomenon: Some, but not all, squirrels can fly from tree to tree.

Individual Performance – 5 minutes
1. Each student observes the flying squirrel video and develops three questions about causes of some species of squirrels to fly from tree to tree.

Group Performance – 20 minutes
2. Use the questions to obtain information for how specific body structures function to enable some squirrels to fly. Use link: *http://www.dec.ny.gov/docs/administration_pdf/squirrels.pdf*
3. Construct an explanation for how the body structures of the flying squirrel function to enable them to survive in forest ecosystems.

Individual Performance – 6 minutes
4. Communicate an explanation for causes of variation among squirrel species in New York State forest ecosystem.

Class Discussion

Explore I
Phenomenon: The wing flaps of flying squirrels are not all the same.

Group Performance
1. Obtain information from reliable resources for how changes in a population have led to some squirrels being able to manipulate their body to fly.
http://evolution.berkeley.edu/evolibrary/article/0_0_0/evo_25)
2. Develop a model using paper to investigate the attributes of wing like structures that have the best proportions of wing dimensions and function to maximize the glide distance. *"Engineering challenge"*
3. Design and build a paper glider from a single sheet of paper with a structure that allows the glider to fly 2X when dropped from a height of 1X.
4. Communicate an explanation for causes of variation among squirrel species in New York State forest ecosystem.
5. Analyze and interpret data from testing of the glider designers to determine which proportions are most effective at maximizing the glide distance.

Individual Performance – 6 minutes
6. Develop an argument for how the evidence gathered during the investigation supports the explanation that specific structures function to provide an advantage for some individuals in the forest ecosystem.

Class Discussion *(Teaching Suggestion: See lesson plan for discussion questions. Use questions to initiate discussion).*

Explore II
Phenomenon: Some organisms have advantages that help them to survive.

Group Performance
1. *Ask questions* to obtain information about *causes* of some organisms being better adapted to survive in a specific environment in which they live but not well adapted to survive in other environments.
2. *Plan and carry out an investigation* to obtain data on the *proportion* of individuals in a population with specific traits that allow these individuals to jump high enough to gather food needed to survive.
3. *Analyze and interpret data* to determine the *proportion* of individuals that survive in the simulation activity environment.

Individual Performance
4. *Construct an explanation* for how variations in the physical *structures* of the organisms (students) affect the individual's ability to reach food they need to survive.

Class Discussion

Explore III
Phenomenon: Flying squirrels can escape predators by flying.

Group Performance
1. *Obtain information* from reliable sources about the *ecosystem* and behavior of the flying squirrels.
https://ecos.fws.gov/docs/five_year_review/doc4177.pdf
https://www.fs.fed.us/ne/newtown_square/publications/other_publishers/OCR/ne_2006_menzel001.pdf
http://www.esf.edu/efb/lomolino/courses/mammaldiversity/labs/nys4.pdf
http://www.esf.edu/aec/adks/mammals/southern_flying_squirrel.htm

2. *Develop a new argument* for how evidence gathered from reliable sources supports an explanation for why *changes* to an environment which *cause changes* in the numbers of organisms able to survive in that environment.

Individual Performance
3. Revise your *explanations* for why variation of traits in a population is necessary for organisms to *change* over time when the environment *changes*.

Class Discussion

Teaching Science is Phenomenal

Phenomenon: Some squirrels are better adapted to forest ecosystems.

Group Performance

1. *Construct an explanation* to describe *causes* of why some individuals in a population are more likely than others to survive and reproduce in forest ecosystems.

2. *Develop an argument* for how evidence you have gathered supports your explanation for why specific *structures function* to help the flying squirrel be successful in the forest ecosystem in which they live.

Individual Performance

3. Revise your *explanation* for why *changes* over time in the physical structures of organisms are evidence of natural selection.

Class Discussion

Elaborate Phase

Phenomenon: Flying squirrels can escape predators by flying.

Group Performance

1. *Ask questions* to obtain information about what *causes* the Uinta Ground Squirrel to be better adapted to survive in Utah and Wyoming than flying squirrels.

2. *Obtain information* from reliable sources on body structures and how these *structures function* enabling Uinta Ground Squirrel to survive in its native habitat.

3. *Use a model (T-Chart)* to compare body *structures and function* of the Uinta Ground Squirrel to the New York Flying Squirrel.

4. *Construct an explanation,* supported by evidence, for *causes* of the difference in structure of the two species, relative to the habitats in which they live.

Individual Performances

5. Revise your *explanations* for why variation of traits in a population led to squirrels in one environment with body *structures* to support burrowing and in another environment structures to support flying.

Phenomenon: Prairie dogs live in colonies of underground dens in the American prairie.

Group Performance

1. Obtain information about how the structures of the American Prairie Dog makes this squirrel well adapted for living on the western prairies of North America. https://naturalhistory.si.edu/mna/image_info.cfm?species_id=54

Individual Performance

2. Develop an argument for how specific structures prairie dogs possess function to enable this species to survive and reproduce in the plains and grasslands of North America, but **not** in the forests of the Northeastern U.S. and Canada.

3. Construct an explanation based on evidence for why genetic variations of traits in the prairie dog population increased the probability of some individuals' surviving and reproducing in response to environmental changes over time.

Reading for Engage Phase: The Flying Squirrel

The flying squirrel: Northern (Glaucomys sabrinus) and southern (Glaucomys volans) flying squirrels are the smallest species of squirrels in New York State, weighing just a few ounces. Flying squirrels do not actually fly, but rather glide. By extending their feet, they cause the large flaps of skin found along the sides of their bodies to stretch tight, forming a wing-like structure. Because of their nocturnal habits, few people are fortunate enough to have seen a flying squirrel in the wild, and many are unaware that these night-time creatures exist. The **key core idea is that natural selection for inheritable traits of one species evolved structures that function to provide the**

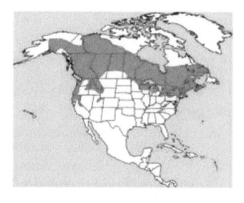

species with the ability to better move from tree to tree. These squirrels are better able to avoid predators, gather more food without going to the ground, survive, reproduce and increase the proportion of squirrels in the population with that trait, and continue that trait in the population).

The **practices of explanation and argumentation** from evidence are two of the science practices that work together. Arguments are the logical rationale for how evidence supports or refutes an explanation. The argument establishes the reasoning that connects evidence to an explanation. Evidence is the basis for argument for a proposed explanation.

Arguing in science is very different from the common use of the word. Arguing, in science, requires a systematic line of empirical evidence logically connecting the best scientific explanation for an observed natural phenomenon. Argumentation is an essential tool to reveal the strengths and weaknesses in reasoning that connects available evidence to an explanation.

The **crosscutting concept of structure and function** is central to the causality of the organism changing over time. An object's structure and shape determine many of its properties and functions.

The structures, shapes, and substructure of living organisms determine how the organism functions to meet its needs within an environment.

Reading for Evaluation Phase: Prairie Dogs on the Prairie

The prairie dog is a rabbit-sized rodent native to the North American prairies and open grasslands. Prairie dogs live in underground burrows, extensive dens of tunnels and chambers marked by many mounds of packed earth at their surface entrances. The dens include defined nurseries, sleeping quarters, and even toilets. Prairie dogs have a keen sense of hearing and build high mounds near entrances to their burrows, where they can stand upright to watch and listen for predators. When the "lookout" sees or hears predator they alert the entire prairie dog colony with a high shrill call of alarm and the entire town goes underground until the danger passes.

These large squirrels emerge from their burrows in daylight to forage and feed on grasses, roots, and seeds. They communicate with loud cries. A warning cry, for example, will send a town's denizens hustling to their holes at the approach of a badger, coyote, or other predator. A second, "all-clear" call alerts the community when the danger has passed.

Prairie dogs spend a lot of time building and rebuilding these dwellings and have strong claws for digging and burrowing. Other animals benefit from their labors as well since the burrows are often shared by snakes, burrowing owls, and even rare black-footed ferrets, which hunt prairie dogs in their own dwellings.

Family groups (a male, a few females, and their young) inhabit burrows and cooperate to share food, chase off other prairie dogs, and groom one another. These group members even greet one another with a prairie dog kiss or nuzzle.

Black-tailed prairie dogs, the best known of the five prairie dog species, live in larger communities called towns, which may contain many hundreds of animals. Typically, they cover less than half a square mile, but may be larger. The largest known prairie dog colony was in Texas, covered over 25,000 square miles, and was home to millions of prairie dogs.

Another prairie dog species, the white-tailed prairie dog, lives in the western mountains. These rodents do not gather in large towns but maintain more scattered burrows. All species hunker down in winter and burn the reserves of fat they have stored during more plentiful seasons. White-tails may hibernate for up to six months on their mountain plains, while their black-tailed cousins sometimes emerge to feed on especially warm days.

Much of the Great Plains has been converted to farming or pasture land, and prairie dogs are generally not welcome in such places. Because of their destructive landscaping, they are often killed as pests. During the 20th century, about 98 percent of all prairie dogs were exterminated, and their range subsequently shrunk to perhaps five percent of its historic size.

https://naturalhistory.si.edu/mna/image_info.cfm?species_id=54

CPSIA information can be obtained
at www.ICGtesting.com
Printed in the USA
LVHW072347201222
735667LV00013B/190